Escape from Dannemora

Escape from Dannemora

Lawrence P. Gooley

Bloated Toe Publishing
Peru, New York 12972

Other books by the author:

A History of the Altona Flat Rock
Lyon Mountain: The Tragedy of a Mining Town
Out of the Darkness: In Memory of Lyon Mountain's Iron Men
The Battle of Plattsburgh Question & Answer Book
A History of the Altona Flat Rock – Silver Anniversary Edition
Brendler's Boys: The House That George Built
Oliver's War: An Adirondack Rebel Battles the Rockefeller Fortune
Terror in the Adirondacks: The True Story of Serial Killer Robert F. Garrow
History of Churubusco and the Town of Clinton, Clinton County, New York
Adirondack & North Country Gold: 50+ New & True Stories You're Sure to Love
25 Diabolical Adirondack Murders: The Twisted, Fiendish Deeds of North Country Killers
Killing in the Kuyahoora Valley—A True Story: The Murder of Poland, New York,
    Schoolteacher Lydia Beecher by Teenager Jean Gianini
People & Places of the Adirondacks & Foothills—VOLUME 1
People & Places of the Adirondacks & Foothills—VOLUME 2
People & Places of the Adirondacks & Foothills—VOLUME 3
People & Places of the Adirondacks & Foothills—VOLUME 4
People & Places of the Adirondacks & Foothills—VOLUME 5
People & Places of the Adirondacks & Foothills—VOLUME 6

Bloated Toe Publishing, Peru, NY 12972

First Edition, Second Printing

ISBN-13: 978-1-939216-42-7   ISBN-10: 1-939216-42-7

Library of Congress Control Number: 2015918128

Copies of the books listed above may be obtained by writing to:
Bloated Toe Enterprises, PO Box 324, Peru, NY 12972

or

Go to: www.bloatedtoe.com   email: info@bloatedtoe.com

Cover photo: New York State Police

Covers designed by Lawrence P. Gooley and
Jill C. Jones of Bloated Toe Enterprises

Printed and bound by Versa Press, Inc., East Peoria, IL
Manufactured in the United States of America

Contents

DANNEMORA'S FAMOUS, INFAMOUS, DANGEROUS, AND UNUSUAL INMATES

Preface

This book was already in progress when the stunning escape from Dannemora occurred in June 2015. Since the plan included extensive coverage of Clinton's violent past and dozens of escape stories, the recent escape that gripped the nation for nearly a month provided the perfect opening chapter.

It was a spectacular breakout, but contrary to what was widely stated in the media, hardly unprecedented. Men went over and under the wall on many occasions prior to 1929, which is the line of demarcation that separates the old from the new. During the eighty-five years following 1929, no one escaped from inside the high wall until Richard Matt and David Sweat did it. But during the eighty-five years prior to 1929, it was done many times in exciting, ingenious, and spectacular fashion.

Included within is the story of the 2015 escape, the long history of violence and horrible tortures at Clinton, a look at escape attempts and more than three dozen breakouts, plus profiles of many famous and infamous criminals who were incarcerated at Dannemora. I found all the stories fascinating, and I believe you will, too.

Special thanks goes to my wife and business partner, Jill Jones, for all the work and support she contributed to one of the most difficult projects we've produced.

And a nod to a dear old friend, Charlie Barney, who encouraged me to write about the prison, and whose dad was once employed there. The fact that Charlie is no longer with us, having died in a tragic fall, confirms that the world is an unfair place.

Escape from Dannemora, 2015

At 10:30 on the evening of June 5, 2015, officers at Clinton Correctional Facility in Dannemora performed the first of several nightly rounds, the so-called "live count" requiring visible confirmation that each inmate was cell-bound. Other scheduled checks were intended to verify that each cell remained occupied throughout the night. This was, after all, a maximum-security prison housing more violent felons than other state facility.

On the fourth level, the top tier in the Honor Block, neighboring cells number twenty-two and twenty-three were occupied by inmates David Sweat and Richard "Ricky" Matt. Shortly after the live count, the two men busied themselves, arranging clothing in their beds to present the appearance of someone asleep. It was a tense, exciting moment, the culmination of events over the course of several years that had recently developed into an escape plan.

Minutes later, after exiting hidden holes in their cell walls, climbing downward to the depths of the prison, and crawling through a large steam pipe, the two men lifted a manhole cover in the streets of Dannemora and peeked out into the free world. How could this happen, and just who were the escapees?

DAVID SWEAT

David Sweat was raised in Deposit, New York, about a half hour east of Binghamton and just four miles from the New York–Pennsylvania border. An atmosphere of drinking and partying pervaded the home, hardly conducive to rearing children. Sweat's mother admitted she didn't know how to handle a child who was forward, arrogant, and often nasty, one whom she said at age nine threw knives at her.

David was sent to Florida to live with his mother's brother, but instead of straightening out, he caused more trouble, even stealing his aunt's car and wrecking it.

He ended up in foster care, and then lived in a group home in Binghamton, New York, where he got into more trouble when he and a friend plotted to steal money and computers from the home. The plan resulted in five years of strict probation and a rebuke from the judge, who called them "teenaged idiots."

But nothing seemed to register with Sweat, and about a year later, at age seventeen, he landed in prison for two to four years, courtesy of a burglary conviction. He was released after serving nineteen months.

His life continued with one burglary after another, working with the same partner as in earlier crimes, Jeffrey Nabinger. They were cousins and kindred spirits, having shared similar family backgrounds.

While living in a cache of stolen vehicles they had hidden in a wooded area, the duo planned more crimes. After robbing a gun shop one night across the Pennsylvania line, they drove to a parking lot to transfer the loot to Sweat's car. Sheriff's Deputy Kevin Tarsia pulled into the lot, prompting Sweat to hide beneath a truck while his two partners ran to the woods.

The officer exited his car, and shortly after, Sweat opened fire with a .40-caliber Glock. Tarsia went down, struggling to reach his service gun lying nearby on the pavement. Sweat quickly got into his Honda Accord and drove over Tarsia, dragging his body across the lot.

Seeing what had happened, Sweat's two partners in crime

David Sweat (2002)

2

came running from the woods. Nabinger shot Tarsia, but when the clip fell from his gun, he grabbed the deputy's own weapon and shot him twice in the face at point-blank range. Holes in Tarsia's hand revealed that his final act was attempting to block the bullets. It was a brutal murder, the kind that made people shudder in disbelief.

The three boys were eventually tracked down, arrested, and brought to trial. After first pleading not guilty, David Sweat accepted a deal to avoid the possibility of a death sentence, admitting guilt to one charge of first-degree murder in exchange for a life-without-parole sentence, but with conditions. Nabinger accepted the same plea the next day. The conditions: all rights to appeal were forfeited, and if their plea status changed at any point, federal prosecutors would try both cases in pursuit of the death penalty.

Less than fifteen months after the murder of Deputy Tarsia, David Sweat was settling into his new surroundings at Clinton Prison in Dannemora.

RICHARD MATT

Richard Matt grew up in the western New York community of Tonawanda, a Buffalo suburb. His childhood in many ways paralleled Sweat's, with poor parenting (his father was convicted of several crimes), life in a foster home, and then in a youth home. He was generally known as a smart, good-looking guy, but committed many crimes during his teen years.

In 1985, at age nineteen, he began a series of eight convictions over the next six years, including assault, possession of stolen property, and criminal possession of a weapon. During that same period he served as a police informant. Matt's proclivity for escape was evident early on, beginning with a breakout from an Erie County cell in 1986, which generated a four-day manhunt.

In the early 1990s, he became involved in a murder-for-hire plot, but turned the information over to the intended victim despite a prospective payoff of $100,000. He claimed to have been stabbed in retaliation for revealing the murder plan, but it would take more than a knife wound to bring down Ricky Matt, a legitimate tough guy. A video posted on YouTube when he was a young man shows him taking a large blowgun dart to the arm without flinching. His escape from Erie County Correctional Facility in 1986 involved clearing a wall topped with unforgiving razor wire, cutting him badly. In both cases, pain appeared to be a nonfactor.

He also exhibited a lack of empathy that was frightening. In the crime that brought Richard Matt lasting infamy, he and partner Lee Bates abducted Matt's former employer, seventy-six-year-old William Rickerson of North Tonawanda, with the purported goal of robbery. According to testimony later provided by Bates, Matt beat his victim with "a long, thin knife sharpener" and rammed it into his ear. After securing him with duct tape, they tossed the pajama-clad old man into his own car trunk and drove around for twenty-seven hours, with Matt yelling at him repeatedly to think about where his money was hidden.

They stopped once, during which Matt beat Rickerson with The Club, a steering-wheel security device. During a second stop, he again struck the victim before bending his fingers backwards until they snapped. Apparently Matt became annoyed at the old man's moaning, and on a third stop, he opened the trunk and snapped Rickerson's neck with his bare hands.

The pair then drove to Tonawanda Island, where they dumped the body. According to Bates, Matt later returned with a hacksaw and dismembered the corpse, tossing the parts into the Niagara River. Police later recovered several of the pieces.

The robbery of Rickerson netted a wedding ring, some credit cards, and less than $100 in cash.

The killer couldn't keep his mouth shut, and when evidence pointed his way in early 1998, Richard Matt deserted America's northern border with Canada and headed south for Mexico. Several weeks after arriving there, he murdered American Charles Perrault in the border town of Matamoros, stabbing

Richard Matt (2008)

4

him to death during an attempted robbery, and earning Matt a prison sentence of twenty-three years.

Because he was an American, and possibly because of his brash attitude, he was abused by fellow inmates and punished severely by guards, who according to Matt held him down and tattooed "Mexico Forever" on his back. It is suspected that he also made connections with members of a powerful drug cartel, but that was never confirmed. Among the souvenirs he collected while abroad were at least one bullet wound suffered during an escape attempt— and a pair of metal front teeth.

After serving nine years in prison, Matt was extradited to the U.S. in 2007. The following year he was put on trial for the murder of Rickerson. Bates had already been found guilty in 1998 as an accomplice and was sentenced to fifteen years to life.

Richard Matt's arrogance certainly didn't help his court case. Among the evidence against him was the "Matamoros letter" that he wrote to the Bates family from his Mexican cell. The missive assured them he would confirm that Lee was innocent if they provided him with $10,000 in cash. Inexplicably, he added, "I was there. [Lee] is just as guilty as me of killing Rickerson." Perhaps Matt didn't recognize that within his offer to help was a written admission of guilt, or maybe it didn't matter to him at the time. It surely mattered in 2008 when he was trying to avoid a prison sentence.

His evil persona led to extreme security measures during the trial. The protective sheets of glass on the lawyers' tables were removed so they couldn't be shattered to produce makeshift knives. A sniper manned the roof in case Matt's associates tried to free him. Corrections Emergency Response Team (CERT) members, the department's equivalent of SWAT-team specialists, shadowed him at all times, including in the courtroom. Beneath the defendant's clothes was a 50,000-volt stun device, with a remote control in the hands of a nearby deputy or CERT man. Between court sessions, he was held in a solitary confinement cell.

But nothing out of the ordinary occurred during the trial, other than disturbing testimony about a vicious crime. After the prosecutor beseeched jurors to "Show him the mercy he showed Bill Rickerson," Matt was found guilty and sentenced to twenty-five years to life. Next stop, Dannemora.

BEATING THE SYSTEM

David Sweat arrived at Clinton in 2003, while Richard Matt, fourteen years older, showed up five years later. Both had spent only a few years of their adult lives outside of prison walls. Despite the horrific crimes that brought them to New York's most infamous prison, both men kept their noses clean long enough to eventually earn assignment to the institution's Honor Block, where good behavior was rewarded.

Lifers have no hope of someday being free, and thus no reason to follow prison rules other than to avoid punishment. Programs like Honor Block serve dual purposes, offering incentives for long-term inmates to improve their own condition, which in turn enhances the safety of officers within the facility, for as corrections insiders know, contented inmates are less of a threat to prison personnel. Perks at Dannemora—relaxed rules on telephone use, cooking, and the wearing of civilian clothing in certain circumstances—make prison life more bearable.

And at Clinton, bearable is about as good as it gets. Located in far upstate New York, the prison in Dannemora is historically reputed as a house of punishment. It has mellowed somewhat from the tortures of long ago, but that isn't saying much. At 170 years old, Clinton is still held over the heads of inmates at other New York prisons as punishment for not behaving.

At a prison where the vast majority of inmates (more than ninety percent) are violent felons, even multiple murderers have a shot at the Honor Block. Staying out of trouble was the key, and that's what Matt and Sweat did. After earning membership, they both found work in the same tailor shop, of which Clinton has several, and a strong friendship developed.

Matt could be a charmer, a trait easily transformed to manipulative, while Sweat was more thoughtful, but friendly, a personality facet he put to good use. By mid-2012, David had developed a very close relationship with a civilian prison employee, Joyce (Clookey) Mitchell, better known as Tillie. As a member of the Civil Service Employees Association (CSEA), she earned more than $57,000 a year supervising in the tailor shop. Her husband, Lyle, was employed in the prison's maintenance department.

Joyce Mitchell (2015)

Eric Jensen, a former inmate who last worked in the tailor shop in 2012, claimed that Sweat, at the time thirty-one, and Mitchell, forty-eight, engaged frequently in sex in a supply closet, something both have denied. But the frequent teasing of David Sweat about his "girlfriend" (they called her his "boo," according to Jensen) was indicative of how close they had become. The relationship continued until suspicions triggered an internal investigation in 2014. No wrongdoing was identified, but as a precaution linked to their closeness and to an unrelated infraction by Sweat, he was moved to a different tailor shop.

Management's decision to move David Sweat nearly precluded the 2015 breakout from ever occurring. By the time his strong ties to Mitchell had raised suspicions, Sweat had already realized that any hope for escape hinged on aid from an insider. She was the key, and separating them had thrown a wrench into the works, perhaps ending any hope of pursuing a getaway plan.

But Matt, who at forty-eight was much closer to her age, came to the rescue, establishing a closeness that equaled or exceeded her relationship with Sweat. An excellent artist, Matt had occasionally gifted paintings to other prison employees, a violation of policy. He had done portraits of Joyce's son, Tobey, and one of her dogs, paintings that she later said were secreted out of the prison for her by a friend, Corrections Officer Eugene Palmer. Matt was also planning artwork for Joyce and Lyle's anniversary, but Lyle wouldn't allow it because it could endanger his employment.

Matt's efforts to charm Joyce were so effective that by December 2014, he felt comfortable enough to approach her about obtaining certain tools for painting projects—items that were actually needed for the escape plan. By some accounts, their alliance was also sexual, something Mitchell later denied to her husband. Investigators said she admitted to a relationship with Matt that was "intimate," a word that left plenty of room for interpretation, but has evolved in modern times to suggest "in the biblical sense."

Whatever the case, Matt's overtures were successful. Tillie Mitchell was deeply flattered by the attention and would get what they needed. Problem solved.

The final piece of the puzzle came on January 20, 2015, when Sweat was transferred to the cell next to Matt's. Almost immediately, David Sweat went to work cutting holes in the quarter-inch steel plating that formed their cells' back walls. According to Erik Jensen, nighttime presented an opportunity: "From 10:30 at night until 5:30 in the morning, you're lucky if you'd see one of those officers one time." Rumors of guards sleeping on the job were prevalent.

By February the job was done, giving both men access to the catwalks—once the sole domain of corrections officers, who used them to spy on inmate conversations, and to cut power to the cells of those who broke certain rules. Inmate complaints about the practice of cutting power ended when prison administrators locked the catwalks and took control of the keys. From that point forward, the area behind the cells was no longer subject to regular patrols, while Matt and Sweat enjoyed sole access to those forbidden spaces. Nothing good could come of it.

David Sweat, facing a life sentence with no chance of parole, suddenly found freedom within the prison that only a few

Hole cut in cell wall (Darren McGee, Office of NYS Governor)

Dannemora inmates in the past century have enjoyed. Night after night he crawled from his cell, descended several levels to the bowels of Clinton Prison, and proceeded to explore. In time, the extensive network of underground pipes, tunnels, and walls became more and more familiar. It took trial-and-error probing to find a possible escape route, and resourcefulness to arrive at solutions to difficult problems.

It took tools as well, including chisels and hacksaw blades provided secretly by Joyce Mitchell. Some deliveries were famously made by hiding the items inside packages of frozen meat. The two men also found a toolbox belonging to outside contractors, and when Sweat managed to pick the lock, they found power tools inside. If electricity could be accessed, those tools could ease the workload and accelerate progress.

For Sweat, a steam pipe that passed through the prison's thick underground wall presented an opportunity, but a daunting challenge as well. Trying to penetrate the wall using hand tools and a sledgehammer (the hammer apparently forgotten underground some time ago by contractors), Sweat found the work difficult and the results disappointing. It was also very hot. While conditions underground are generally cooler, the twenty-four-inch steam pipe

Cell-wall holes viewed from catwalk (Darren McGee, Office of NYS Governor)

that passed through the prison wall emitted a tremendous amount of heat.

But on May 4, that annoyingly hot pipe suddenly went cold, providing a solution. Instead of penetrating the wall, they would bypass it. Cutting into the pipe and cutting out again on the prison wall's opposite side precluded any need for bashing through the solid barrier. Warm weather meant the steam pipe would be out of use until fall, so it was important to act soon. After several weeks of noisy, dirty work, handsawing through the pipe, the job was done. They could now access the tunnels beneath village streets and exit from any connected manhole.

The solutions to some impediments they overcame may have been Richard Matt's doing, but only Sweat survived to tell the story and claim the credit, so the full truth will never be known. The most important thing to know was how; the who of it all was secondary, except for Sweat, who later defined himself as the mastermind. It is true that historically, he was much more the planner than Matt, whose impulsiveness frequently worked against him.

The noise from sawing through the cell walls, and any other loud work involved in planning and preparing the escape route, was never an issue for Sweat. The Honor Block was a very noisy place in the daytime, and he later claimed with confidence that the guards on duty at night would be asleep. When inmates themselves questioned the noises, Matt put them off the scent with a story about preparing canvases for painting.

What apparently *was* an issue was Ricky Matt's weight. He was too large to fit through the twenty-four-inch-wide steam pipe, so a crash diet was necessary. What followed was a month of working, dieting, planning, and ensuring that Joyce Mitchell remained on board. She was, even to the point of discussing her role in Lyle's murder during the escape.

There were other signs as well. Between mid-October 2014 and May 1, 2015, she had texted Matt's daughter and made phone calls to the families of both men, but not in relation to the escape plan. Her deep involvement, even helping them with personal matters, signified Joyce was fully committed. The plan was for her to pick them up in Dannemora and drive seven hours to a safe place Sweat knew of in West Virginia (a trip that would likely have taken longer).

Hole cut in steam pipe (Darren McGee, Office of NYS Governor)

At some point they would continue to Mexico, with Richard Matt guiding the way across the border. An alternative later mentioned by Mitchell was splitting up after hiding out in West Virginia, with Matt going off on his own and Joyce remaining with Sweat.

The job of cutting through the pipe was finished in early June, and on the night of June 4, Sweat made the now familiar descent, entered the pipe, exited outside the prison wall, and made his way to a manhole. At that point he could have simply escaped on his own, but later claimed he didn't for two reasons: there were too many homes nearby, and he needed Matt to ensure safe passage into Mexico. Sweat retreated to his cell, after which they finalized plans for the great escape, just twenty-four hours away.

In the morning, Matt approached Joyce Mitchell and told her it was go time. She was to pick them up at the powerhouse at midnight after immobilizing Lyle with the two pills provided by Matt.

After the routine standing check later that evening, the inmates made their move. The other nightly checks to follow, having been thwarted so many times already, were hardly a concern. Shortly before midnight, with their familiar bed-dummies in place, the two men entered the catwalk and descended six stories to the underground pipe, to which they attached a sticky note with a Chinese caricature bearing the message, "Have a nice day!" Making their way to a manhole at the intersection of Bouck and Barker Streets, they cut the chain locking the cover shut and exited into the streets of Dannemora.

THE MANHUNT

There was no getaway car waiting, but parking for several minutes late at night on a village street might have attracted unwanted attention. It was an hour's drive from the Mitchell home, so pinpoint timing was unlikely. Surely Joyce would show up any moment now, and they would finally taste real freedom.

But twenty-nine miles northwest of the prison, their worst nightmare was playing out. During dinner with Lyle that evening at a Chinese restaurant in Malone, the enormity of the situation— helping two murderers escape, seeing her husband die, running off with two ruthless killers—triggered extreme anxiety in their accomplice. After the short drive home, Joyce wasn't feeling well, so she took a nap. When it didn't seem to help, Lyle asked if she wanted to go to the emergency room, and when Joyce said yes, he drove her to the Alice Hyde Hospital in Malone, where her discomfort was diagnosed as a panic attack.

According to David Sweat, they soon realized there would be no getaway car. It was a jolting moment for two con men known for having brass balls—for all their nerve, acuity, and manipulations, they had misread Joyce Mitchell.

But there was no time to worry. Rather than call off the escape, they made a run for it. Matt carried a canvas bag and Sweat a guitar case (another perk allowed on the Honor Block), both containers holding tools and supplies they would need.

Moments later, months of hard work and planning nearly all went for naught. Leaving the intersection to avoid notice, they crossed nearby backyards, where an annoyed resident, Leslie Lewis, challenged them. Sweat quickly offered an apology, saying they were accidentally on the wrong street. Anyone taking the guitar case into consideration might think little of it—probably a couple of guys coming home a little drunk after a gig or a party. They immediately headed south on Barker Street towards the powerhouse, a crisis narrowly avoided.

DAY 1

Hours later, at 5:30 a.m., corrections officers discovered the two inmates were missing from their cells, prompting an immediate prison lockdown and a facility-wide search. The terrible, embarrassing truth was soon evident, and well before noon there was a heavy police presence in Dannemora, complete with their own Special Operations Response Team, the Bureau of Criminal Investigation (BCI), the Forensic Identification Unit, helicopters, and K-9 units. Roadblocks were established, manned by police officers carrying rifles and wearing bulletproof vests. Others soon to enter the mix were the FBI, the U.S. Department of Homeland Security, the U.S. Marshals, New York State Forest Rangers, the Clinton County District Attorney's Office, and the sheriff's departments of both Clinton and Franklin Counties. Within hours, more than 200 lawmen were involved in the search, which was led by Major Charles Guess of State Police Troop B in Malone.

Without proof the inmates had left the area, the working assumption was that they were nearby. Dannemora village is a mix of new, old, and very old structures, all of which needed to be checked as soon as possible. Since any one of them could hold the escapees, police began a door-to-door, building-to-building campaign. In a region filled with hunters and gun enthusiasts, bravado and confidence were expressed by some folks. Thousands of others were just plain scared.

DAY 2

Day 2 of the manhunt only served to heighten fears as details of the escape were revealed. Dummies had been left in the inmates' beds, certainly no novelty in prison escapes—but how could it have worked in Clinton, a facility notorious for tight security? Holes had been cut in cell walls and heavy pipes, possibly with power tools, which was simply inconceivable. Worse yet, all the prison's tools had been accounted for, suggesting that people on the inside or outside had aided in the escape. And somehow, the absence of Matt and Sweat had gone unnoticed for about six hours. The trust that even residents in the shadows of Clinton's wall had felt for so long was shaken by such surprising revelations. Was no one safe anymore?

With nerves already on edge, the public became privy to details of the two inmates' crimes—an innocent old man tortured and strangled by Matt, and a young police officer shot at least fifteen times by Sweat, then run over and dragged by a car. Imagine what the rest of Clinton's population was like if those two guys were serving in the Honor Block.

Inside the prison, the dangers of being a corrections officer at Clinton were elevated. With a guard-inmate relationship that was mostly adversarial, the escape was just the excuse inmates needed to taunt officers, which they began to do openly. Some guards confided that physical attacks upon them increased in the wake of the escape. In laymen's terms, they had lost their mojo, and it would be tough getting it back. The most violent prison in New York State was getting worse, at least for the guards—and possibly for the inmates as well. Rumors floated on the village grapevine that physical violence was a component of interrogations that were being conducted by corrections officers.

DAY 3

By Monday, Day 3 of the manhunt, the escapees' whereabouts remained a mystery. With public safety at risk, the state offered rewards of $50,000 for information leading to the arrest of each inmate. The expanding manhunt received additional manpower from the State Department of Environmental Conservation, U.S. Immigration and Customs Enforcement, and the U.S. Border Patrol.

Early in the day, word began filtering through several media outlets that Joyce Mitchell, a civilian employee in the prison's tailor shop, was being questioned, and that her husband also worked at Clinton. Her friendship with the two escapees was mentioned, adding intrigue to the mystery surrounding the breakout. But it was all unofficial, with no confirmation by police and no names provided. The full story was withheld from the public as investigators dug deeper. In doing so, they opened wounds that for Lyle Mitchell might never heal.

After Joyce's night in the hospital for the anxiety attack, Lyle joined her there the next morning. At about 11 a.m., she became aware of several messages on her phone indicating that police were looking for her. Having heard about the escape, Lyle assumed it was a routine check on all prison employees. They went to the police station at 1 p.m., where she was interviewed.

But investigators questioned Joyce again the following day. Lyle, meanwhile, had learned the identities of the escapees, but didn't fully grasp the confluence of recent events and why Joyce was being targeted. Investigators began sharing with him bits of what she had admitted thus far, leaving Lyle stunned, hurt, and disbelieving. But for now, the public only knew that Joyce was being questioned.

While speculation continued on all fronts, New York Governor Andrew Cuomo branded the escape a public safety crisis. No one knew if the inmates had an alternative plan, but if someone else picked them up, they might well have reached New York City by the time their absence was discovered.

The story caught fire on social media and on television stations across America, including breathless coverage during nightly news broadcasts on every major channel and several minor ones. Other stations operating 24/7 brought in a wide range of "experts" to speculate on how the escape could have been executed, where the

Dannemora village. The pushpin marks the manhole at Bouck and Barker Streets.

escapees might be, what law enforcement was doing, and what law enforcement *should* be doing. Day by day, as the story played out, coverage only increased. The North Country, which at Lake Placid in 1980 had hosted one of the most famous Winter Olympic Games ever, had never seen anything like it.

On Monday night, during a heavy rainstorm, two men were sighted on a secondary road in the town of Willsboro, about thirty miles southeast of Dannemora. At around 10 p.m., a report came in of a disabled vehicle a few miles south of Willsboro, at Essex, the site of a short ferry crossing across Lake Champlain to Vermont. A team was dispatched immediately, and by Tuesday morning more than a hundred searchers were working the fields and woods of Willsboro. The hunt continued through the afternoon despite dangerous lightning storms and heavy rains. About two hundred other lawmen continued the search near Dannemora.

In the meantime, more details surfaced about their quarry. Sweat had been a terrible child and earned a life sentence at age twenty-one. Matt was a dangerous man with a history of escapes, as revealed by his estranged son, Nicholas Harris, in an interview with the *Buffalo Daily News*. Some of Harris's comments added to the legend building around Ricky Matt, who, during an attempted escape in Mexico,

> ... made it up to the roof of the prison and got shot in the shoulder.... This guy has bullet holes on his body. He's been shot like nine times. It's like they can't kill him. He showed me the scars [from razor wire] on his forearms from another time he escaped.

If razor wire and bullets hadn't stopped him, what could? As Governor Cuomo would reiterate many times, these were not men to be trifled with.

News updates shed light on the role Joyce Mitchell had played in helping the two criminals escape. The media used her name freely, but police would only say that an as yet unnamed female civilian employee had smuggled certain tools into the prison. The same employee, they said, may have been the intended getaway-car driver who failed to show up. The story was getting juicier by the minute, devouring hours of daily television coverage on a number of channels, and sending social media into a frenzy of news updates, conjecture, and outright fabrications.

DAY 4

On Tuesday, Tobey Mitchell, Joyce's son, appeared on *NBC Nightly News,* confirming that his mother had suffered a panic attack over the weekend and was treated at a Malone hospital. He publicly defended her as not the type of person to mix with such dangerous company as Matt and Sweat, but left the door open to her doing so under threats or duress. Tobey's wife, Paige, took the same stance on social media and in newspaper interviews. The response in general was not sympathetic.

At noon in Dannemora, Vermont Governor Peter Shumlin joined New York Governor Cuomo for a joint press conference, addressing the supposed plan of the escapees to hide out in a cabin in Vermont, New York's neighbor to the east. Lawmen there began methodical searches of private camps and area campgrounds within several miles of Lake Champlain's eastern shore.

Television commentators frequently suggested the escapees might be heading north to Canada, as if it represented salvation of some sort. That notion may have occurred to Matt and Sweat, but for many of those living in close proximity to the international boundary, such a move was laughable and meant almost certain capture. New York and Quebec cooperate on tourism, share a regional economy, and fight a daily battle against smuggling of illegal aliens and countless commercial products. Both sides of the border are manned day and night by customs and border patrol officers from the two countries, and security on the line had increased drastically since the terrorist attacks of September 11, 2001. Besides manned stations and roving patrols, electronic sensors guard portions of the line, detecting any motion. Of all the places Matt and Sweat might go, the U.S. border with Canada represented the highest risk of detection.

DAY 5

On Day 5, a story surfaced about a recent fight at the prison involving thirty to sixty inmates, a battle ended by canisters of tear gas. The normal aftermath included a full prison lockdown and the type of search that would have revealed holes in the cell walls of Matt and Sweat. However, Albany officials reportedly opted for only a partial lockdown because of excessive overtime costs.

After five days of fruitless searching, state police took action on a wider scale in case the inmates had quickly distanced themselves from the prison after escaping. Across Massachusetts, New Jersey, New York, and Pennsylvania, more than fifty digital billboards featured photographs of the escapees, along with pertinent information.

For those living within the search perimeter, there was no denying that life was a mess. Kennedy Road, Trudeau Road, and parts of Route 374, the area's main artery, were closed at different times. Residents received robocalls outlining safety procedures, and advising that anyone leaving their homes could not return without permission from authorities. Many remained, but others left to board with friends or family. The fear of a home invasion by desperate murderers was unsettling, even to confident gun owners. Remaining inside, avoiding windows, and carrying weapons from room to room became a way of life for some. Those on closed roads had no access to school buses, stores, or mail delivery. Their one comfort through it all was the constant presence of police, guarding homes and ensuring everyone's safety.

New energy infused the manhunt when forest rangers at the Mobil Station/Subway Shop (Maplefields) on the eastern outskirts of Dannemora village noticed a path into the woods leading to an area of flattened grass, where a deer—or a fugitive—could have slept. Bloodhounds detected a scent and followed it east of the store, prompting many to believe the chase was on and was about to end. Because the path led southeast towards Cadyville, a small village four miles from Dannemora, lawmen lined Route 3 along the Saranac River, effectively cutting off any escape route south. With excitement building among observers, police sources told Plattsburgh's *Press-Republican*, "Best lead so far. We are close. This could be it."

As more than five hundred lawmen swarmed the wooded areas near Cadyville, reports came in of sightings on Barton Island on the Vermont side of Lake Champlain, and from as far away as Philadelphia. But all the leads, including the one at Cadyville, eventually fizzled. No hard evidence linked to the escapees was found.

More road closures followed as hot spots developed between Cadyville and Dannemora, at times affecting the Buck's Corners, Cringle, Kennedy, Ryan, and Trudeau Roads. Helicopters passed overhead day and night, providing many tense, anxious moments for those huddled in their homes, wondering what would come next.

DAY 6

On Thursday, Saranac Central School, four miles down the valley from the prison, closed until Monday, and roadblocks at many locations caused traffic backups. Things heated up again as the scent originating at Maplefields was pursued once more. Near Cadyville, ground troops, men on ATVs, aviation units, and K-9 teams focused on an area of about five square miles. Shoulder-to-shoulder grid searches were conducted, and at one point flash grenades were employed, but to no obvious effect.

Much of the search so far had been conducted in terrible weather, with rain a daily occurrence for twenty-five of the past thirty days. Downpours exacerbated the bug problem, creating perfect breeding conditions for mosquitoes, a miserable blight on hikers, day or night. During daylight hours, swarms of deer flies helped redefine irritation, while also packing a powerful bite. Against the variety of bugs, insect repellent was only marginally effective.

DAYS 7-8-9

On the morning of Friday, Day 7, intense excitement was generated when two men were reportedly seen jumping a stone fence on the Cringle Road, less than four miles west of Cadyville. Police swarmed the area and lined the roads as on-the-spot accounts lit up social media, presenting live "news" as it happened from the view of the common man.

Two men jumping a fence where hundreds were searching for a pair of escaped murderers? To thousands, perhaps millions, following the story, this had to be it. Clinton County District Attorney Andrew Wylie, appearing on CNN, said, "If this is an actual true lead that the dogs are following on, we hope to be successful in the next twenty-four hours." But the lead wasn't true and nothing was found.

Through it all—rainstorms, thick brush, biting insects, long

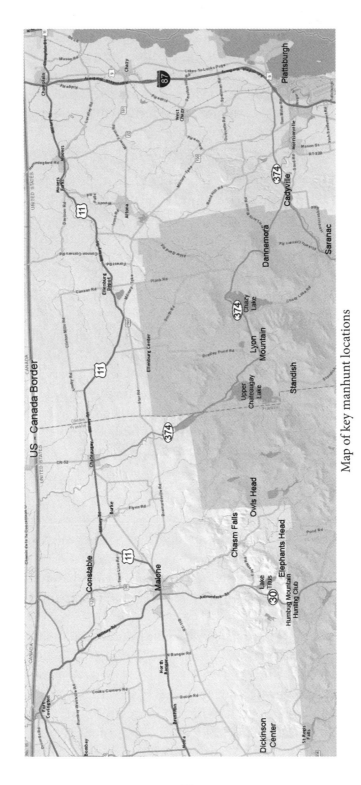

Map of key manhunt locations

shifts, and near exhaustion—eight hundred searchers trudged on, showing little interest in taking a breather. As police spokesperson Jennifer Fleishman told *Press-Republican* Editor Lois Clermont, "Attempts to provide relief have been met with resistance."

Despite the tense moments surrounding the Cringle Road early Friday morning, the biggest news of the day was the arrest of Joyce Mitchell. She had been increasingly cooperative over days of questioning, but the time had come to file official charges. For promoting prison contraband in the first degree, a felony, bail was set at $100,000 cash or $200,000 bond, and for fourth-degree criminal facilitation, a misdemeanor, bail was $10,000 cash or $20,000 bond.

Joyce's ex-husband, Tobey Premo, said he wasn't surprised she had become involved in such a sordid story—their marriage had ended in divorce long ago when she cheated with Lyle. Other family members who previously defended Mitchell swore to stick by her side. Husband Lyle said nothing.

A truly bright side of the story was the reaction of North Country citizens to the manhunt. For most area residents, this was "their" prison, long regarded proudly as inescapable. But now it had been breached, its reputation tarnished, and thousands of lives disrupted. Nearly everyone endured some level of anxiety with killers on the loose, but there was little griping about any of it. The response was unwavering support for the men and women blocking the roads and searching the hillsides. Despite the hassles of multiple roadblocks, people ventured forth, waiting in long lines to deliver food, clothing, raingear, and anything else to sustain the searchers more comfortably. Families of local officers, aware of the difficulties associated with similar deployments, stepped up and filled a need, visiting sites where searchers were housed and providing a range of amenities like toothpaste, shampoo, and dry socks.

Businesses chipped in as well, sending food to headquarters for distribution to outposts. EMTs tended to minor injuries, and the local hospital supplied towels and linens. It was an impressive effort, epitomizing the goodness that drew so many to the North Country as the home of their choosing.

A campaign of moral support also developed, informally launched among a group on Facebook. Blue ribbons began showing up, tied to mailboxes, power poles, and porch posts. When demand caused some Plattsburgh stores to sell out, blue balloons were substituted. No matter what the form, the message was clear: we support you and we're proud of you. It was a wonderful morale booster.

Except for local stations, televised media paid little attention to the demonstrations of support. They were more interested in speculating on what led to the escape—perhaps lax security, guards misbehaving, a deaf administration, or inmate-sympathetic rules generated at the state level by pressure from prison reformers. Such topics were newsworthy, but could hardly hold a candle to what came next, at least in terms of shock value.

Further interviews with Joyce Mitchell verified some terrible truths, many that had flooded the media but remained unofficial until now. It was confirmed that the escape had been in the works for some time, with the two inmates freely exploring the depths of the prison for several weeks prior to breaking out.

As hard as that was to fathom, the real blockbuster followed. While working with them in the tailor shop and developing very close (possibly sexual) relationships with both men, she had decided to leave her husband and run off with the fugitives. Mitchell confirmed not only supplying the tools to effect their escape, but agreeing to drive the getaway car. As if that weren't enough, the scheme also involved Ricky Matt murdering her husband before they left.

DAY 10

On Monday morning, local and national reporters filled the Clinton County courthouse as Joyce Mitchell appeared with a new attorney, Stephen Johnston of Plattsburgh. On behalf of Mitchell, he objected to allowing cameras in the courtroom, but was overruled by City Court Judge Mark Rogers. When questioned about her need for a new attorney, Mitchell offered only yes and no answers.

While Joyce had little to say, Governor Cuomo spoke for her later, saying that Mitchell backed out of the escape plan due to a last-minute case of cold feet, realizing she couldn't go through with it because of feelings for her husband. Turning to the manhunt, Cuomo admitted that with tips coming in from as far away as Mexico, no one knew for certain where the escapees were.

DAYS 11-12

By Tuesday, Day 11 of the manhunt, eight hundred lawmen had addressed more than twelve hundred tips and searched more than ten thousand acres. But the most important number of all was also the most depressing: zero honest-to-goodness leads had been generated.

The following day brought a change in tactics and a reduction of the search team by two hundred corrections officers, who returned to prisons across the state. The focus now was on local patrols and following up on tips, while keeping a close eye on all sites that had already been searched. More than six hundred miles of ATV trails, abandoned railroad beds, and snowmobile trails would be examined during the next several days.

Lyle Mitchell, who had visited Joyce in the Clinton County jail at Plattsburgh earlier in the week, was summoned Thursday to the Franklin County jail for questioning. As yet, no one knew what role he might have played in the escape plan. After three hours of questioning, he left through the back entrance in early afternoon without making a statement. Lyle's attorney had little to say except that his client was not facing charges.

However, Joyce's attorney appeared in a news clip that was widely broadcast on television, stating that Lyle had professed support for her after their meeting on Monday.

Mr. Mitchell was quick to issue his own statement to the contrary, asserting that he remained confused and unsure what to believe after meeting with Joyce, who explained she had gotten in too deep with the inmates. When she tried to back out of the escape plan, they had threatened to have Lyle killed, she said. It was a new twist, something she hadn't told investigators in any of her confessions.

Lyle Mitchell (Facebook)

Was it true, or was it a legal ploy establishing a defense for Joyce's future court case? The suggestion of forced participation made her a victim of sorts. Like the hacksaw blades and chisels, she was portraying herself as just another tool they used to break out of prison.

But Joyce was with them almost to the end, dropping out only at the last minute, which was deeply disturbing to Lyle. Yet he chose not to believe widely reported stories that his wife had sexual relations with one or both of the escapees. He knew both inmates personally, and during the 2014 internal investigation into Joyce's relationship with Sweat, David had assured him nothing was going on.

But now, with his previously quiet, unassuming life turned upside down beyond all imagination, Lyle Mitchell stated publicly he didn't know what to believe anymore.

Days 13-14

Thirteen days after the breakout, repairs were completed to all escape-related damage, including the cell walls, steam pipe, and manhole cover, and the Clinton lockdown, enforced since June 6, was lifted. Under orders from Governor Cuomo, State Inspector General Catherine L. Scott arrived with a team to begin a thorough investigation into the escape.

At the federal level, Stacia Hylton, the U.S. Marshals Service Director, announced that the escapees had been added to an important roster. "The agency's 15 Most Wanted fugitives list is reserved for the worst of the worst. There is no question David Sweat and Richard Matt fall into this category." They offered a $25,000 reward for information leading to the arrest of either man.

Day 15

On Saturday, Day 15, hopes were suddenly elevated with the reported sighting of two men fitting Matt and Sweat's description. Rather than in the vicinity of Dannemora, the location was three hundred fifty miles away in western New York, in the Allegany County town of Friendship. Officers were quickly deployed to pursue what appeared to be a credible incident. Residents of the Friendship area were warned to stay inside, lock their doors, and await the outcome. The focus was on a railroad bed where two men were seen scurrying away from view.

As the search was launched, authorities revealed similar sightings from a week earlier in Steuben County. Two men matching the escapees' description had been seen in a rail yard in Erwin, and the next day at Lindley, apparently bound for the Pennsylvania border. Unfortunately, the incidents weren't reported until a few days after they occurred, making follow-up difficult. Surveillance video was being analyzed, but search teams were not deemed necessary at the time.

It was a different story in Friendship, where helicopters, ATVs, and lawmen with rifles combed the area, reminiscent of recent scenes at Cadyville near the prison. Media coverage was heavy in Rochester and Buffalo to the north, generating excitement and anticipation that the end was near.

In the meantime, back on the home front, the search continued near Dannemora, overshadowed by the news that corrections officer Gene Palmer, 57, a veteran employee of twenty-eight years, had been placed on administrative leave for possible culpability in the escape. Defenders of corrections officers routinely blamed most of Clinton's problems on Albany, meaning Department of Corrections administrators. It was disheartening news that Palmer, a respected member of the corrections family, faced blame and punishment for the ongoing ordeal. The word scapegoat was bandied about, but it soon became clear that Palmer's actions, whether intentionally or unintentionally, had aided the escape effort.

After fifteen days of fruitless searching that extended more than three hundred miles from the prison, doubt had entered the minds of many. Could the fugitives really be somewhere near Dannemora? What if they actually *were* in Mexico, as suggested by some in the media, and even Governor Cuomo. Search leaders recognized the importance of maintaining morale, but in the face of it all, staying upbeat and focused was not an easy task.

With the lack of results near Dannemora, Cadyville, and Friendship, plus the demoralizing news about Gene Palmer, Saturday, June 20, was shaping up as the worst day yet of the manhunt—but that was about to change in dramatic fashion. Amid the ongoing tension, North Country folks craved some sense of normalcy. Typical was a Lyon Mountain couple, John and Nancy Stockwell, who planned a casino visit to celebrate their anniversary, but delayed it for a day so

John could take advantage of the unusually sunny weather during a very wet summer.

His plan was to ride an ATV to Twisted Horn camp near Mountain View, some fifteen miles west of Lyon Mountain, to check on the place and make sure everything was okay. Stockwell (a corrections officer at Malone) and other guards leased Twisted Horn for use during hunting season, just one of many such camps in the area. With known killers on the loose, he grabbed a handgun for safety. His black Lab, Dolly, accompanied him on the long ride.

As the ATV crept slowly along the final stretch, Dolly ran ahead, and when John arrived, she stood at attention in front of the camp. Sensing something was wrong, he looked towards the cabin about fifty feet away and saw movement. Drawing his gun and moving a bit, he caught sight of either the same person or a second intruder, and then shouted for them to come out. The person or persons ran from the back deck and entered the woods in a hurry.

With no cellphone reception, Stockwell rode back to the Wolf Pond Road, returning to the camp forty-five minutes later with two state troopers and a sergeant. To maintain the integrity of the manhunt, the full story of what they found wasn't revealed until days later: a peanut butter jar on the table, a coffee pot, and some bloody socks. Missing from the camp were a wall map and, alarmingly, a .20-gauge shotgun that had been hidden between mattresses.

The intruders had left in a hurry, dropping a water bottle, toothbrush, and a pair of Corcraft-brand, prison-issue underwear in the woods. Inmates and officers alike had access to Corcraft products, so it wasn't certain that Matt and Sweat had been present. But on a simpler level, who else would be running off from a remote camp and dropping a toothbrush? Certainly not kids or local thieves.

To support several roving patrols already active in the area, reinforcements were called in while the physical evidence was rushed to the State Police Forensic Investigative Center in Albany. Aside from the K-9 pursuits between Dannemora and Cadyville, this was the most promising lead yet.

But the prospects were also daunting. Terrain searched elsewhere was like a city park compared to the vast wilderness surrounding Mountain View. If one wanted to disappear, this was the place to do it.

DAY 16

Sunday, June 21, provided the pivotal moment of the entire escape story: confirmation that DNA from items at the cabin matched that of Richard Matt and David Sweat. Two very different stories now converged—the long, frustrating journey of searchers, and the meandering trek of two fugitives.

From the start, nearly all assumptions about the escapees had been wrong. Perhaps most surprising was that every single lead—upwards of two thousand during the past twenty-two days—had been false, and nearly every theory by amateurs and professionals alike had been wrong. Throughout the manhunt, peripheral searches were done in all directions from the prison, but the focus was on areas to the east, where literally thousands of heart-pumping moments were expended in pursuit of a quarry that was never present.

David Sweat later explained that within minutes of exiting the manhole, they came to the realization that Joyce Mitchell had jilted them. Walking west, they ascended the steep stretch of Route 374 beginning at the village limits. About three-tenths of a mile up the hill, they turned left on the Hugh Herron Road, where the transition is unusually stark even by North Country standards, switching suddenly from a main highway to a very rural road—narrow, sparsely populated, and traveled mostly by those who lived there. With a primary mission of simply staying out of sight, it was just what they needed. As long as no one saw them, they were as good as gold.

Traveling mostly at night, they avoided roads, bushwhacking westerly through miles of rugged terrain. It was slow going, covering just twenty-four miles in twelve days before settling in at Twisted Horn for a few days. Sweat described his relationship with Matt as growing more contentious as time dragged on, David wanting to keep moving, but Matt preferring the comforts found at various cabins—booze, food, a little marijuana, and toilets. They disagreed about strategy, convincing Sweat he was better off on his own.

DAYS 17-18-19-20

A few days after they were driven from the cabin by John Stockwell, a noisy fall by Matt that might have exposed their location was the last straw. Sweat ran off, ending one of the most infamous partnerships in Clinton Prison's history. Richard Matt—tired, ill, with no map or compass, and carrying a loaded shotgun—was on his own.

He remained on the move, dropping food wrappers and peppershakers along Webster Street, which extends more than six miles through the countryside south of Malone, and leaving DNA on underwear and an outhouse door handle at a camp on the Fayette Road. The peppershakers were used for sprinkling on their shoes and on certain trail sections to confuse K-9 pursuers—straight out of *Cool Hand Luke*, one of Hollywood's most famous prison movies, where Paul Newman's character used the same tactic. (Experts say it actually doesn't work, for a dog will simply dismiss it or "sniff through it.") As Sweat later mentioned, it also wasn't lost on them that crawling through a pipe to escape Clinton paralleled another prison-movie favorite, *Shawshank Redemption*.

Despite his less-than-optimal physical condition, Ricky Matt could still move quite well, for a day or so later he had traveled three miles south through some rugged terrain and plundered another camp. But he was much less careful than Sweat had been, choosing the Humbug Mountain Hunting Club cabin, which was just eight hundred feet off Route 30. Cabins so close to surfaced roads were visited more often by owners and members, and the location placed him perilously close to any lawmen traveling the main highway. As a desperado's hideout, Humbug shared none of the advantages of Twisted Horn's remote location.

Days 21-22

Humbug is owned by Robert Willett Jr. and Paul Marlow, who live in the area and are both corrections employees. Willett visited the camp on June 26 and thought a bottle of grape gin, partially spilled on a kitchen counter, seemed out of place. He conferred with Marlow, and they called police to report the camp had been burglarized. While the lawmen were interviewing them, five shots rang out nearby.

A passing fifth-wheel camper was struck, but nothing further came of it. The gunfire seemed nonsensical except for the theory that perhaps the fugitives were attempting to hijack a vehicle. Police converged upon the area where the shots were fired and drove about two hundred feet down a trail, stopping about a hundred feet short of an old camper trailer. Smoke emanated from it, and a door swinging back and forth suggested someone had just rushed off. A closer look revealed boots on a nearby trail, and a knife jammed into the ground near the camper.

Tactical team leaders were consulted, and as police lined up along Route 30, coughing was heard in the woods near the Elephant's Head Trail, not far from the Humbug cabin. Helicopters moved in, but were waved off because the noise was drowning out the coughing sounds.

Shortly after, the National Tier One Team of the Border Patrol Tactical Unit (BORTAC) out of El Paso made a dramatic helicopter landing in the middle of Route 30 and began the hunt, pursuing the sounds of someone moving through the woods. Finally, amid the quiet, troopers on the road heard a voice say, "Let me see your hands. Let me see your hands. Drop the gun." The Border Patrol team had spotted Ricky Matt lying in a thicket, his head and shoulders visible. There was no verbal response to the orders, and Matt reportedly turned the shotgun toward his pursuers. Christopher Voss, a combat veteran and former Army Ranger, killed him on the spot with three quick shots to the head. Toxicology results later revealed Matt's blood-alcohol content (BAC) was 0.18, well beyond the legal threshold defining intoxication. Severe skull fractures and brain injuries were the cause of death.

Since Sweat was believed to be nearby, the kill site was secured as quickly as possible, allowing searchers to establish a perimeter, hopefully trapping him within. For two days, a high level of tension endured while lawmen probed the thick woods, but found nothing. No one knew where he was, and for good reason.

Several days earlier, David Sweat had made the smartest move of the manhunt by ditching his partner. Matt, heading south and displaying reckless behavior at hunting camps, had served as the perfect decoy. While lawmen were busy hunting him down and finally killing him, Sweat had moved north, well outside the perimeter established south of Lake Titus.

He was, in fact, fourteen miles north of the search area, but soon realized he hadn't outrun his pursuers. With the belief that Sweat sought some sort of respite by crossing the border into Canada, officers on both sides had been placed on high alert as search teams worked the area south of the line.

DAY 23

Sweat was aware of this, having made it north of Malone to the Constable area, less than two miles from the border. He later claimed to have spent the better part of two days hiding in a tree stand, even observing lawmen directly below his perch. It was possibly an embellishment to the story, intended to make his adversaries appear foolish. If Sweat was being truthful, he was very lucky and the tree stand was a risky gambit. Any North Country hunters on the search team would have certainly looked up, down, and all around as they scoured the woods. Successful hunting, whether for deer or small game, results from exercising keen powers of observation. Had he been detected in a tree, the chase would have ended immediately. On the ground, at least he could have run. Up a tree was equivalent to up the creek without a paddle.

When he finally decided it was time to move, Sweat became careless, later admitting that desperation overcame him as the number of searchers increased in the Constable area. Rather than continue the effective method of moving under cover of darkness, he headed for the border in broad daylight.

At about 3:30 on Sunday afternoon, June 28, while walking in a roadside ditch, he was spotted by Officer Jay Cook of Troop B in Malone. Sweat, dressed in camouflage for reduced visibility in the woods, left the ditch and entered an alfalfa field by about sixty feet. When Cook drove closer and called out, Sweat turned and replied with a casual wave. Cook tried again, but Sweat said only, "I'm good, bro," casually waving him off as if indicating *he* wasn't the guy they were looking for.

The officer knew otherwise and attempted to further the conversation, but Sweat broke into a run. After a quick radio call to report the sighting, Cook gave chase with gun in hand, yelling warnings that he would shoot if necessary. Sweat, with a big head-start, discarded his backpack and continued running. Cook was in good physical condition, but ninety yards away was a tree line, and

Officer Jay Cook (NYS Police)

Sweat was already halfway there. It appeared he was going to reach the woods.

The odds of using a pistol to hit a moving target fifty yards distant would seem to favor the target. But as a former firearms instructor, Cook wasn't your average plinker. Still, it was fifty yards—half a football field!—and with a handgun, not a rifle. Cook fired once and hit paydirt, but Sweat stumbled and kept going. A second shot dropped him in his tracks. So much for the odds.

Both bullets struck his torso, causing injuries that included a collapsed lung. After EMT treatment at the scene, he was taken to the Alice Hyde Hospital in Malone, ending the escape saga right where it had begun twenty-three days earlier, when Joyce Mitchell checked in with a panic attack instead of driving the getaway car.

After a trip to the hospital in Albany, it was determined he was going to be okay—if "okay" is defined as living in a very small, solitary-confinement cell for anywhere from a decade to the rest of his life. Officially it's known as Special Housing, but in prison lingo, it's known as the hole. Which is fitting in Sweat's case. He got there, after all, by crawling out of one.

THE AFTERMATH

When David Sweat was first imprisoned at Clinton many years earlier, he and his mother exchanged letters weekly, a practice that stopped shortly before the 2015 escape. Mrs. Sweat spoke out publicly several times about the grief her son had brought her since his childhood.

> I don't want nothing to do with him. He has tormented me since he was nine years old. Now he's thirty-four and I feel like he's still doing it. He's making my life miserable. My son knows if he woulda come here I would have knocked him out and … had them take him to the jail themselves, cuz that's just

the way I am. I've always done it to him when he's bad…. He always got into trouble, and I would grab him by the ear and take him to the police station…. I'm relieved he was captured alive…. I love him and I miss him. I'm so tired of all the stuff he's put me through. It is all because of him. He is always doing shit that hurts me.

David Sweat's hospital room in Albany was frequented by investigators looking for answers after the manhunt, and New York's infamous escapee was happy to accommodate them, portraying himself as the mastermind behind the breakout. He also maintained that Joyce Mitchell had been a very close friend, but that nothing of a sexual nature had transpired between them.

Mitchell, meanwhile, was facing charges and prison time for her role in the escape. A plea deal was reached, hinging on her confession, which included stunning revelations from statements she had given police on June 7, 8, and 11. Some of it played in the media during the manhunt, but other parts remained confidential until her plea deal was announced.

Confession #1, June 7, 2015

After confirming that she had been charmed by both inmates, Mitchell expanded on previous revelations. Following Sweat's reassignment in September 2014, she had become very close with Richard Matt, texting his daughter many times at his urging. Those contacts were generally personal, discussing paintings he sent to his daughter, and mentioning his frequent back pain.

According to her statement, Mitchell's curiosity led her to check out his paintings on the Internet. Impressed with what she saw, Joyce asked him to paint a portrait of her three children as an anniversary gift for her husband. In exchange, she provided him with a pair of speed-bag boxing gloves, her first gift to him.

Richard Matt was playing her, and evidently playing her well, for all Mitchell could see was that he made her feel special. Emboldened, he asked her in December to procure two pairs of eyeglasses with lights, ostensibly for nighttime painting, but actually for working after dark to prepare the escape route. She purchased them on eBay, using husband Lyle's account without his knowledge.

The painting she had requested wasn't ready by Mitchell's anniversary date, but Matt explained that he had spilled something on it and needed to start over. Said Mitchell, "It was around this same time that I started bringing more stuff in to Inmate Matt. I brought in cookies, brownies, peppers, and other food items," further enhancing their bond.

Matt continued pouring on the charm, and near the end of April 2015, while procuring a machine part from a different tailor shop, the two found themselves temporarily alone. Their relationship entered the physical realm as Matt embraced Mitchell and kissed her passionately.

Said Joyce,

> It startled me. He kissed me with an open mouth kiss. I didn't say anything because I was scared for my husband, who also works in the facility.

Not long after the kiss, Matt asked her for a specialized screwdriver bit, which she supplied without question, purchasing it with her own credit card at "either K-Mart or Walmart."

Then, in early May, when Mitchell and Matt were once again alone in a different shop (she supervised in Tailor 1, but went with him to Tailor 9), their relationship took on a sexual component. Matt told her to perform an act on him, and she complied.

> I was scared. He pulled his [penis] out and I put my mouth on it for maybe a minute. He did not ejaculate. We left and went back to Tailor 1. After this, inmate Matt would come over to my desk, with his big coat on. He asked me to squeeze his [penis]. He had cut a hole in the inside of his coat pocket and had it sticking in his pocket. He told me to pretend I was going to give him a piece of candy and reach into his coat pocket and squeeze his [penis] really hard. This happened two or three times. The only other physical contact I had with inmate Matt was when he kissed me at the bottom of the first set of stairs. He never touched any of my private areas.

At about that time, for the supposed purpose of making picture frames, he asked her to obtain two hacksaw blades, which she purchased at Walmart. She also provided him with batteries for the glasses with lights.

Joyce noticed that Matt was coming to work tired, which he explained was because he was up all night. But a few days later, he told her of the nightly trips into the prison's piping system. Fully a month before their escape, she admittedly knew what they were doing. But, said Joyce, "I was already bringing stuff in to him, and didn't really feel I could stop."

She became privy to details, like the toolbox containing power tools, which Joyce said they used to cut through pipes. At that point Matt involved her in the escape plan. "Inmate Matt told me they were getting out and we were all going to be together. By this he meant Inmate Sweat, him, and I."

On May 12 and for three days thereafter, using information provided by Matt, she tried several times to make phone contact with unknown persons. The calls involved one or more mysterious packages arriving at Alice Hyde Hospital in Malone. She finally did make contact but bungled the call, forgetting to provide her own vehicle information so the delivery person would be able to find her. Joyce then told Matt she was uncomfortable with the subterfuge, so he said not to worry about it. It remains unclear why she was comfortable helping two murderers escape, comfortable planning to leave her job, and comfortable deserting her family, but resisted the comparatively easy task of making telephone calls. On June 4 he told her to try again, but she had no luck making contact.

On Friday, June 5, shortly after arriving at work, Mitchell was approached by Richard Matt. He informed her that the breakout was later that night, and

> ... we were all going to be together, me, him, and Inmate Sweat. He told me to pick them up in Dannemora, near the powerhouse at midnight. The plan was that I was going to leave my husband and meet him there and we were all going to leave together. He did not say where we were going to go. He asked me to bring a shotgun he could saw off.

During work that day, Joyce had an argument with a corrections officer about workers standing around idle, and argued again over the same subject on a telephone call with her supervisor. She and

Lyle stopped for Chinese food after work, across from the Malone state police station. Said Joyce, "When we got home, I was not feeling well. I laid down and was having a panic attack." After a nap, she went with Lyle to the hospital emergency room, and remained there from around 10 p.m. until 2 a.m., when it was decided she should be admitted overnight.

Lyle went home to let their dog out, and when Joyce called him later, it was decided that he would stay home and get some rest. He arrived back at the hospital at about 8 a.m. on June 6. Joyce checked her phone at around 11:30 a.m., discovering "a bunch of messages from my family that the police were looking for me." She went to the police station at about 1 p.m. "I was questioned, but did not tell the whole truth."

Confession #2, June 8, 2015

On June 8 she met with police for a second session, signing a statement that said, "I would like to explain the details of the escape plan Inmate Matt, Inmate Sweat, and I had agreed to." She described buying all the tools that Matt asked for, adding,

> I was aware these tools were being used by Inmate Matt and Inmate Sweat to escape. The day they were supposed to escape, I was supposed to give my husband, Lyle, two pills. These pills were intended to knock Lyle out so I could leave the house. After Lyle was asleep, I was supposed to drive to Dannemora and meet them by the powerhouse. The agreed upon meeting time was midnight. I was to drive my jeep and bring my cell phone, GPS, clothes, a gun, tents, sleeping bags, hatchet, fishing poles, and money from a package I never picked up. [Her statement the day before said she did not know what was in the packages, but now acknowledged it was money.]
>
> After I picked them up, the plan was to drive to my home, and Inmate Matt was going to kill "the glitch." Inmate Matt referred to Lyle as "the glitch." After Inmate Matt killed Lyle, we were going to drive somewhere.

She didn't know the specifics of where they were going except that it was six or seven hours away.

Mitchell went on to explain that she enjoyed the attention

showered upon her by both inmates, along with the prospects of a new life, adding that despite everything she did to help the two men escape, "I really do love my husband and he's the reason I didn't meet Inmate Matt and Inmate Sweat."

That information was in the hands of investigators just two days after the escape, but as police would soon learn, Mitchell was still not telling all that she knew.

CONFESSION #3, JUNE 11, 2015

Three days later, in a third confession, she admitted to withholding information earlier.

> During the course of those statements, I did not provide all the information I knew about how they escaped and the plan the three of us had made. I had previously stated I brought hacksaw blades into the facility and gave them to Inmate Matt. I originally brought in two blades, by bending them in half and putting them in some hamburger, which I then put in the freezer. I brought the frozen hamburger into work and put it in the freezer where I work.

She confirmed that upon Matt's request, Corrections Officer Gene Palmer transported the meat to his cell, and that Matt had added a couple of paint tubes to the package. Had the metal detector been triggered, the tubes would have been the presumed cause. She also confessed to providing Matt with rum and Coca Cola in separate containers, and said he boasted of having shared drinks with Palmer.

Later, in a second meat package, Mitchell provided a punch, two chisels, and hacksaw blades in the same manner, items that made the hamburger noticeably heavier. She brought the package in on a Friday, but noted that Palmer didn't work until Saturday. Matt told her to leave the freezer unlocked and he would ask Palmer to deliver the package. Mitchell assumed he did so, for Matt later confirmed he had received the items.

She then turned to the subject of sedating Lyle.

> Another thing I was not totally truthful about was the pills I was supposed to give to my husband, Lyle. Sometime

around Monday, May 25, 2015, inmate Matt gave me two pills to drug my husband Lyle with. I took the pills home and put them in a drawer, next to the medicine cabinet, in my bathroom.

But when she didn't go through with the plan, the pills were forgotten, said Joyce. As a follow-up, she added,

Sometime this week, since I have been speaking with the police, I took the pills and flushed them down the toilet. I do not know what the pills were and can only describe them as small round pills.

By destroying the evidence, she left no room for prosecution on possible charges of conspiracy or solicitation related to the planning of her husband's murder.

Finally, Mitchell conceded that her physical contact with Matt wasn't the only interaction she shared with the two men.

I had also previously mentioned that I had passed notes to Inmate Matt to give to Inmate Sweat. Some of those notes were of a sexual nature, but I never had any sexual contact with Inmate Sweat, only Inmate Matt. I did take some naked photos of my breasts and vagina and gave them to Inmate Matt to give to Inmate Sweat. I do not know what they did with the photos. This is all I can remember.

The Matt Lauer Interview, September 18, 2015

Perhaps it *was* all she could remember, but with a few months to think things over, Mitchell recalled things a bit differently while speaking with *Today* host Matt Lauer in a prime-time, two-hour television special. In her comments to Lauer were additions and modifications to statements she provided earlier to police. The newer version of events was far more self-serving, emphasizing repeatedly how she had been victimized and had done everything to protect her family.

Joyce's confessions, signed two weeks *before* Richard Matt was shot, confirm that she fulfilled each request for tools and knew they were to help the inmates escape. But on television three months later, with Richard Matt deceased, she added a reason: he had full control of her, and threatened to hurt Lyle if she didn't comply.

Why wasn't that critical, exculpatory information included in any of her three confessions? Lauer didn't ask, and she didn't offer. Had Joyce told police early on that Richard Matt made such dire threats, she would have appeared much less to blame for the escape and manhunt. But Matt was still alive when she made her "confessions," and could have rebutted her claims were he captured. Once he was killed, the obvious best plan from Mitchell's perspective was to blame the dead man.

It was quite the turnaround, from confessing blame as an accomplice to becoming not only a victim, but heroic for standing up to a monster and protecting her husband from harm. As if to cover all her bases, but without substantiation of mental issues, she added that depression played a role in her behavior as well.

It's notable that in seven pages of Mitchell's confessions to police while Richard Matt was still alive, nowhere do the words force, coerce, or threaten appear. But after he was dead, Joyce said of Matt, "He could have beat me, he could have done whatever he wanted to me, but I wasn't going to let him hurt my family." In her signed confessions, she never said he actually threatened to do any of those things—but a dead man makes the perfect scapegoat.

She did say earlier that, after Matt kissed her, "... I was scared for my husband, who also works in the facility." It's not clear if she was scared Matt would hurt him, or scared Lyle might lose his job because she was consorting with inmates. The fact that she eventually planned to run off with them and leave her murdered husband behind suggests she overcame any fears regarding Lyle's safety.

And it's at least interesting that Joyce placed no blame for anything on David Sweat, who not only survived, but claimed to be the mastermind behind the escape. After his capture, Sweat said it was Mitchell's idea to kill Lyle, something she has denied. That aside, Joyce's different statements regarding the pills to knock out her husband were worlds apart. She told Lauer before a national television audience that she took the pills home and flushed them, implying that it was an instant reaction, a no-brainer. Had that been the truth, it would have strongly supported Mitchell's assertion that she never intended to carry the escape plan to fruition.

But in her third confession, Joyce said she received the pills on May 25, and only between police interrogation sessions fifteen to eighteen days later—*after* the escape—did she flush them down the toilet, destroying evidence. The explanation? She forgot about them. It challenges credulity that one would forget pills provided to initiate the murder of a beloved spouse. The modified claims made on television were again self-serving and deeply misleading.

Mitchell's most memorable statement during the broadcast was made as tears flowed uncontrollably: "I'm not the monster that everybody thinks I am. I'm really not. I'm just somebody that got caught up in something she couldn't get out of."

That's a pretty simple explanation for such a convoluted mess, begging several questions. What *do* you call someone who released onto her friends, family, co-workers, and North Country neighbors two brutal, dangerous murderers? What *do* you call someone who abused the public trust, betrayed the corrections system, embarrassed the employees of Clinton Prison, endangered the lives of corrections officers, and for twenty-three days disrupted the lives of more than 100,000 people? What *do* you call someone who dropped on New Yorkers a bill of more than $22 million as the price for her fantasy? What *do* you call someone who held a state job with excellent benefits, who with her husband's income totaled more than $114,000 per year, yet asked Clinton County taxpayers to pay the cost for her defense? What *do* you call someone who began assuming responsibility for the entire mess, but when one of the participants was killed, laid nearly all the blame on him—not on herself, and not on David Sweat, the self-professed mastermind?

What Joyce Mitchell did could be described as frightful, atrocious, egregious, dreadful, and horrendous—all synonyms for monstrous. For her to appear on national television saying, "I'm not the monster people think I am. I'm really not," suggests perhaps she's just lacking a dictionary.

For most of those affected, especially in far northern New York, "I'm just somebody who got caught up in something" hardly cuts it. And with the plea bargain, her sentence was two and a half to seven years. She can still retire with her full state pension intact.

Especially painful to watch was how Mitchell dismissed the entire saga by revealing what she perceived as the inherent lesson:

"You have to learn to not be as, I guess like me, a caring person.... Unless you're going to be someone that's completely coldhearted when you go in there, it's going to happen to someone else."

How better to trivialize what happened than with self-comfort, bolstered by the suggestion that it was all inevitable, and she was just the conduit. That's an insult to the thousands of employees at Clinton Prison over the years who took seriously their mandate to protect the public. The accomplice to an unthinkable horror foisted upon her neighbors tried to publicly recast herself as a victim, and with the simple explanation that she was a caring person.

The reality is that she impacted more than 100,000 victims of her own in various ways. This "caring person" ignored friends, family, and North Country neighbors, instead fulfilling her own emotional needs through two vicious killers that she then helped to escape. As the cause of all hell breaking loose in northern New York for three weeks, wishing "that it hadn't happened" and saying "sorry" doesn't make one a caring person. Rather, it defines a person who got caught.

At her sentencing on September 28, Mitchell sobbed continuously while making a statement to the court.

> I know I should have told someone, but Mr. Matt had others watching and reporting to him about what my husband and I were doing at all times. I was fearful of Mr. Matt threatening to kill my husband.

But she had no proof to back up those claims, which were not made in any of her three confessions. They only began to appear after Richard Matt was confirmed dead and could not contest them. She made no such claims about the surviving murderer, David Sweat.

Judge Kevin Ryan dismissed her claims as not credible, and chastised Mitchell for complaining earlier that the terms of her plea bargain were too harsh. It's a safe bet that, other than perhaps her own family members, not a soul among the other 133,000 residents of Clinton and Franklin Counties would agree with her. The consensus is that she got away with idiotic, irresponsible, and extremely dangerous behavior that cost the taxpayers dearly.

Her sentence was two and a third to seven years and a $5,000 fine for first-degree promoting prison contraband. For fourth-degree criminal facilitation, she was fined $1,000 and given a concurrent jail term of one year, which will result in no extra prison time on that charge. Mitchell is serving her sentence at Bedford Hills Correctional Facility for Women in Westchester County.

The providing of assigned counsel for Mitchell led to a huge public outcry. The county legislature contested the cost, and the Mitchells reimbursed nearly $3,000 to Clinton County.

Gene Palmer, facing charges related to performance of duty, appeared to be in worse trouble than the woman whose collaboration with murderers allowed the escape to happen. He burned and buried paintings received from Richard Matt, and bypassed certain procedures in delivering items to his cell.

Palmer's official statement conceded several violations:

> Matt provided me with elaborate paintings and information on the illegal acts that inmates were committing within the facility. In turn, I provided him with the benefits such as paint, paintbrushes, movement of inmates, hamburger meat, altering of electrical boxes in the catwalk areas. I did not realize at the time that the assistance provided to Matt and Sweat made their escape easier.

His case was certainly weakened by Mitchell's revelations about sneaking paintings out of the prison for her and allegedly drinking with Matt, but Palmer turned down an initial plea offer, opting instead for trial unless a better plea is presented down the road.

Others at Clinton faced possible punishment as well from a close examination of security procedures by the state inspector general, and an FBI investigation into corruption and possible drug trafficking at the prison.

On June 30, 2015, three members of the prison's executive team were suspended. At the top was Clinton Superintendent Steve Racette, with thirty-seven years in corrections. He was also supervising superintendent of the Clinton Hub, encompassing six local correctional facilities: Adirondack at Ray Brook, Altona, Bare Hill at Malone, Clinton at Dannemora, Franklin at Malone, and Upstate at Malone.

Faced with the options of demotion or retirement, Racette chose to retire effective July 31. James O'Gorman, Assistant Commissioner of Correctional Facilities, was appointed to oversee operations at Clinton until the replacement superintendent, Michael Kirkpatrick, was ready to assume control.

The other two suspensions were deputy superintendents Donald Quinn and Stephen Brown. Nine members of the prison's security staff were placed on administrative leave, but no specific charges were revealed to the public. A source inside the prison intimated that security lapses may have occurred when violent incidents went unreported, suggesting that officers may have been avoiding the attendant paperwork, thus allowing unqualified (rebellious and/or disruptive) individuals into special-privilege sections like the Honor Block. The Honor Block itself, considered a valuable corrections tool, was shut down indefinitely following the escape. Among the other security lapses mentioned was sleeping on the job.

Meanwhile, several procedural changes were introduced at the prison, including the reinstatement of tasks that had previously been abandoned. Security gates were added to the tunnels, and inspections of those areas were changed to monthly instead of biannually. A heartbeat-detection device was added to aid in searches. Job boxes in secure gated areas were provided for the storage of contractors' tools. Random bed checks were instituted. The number of cells searched daily for contraband was tripled, and a requirement was added that every cell must be searched every two months. Executive staffing was added to the graveyard shift, and was also required for overseeing head counts and other security procedures.

Just as the hubbub from Mitchell's statements began subsiding, Clinton Prison was again in the headlines because of ongoing investigations. Prisoners Legal Services of New York cited seventy-one claims by inmates that they were beaten in the days and weeks following the escape. Others said they were suddenly removed from their cells in the middle of the night and transferred to other facilities.

Such claims, whether true or false, are common in the history of New York State prisons. After riots, uprisings, or other major events, inmates who are deemed possible witnesses are whisked off to other facilities and placed in solitary confinement until investigators meet with them. There's no contact with the outside world from solitary, and thus no opportunity for testimony to be tainted by inmates consorting with others and "getting their stories straight." The move also precludes any chance of inmates in Clinton attacking suspected snitches, or guards abusing them for speaking out. Some complained of sitting in solitary for extended periods, which would be no surprise from the corrections' perspective. A possible informant might be more inclined to talk as a prelude to escaping such stringent conditions.

From the standpoint of inmates' rights, it's abusive, unfair, and perhaps illegal to lock potential witnesses in solitary, but the likelihood of substantial change resulting from the complaints is not strong. During past crises, after investigations were completed, the general response was that such treatment was necessary, or was an overreaction in the heat of the moment. Outside of prison reformers, citizens historically have supported the notion that avoiding such mistreatment is achieved by one simple rule: abstain from criminal activities that lead to incarceration at Clinton.

As for the charges of physical violence during interrogations in the wake of the escape, there are again two perspectives. One is the violation of prisoners' rights. The other is the urgent need for information when an innocent citizenry is threatened by two dangerous killers on the loose, prisoners who somehow escaped without even cell neighbors just a few feet away being aware anything was afoot. That is not to excuse the physical punishment said to have been dished out, but to instead explain it as it has been explained in the past.

The reality is that there is no place for Pollyanna-type thinking in a maximum-security prison. About ninety percent of Clinton's inmates got there by committing violent felonies. None of them are to be trusted to any great degree, for as the past has proven, they will take advantage. It's exactly what Matt and Sweat did—two convicted murderers who were justifiably denied access to the outside world, but were otherwise provided with relaxed care in a facility known for strict control. Despite those perks, they created an opportunity and took full advantage of it.

It's the same thing "trusties" did in decades past. At Dannemora, trusties were usually "short timers" whose sentences were almost up. Those men were considered the lowest risk for escape, and as such were entrusted to work on highway jobs, lumber jobs, and the prison farm, employment that kept them mostly outside of prison walls. In spite of all the advantages granted to them, more than a hundred trusties escaped in a forty-year period, prompting manhunts that nearly always landed them back in prison within a few days—but no longer as a trusty.

There's no question the 2015 escape was an embarrassment to the corrections system, and particularly to officers at Dannemora. In the aftermath, there was also a question of dominance. It's a scary world inside places like Clinton, and the taunting of officers after the escape was a challenge to their authority. Based on the past, there's little doubt retaliation would follow.

It is, after all, the nature of the beast. Clinton has always been New York State's house of punishment. Perhaps it can't be so by law, but that's what it is. Troublemakers elsewhere have long been warned that misbehavior might result in a transfer to Clinton. It was held over Sing Sing and Auburn inmates' heads one hundred fifty years ago, and was repeated frequently by Governor Cuomo in 2015.

It's generally said within New York's prisons that the inmates run most facilities, but Clinton is run by the guards—for their own safety, and for the public's as well.

Note left by the escapees (Darren McGee, Office of NYS Governor)

Clinton Prison History:
A Culture of Violence

Not everyone with connections to Dannemora was surprised at the claims of brutality in the wake of Matt and Sweat's escape. With a pride admittedly perverse, northern New York residents always pointed to Clinton Prison as inescapable—the toughest, most dangerous prison in a state boasting the likes of Auburn, Sing Sing, and Attica. Clinton was your worst nightmare, the hellhole that prisoners everywhere feared, and for good reason—but for not-so-good reasons, too. Claims of torture and beatings by guards have dogged Clinton throughout its long history.

The violence is nothing to be proud of—but with inescapable, now you've got something. Even Alcatraz had a famous escape story. Clinton had none. In a country where number one is worshiped and all others are losers, hosting the toughest prison in New York at least *felt* like being number one. Then, with the clank of a manhole cover in 2015, inescapable no longer applied.

The widely held notion that no one had ever escaped from inside Clinton's wall was actually incorrect, but no one had done so during the past eighty-seven years of guarding mobsters, rapists, murderers, and serial killers. With that reputation lost, it was time to pick up the pieces, find the escapees, and recapture the past. But was it really worth recapturing?

CLINTON'S ROOTS

Clinton is New York's third-oldest existing prison behind Auburn, founded in 1818, and Sing Sing, originally named Mount

Pleasant, established in 1826 at Ossining—about twenty miles up the Hudson River from New York City, which is where the term "up the river" originated. When those institutions were founded, the Pennsylvania system of incarceration focused on inmate segregation: prisoners slept, ate, and even worked alone in their cells while undergoing regular religious instruction. The goal was contemplation and penitence, adding the word penitentiary to the lexicon.

New York opted for what became known as the Auburn system—solitary confinement, harsh discipline, and strict silence while working in prison shops. Products from in-house industries helped finance prison operations, a plan that proved to be deeply flawed.

Capitalists recognized in the Auburn system a ready source of cheap labor. Multi-year contracts employing low-paid inmates reduced company overhead, allowing depressed retail prices that drastically impacted rival businesses.

Other capitalists—those not employing inmates—called it unfair competition funded by their own taxes that supported public prisons. The argument persisted for decades, joined by a movement of workers and craftsmen referred to collectively as "mechanics," who were injured financially by the use of virtual slave labor to compete against them in the private sector.

As a possible solution, New York's legislature commissioned a study in 1842 on the potential use of state land for mining operations staffed by convict labor. Since the state's natural resources were underutilized, there was room for everyone in mining, which tempered the perception of government competing with business.

Ransom Cook of Saratoga, a furniture maker and inventor (with a partner, he shared a patent on the first electric motor), was tasked with studying the plan's feasibility. Cook's tour of the state's natural resources found promising candidates in the far north, where remoteness carried with it the attractive prospect of prison placement far away from public view. With few roads and rail lines in the region, access from outside was by water on Lake Champlain, fifteen miles east.

In this rough, mountainous region were iron-ore beds, the same mines used to build weapons during the Revolutionary War and every conflict that followed. There was quantity as well as quality here, valuable resources for a country looking to reduce dependency on foreign imports.

Near Lake Champlain's northern extremity lay the town of Plattsburgh, located on the mouth of the Saranac River. Forge fires dotted the riverbanks for nearly thirty miles, fed by numerous mining operations. Nearly four miles upstream from Plattsburgh, and a thousand feet in elevation above the river, were several promising sites yielding quality ore samples. Two of these, the Averill and Skinner ore beds, were chosen by Cook as the best options available.

General John Skinner, owner of the surroundings, had named the area after Dannemora, Sweden, where iron ore of great purity was mined and used for making quality steel. It's somewhat ironic that Skinner applied the name to a site that never panned out as intended, while nine miles due west, at Lyon Mountain, were discovered massive underground deposits of the world's purest iron ore, equal to that of Sweden's Dannemora. Lyon Mountain ore was eventually used in hundreds of products, including Henry Ford's Model T's. Steel made from the same ore, which was successfully mined for a century, comprises many of the cables supporting America's suspension bridges, including the George Washington and the Golden Gate.

Cook presented his recommendations to the state, bolstered by claims that superior-quality ore from Dannemora's mines would produce excellent cast steel, which the United States was importing from England. This reinforced the idea that, unlike other prison industries, Clinton's mines wouldn't compete with domestic manufacturers.

New York's legislature funded Cook's plan, granting him sweeping powers. As the new prison's agent and warden, he could purchase land, water rights, and anything else deemed necessary for building the prison and developing the mines.

The demanding physical work of laying out the prison grounds in five feet of standing snow began in February 1845. By May, wooden pickets twenty-five feet tall, buried four feet in the ground and encompassing about fifteen acres, formed the first outer walls of Clinton Prison.

In early June, Cook visited Sing Sing and left with fifty convicts who became Dannemora's first inmates. They were no strangers to mining, having been chosen from Sing Sing's marble quarries. By month's end, when a similar foray netted Cook forty-four Auburn convicts, he had enough manpower to begin operations at Dannemora.

Among the few buildings already in place was the prison's first cellblock, two hundred fifty feet long. Down the center was a ten-foot-wide path where guards could pace back and forth. Inmates slept on the floor on both sides of the path, their feet to the center of the room, each with an ankle shackled to the floor by a three-foot chain. Four guards monitored the room throughout the night.

By day the men worked at clearing the rugged landscape, adding new buildings, and preparing the mining operations. Manpower reinforcements would gradually arrive, courtesy of a new state mandate that all future convicts from the Third, Fourth, and Fifth Senate Districts, comprising twenty-four counties, would be incarcerated at Clinton Prison.

STATE-SANCTIONED TORTURES

From the very start, Dannemora was a violent place. Underground iron mining by nature was dangerous, involving hand drills driven by sledgehammers, intense manual labor, and dynamite to blast the ore free. Deaths and serious injuries were routine. Worse than the mines were the brutal punishments that awaited inmates who rebelled against prison rules or refused to work.

Prison punishments were rooted in New York State's first experiment with incarceration, which was previously used only for orphans, paupers, the insane, and debtors—in general, those perceived as victims of circumstances, a category that exempted criminals. People who broke the law weren't locked away, but were instead punished harshly, with the intent to dissuade or prevent recidivism.

Previously, under British rule, those convicted faced any number of painful, public, and humiliating consequences: whipping, branding, the pillory, the stocks, cropping of the ears, or death. Under that scheme of dealing with convicts, prisons were unnecessary. Only jails were needed to temporarily house defendants until guilt or innocence was established.

Under New York's new rules, preventing recidivism was accomplished with the death sentence for burglary, counterfeiting, forgery, murder, rape, robbery, and ten other crimes classified as felonies. For other offenses, the goal of punishment was deterrence, accomplished by hard labor or solitary confinement for non-capital crimes—fourteen years for the first violation, and life for a second.

In 1796, New York's penal code was modified, leaving only murder and treason as capital offenses. For other crimes, the penalty was incarceration, which required taxation in order to finance the building of prisons, pay management and guards, and provide inmates with the daily necessities of life.

Incarceration carried with it many vexing problems, some that were battled over for a century. Citizens resented paying taxes to babysit criminals, who sat idle at the public's expense. Putting convicts to work seemed the obvious solution, but when prison products hit the open market, a problem became apparent: the taxes of honest workmen were funding their own competition.

The lofty goals of New York's first prison, Newgate, were inmate education, moral instruction, and prison industries that taught convicts the value of hard work while paying the prison's operational costs. But prison industries needed business managers, while most prisoners needed wardens who strictly enforced rules. Politics muddled the role of prison management, and kinder, trusting treatment of inmates by well-intentioned reformers proved disastrous. At every opportunity, inmates took advantage, and by the time Newgate closed in 1828, prison enforcement had devolved to floggings, beatings, and other drastic punishments.

The Auburn method of incarceration was then adopted. After evolving for another seventeen years, it was applied at New York's newest prison, Clinton. Although the state's other two prisons had decades of violent disciplinary experience by the time Dannemora was built in 1845, it didn't take Clinton long to surpass the competition. Within a few years, the Correctional Association of New York, a watchdog group founded in 1844, cited Clinton as a house of horrors, already equal to Auburn and Sing Sing, where life had been hellish for decades.

From the outset, several state-sanctioned tortures were used in New York's prisons. The methods of punishment favored at Dannemora were the ball and chain, solitary confinement, the cat, the shower bath, electrical shocks, and the dark cell. A brief description of each helps define their potential impact.

The ball-and-chain units were heavy, cumbersome contraptions consisting of twenty-five-pound iron balls shackled to the ankle. Solitary confinement speaks for itself, and usually involved reduced food and water rations. Electrical shocks might be applied fifty to a hundred times to an inmate who was naked and shackled to a wall in a standing position.

The more benign names in the group—the cat, shower bath, and dark cell—suggested little about their inherent brutality.

Ball and chain

An official state report in Clinton's early years referred to the cat as "a time-honored, antiquity-hallowed instrument. ... it maintained its position in the affections of the prison officers." The same report acknowledged death resulting from application of the cat in at least one instance, and probably more.

And just what was the cat? The dreaded cat o'nine tails—a cord about thirty inches long, with the strands separated at one end to create a whip with nine tips. Knots were sometimes tied in the strands to intensify the pain inflicted upon the victim. Twenty strokes delivered up to a hundred eighty lashes.

The rather delicately named shower bath was an insidious form of water torture, partner to modern waterboarding. The bath had many variations, the most common of which found the victim stripped naked, seated, restrained in stocks, and for an arbitrary period decided on by the guard, water was poured upon the head from above. The impact alone soon became mind-numbing, and the water temperature, as close to freezing as possible, was extremely debilitating. Effects from the water bath were often suffered even months later.

Cat o'nine tails

Several of New York's inmates died from the practice. Such deaths were generally attributed to inartful application of the method by inexperienced practitioners.

Auburn Prison's doctor described the physical effects of the shower bath:

> The muscles involuntarily shrink upon the application of cold, but here they must bear the shock in all its severity. The first effect is strangulation to a most painful degree; the next is aberration, convulsions, congestion of the brain, liver, and bowels. The blood receding from the surface is thrown suddenly and violently upon the organs.

Besides the great pain inflicted on the body, New York State annual prison reports described an addition suffering.

> With his head contained in a sort of a trap, the bottom of which encircles his neck so closely that the water will not run off as fast as it can be let on, the water being under the control of the keeper by means of a cord attached to a valve in the bottom of the reservoir.

The result was the same as waterboarding, controlling the flow of water to produce near-drowning, applying more or less water based on the victim's frantic choking and gasping for air.

Shower bath (*Harper's Mag.*, 1858)

The dark cell, or dungeon, was among the most horrifying and dehumanizing punishments ever devised. Insanity and pleas for death were common outcomes. Such accommodations, better known as "the hole," still exist today in New York's prisons, although falling short of the terrible original, which allowed daily rations of just one or two slices of bread and four ounces of water (about one-third of a modern soda can). And that was just the beginning.

In dark cells, a naked or nearly naked inmate starved and thirsted for the first few days, becoming weaker and more miserable as cold from the stone surroundings penetrated the body. No bed or bedding was provided. Dark cells, completely devoid of light, often had no furnishings other than a pail for urine and excrement—the slop bucket. Nature's only mercy was the virtual shutting down of the excretory system, reducing the need to urinate or defecate. But by that time, the bucket's contents exuded a nauseating stench that couldn't escape the room. Those held in dark cells breathed a toxic atmosphere for the duration, or until death brought relief.

In annual reports to the state, Ransom Cook, the warden at Clinton from 1845 through 1847, portrayed himself as a strong believer in treating prisoners humanely, opting for reform through kindness and rewards (whenever possible) rather than punishment. He expounded on the theme at length, which begged the question: if Cook was compassionate, what would a regime led by a stern taskmaster look like? Unfortunately, the answer would come within a few years.

Under Cook in 1846, the prison's second year, Clinton housed 181 inmates. His humane system doled out thirty-two punishments to twenty inmates. The most persistent offenders were Morris Mayhew, John Lincoln, and Joseph Thompson.

Mayhew's four punishments consisted of one, two, and one day in the dungeon, plus three strokes of the cat.

Lincoln was an incorrigible, constantly rebellious no matter what discipline was imposed. For breaking his cell door he received fifteen lashes with the cat. Three weeks later, after an escape attempt, one side of his head was shaved (intended as humiliation), and he dragged around a ball and chain for thirty-one days. A week after that punishment ended, he again tried to escape, which led to solitary confinement in shackles. Lincoln somehow broke free, but was recaptured, strapped into an iron harness for thirty-six hours, and then confined to his cell for twenty-five days. Three months later, he refused to work and was confined to his cell for seven days on bread and water. After another two months, he again refused to work, leading to five days in the dungeon and one day with a ball and chain. Such was life for those who defied Clinton's rules.

As bad as Lincoln's punishments were, Thompson's were

worse. For "insolence and assault on his keeper," Joseph "Gassy Joe" Thompson was kicked, caned, and given a hundred fifty lashes. Then, with his hands manacled to a wall, he received "lightning" (electrical shocks) eighty-five times. Thompson piled up four more punishments later in the year: four days in the dungeon for stealing tools and lying, six days in the dungeon for refusing to obey orders and resisting officers, and two days in the dungeon for beating another inmate. Upon release from the last incident, he immediately beat the inmate again and received another two days in the dungeon.

In 1847, the state outlawed all punishments other than solitary confinement, and prohibited "the infliction of any blows whatever upon any convict, unless in self-defense, or to suppress a revolt or rebellion." But semantics made the new law toothless, for the phrases "unless in self-defense" and "to suppress a revolt or rebellion" were all the prison guards needed—excuses conveniently built into the new law. Even minor resistance by an inmate could constitute rebellion or the need for "self-defense," thus opening the door to arbitrary discipline.

Some guards simply ignored the order outlawing certain punishments, while others seized the opportunity to devise new tortures that weren't specifically prohibited. It was the type of thing that helped Dannemora build a reputation as the state's house of punishment.

The Hooks, hoisted above floor

Clinton and Sing Sing guards improvised with "the hooks"— binding a convict's hands behind his back in irons, which were in turn linked to hooks driven into the wall. By this apparatus, he was then hoisted until his toes barely touched the ground, inducing pain that often proved unbearable, causing the sufferer to faint after a few minutes of agony. Painful, lasting injuries sometimes occurred from being suspended in such a contorted position.

Yoking became another Clinton favorite. The yoke, commonly referred to as the crucifix, was a flat, iron bar five or six feet long, with adjustable shackling mechanisms in the middle for the neck and near each end for the wrists. The arms were extended to their fullest, and the tightened shackles caused the hands to turn purple and swell profusely. But the primary intent of the yoke, which ranged

The Yoke (*Harper's Mag.* 1858)

in weight from thirty-four to forty pounds, was to virtually crush the neck bones. Most inmates collapsed under the pressure and struggled vainly to free themselves, suffering terribly. It was a torture device straight out of the Inquisition, one that Clinton guards used regularly for fifteen years before modifying it to a lighter format.

No matter what the guards did to them, inmates had little recourse, which made the case of John Thurston so unusual. Shortly after the new law of 1847 was passed, George Throop took over as warden at Clinton, and instituted changes—at least on paper.

> The lash and other instruments of torture, which were calculated to inflame the passions and engender hatred and animosity, have been supplanted by methods of correction more consistent with the dictates of humanity.

His stance on violent punishments was similar to that of his predecessor, Ransom Cook. Both men disavowed the use of whipping and other severe punishments as useful or productive. Such measures were reserved for a very small number of prisoners, estimated at three to five percent—men who were rebellious at every opportunity and could never be trusted.

Despite that claim, officers under Throop disciplined inmates as they saw fit. John Thurston faced punishment for speaking to another inmate, which was strictly forbidden. When the guards came for him, Thurston claimed illness and refused to leave his cell. The guards forcibly dragged him to the punishment room, where he ignored an order to strip. Three guards then took him to the floor and tore the clothes from his body. Clad only in shoes and socks and held down by guards, he was struck and kicked repeatedly by Sergeant George Sanborn. Finally, he was forced into the stocks and given the shower bath.

Thurston took the matter to Clinton County court, citing the new law that "prohibited the infliction of any blows whatever upon any convict." Remarkably, the judge found Sergeant Sanborn guilty and fined him $25 for the kicks and punches. Discussion in court was not allowed regarding the stripping and water torture, which were determined to be lawful actions.

Thurston's case was remarkable only for having landed in court. The handling, abuse, and punishments he received were not unusual. By state law, physical discipline was forbidden, except that wardens could allow any methods necessary to obtain the submission of disruptive inmates. In effect it was carte blanche, and wardens were known to run the state's prisons as they saw fit.

Over time, Clinton Warden George Throop developed a strong preference for the water bath as a disciplinary tool, confirming for himself its usefulness over a two-year period. In 1849, his second year on the job, 168 punishments were meted out: 78 shower baths and 79 solitary confinements on bread and water. The following year, Clinton had only fifty punishments, thirty-seven of which were water baths.

Inmates at Dannemora faced a truly dreary existence: heavy manual labor, physical tortures for a variety of reasons (correction, punishment, or outright sadism), extremes of hot and cold inside the cells due to the region's weather, and poor medical treatment.

A daunting affliction in the face of it all was rampant diarrhea, weakening otherwise strong men and reducing their work output. It also worsened conditions in the cellblock, where a slop bucket was one of the few furnishings in each seven-by-four-foot cell, so small that there was no escaping the terrible and unhealthy stench. The problem was at least partially addressed in 1850 by the prison physician, who deduced that a daily diet featuring heavy doses of molasses was the culprit behind the chronic diarrhea.

But Clinton, like other prisons, had ongoing problems related to the system of management imposed by the state. A facility's "personality" was based on who the warden was, and therein lay a problem that endured for decades. Prison warden, like postmaster, was a position filled by the ruling political party. During a Democratic administration, a Democrat filled the top post and awarded keeper and guard positions to his supporters. If a Republican won the next election, a new warden was installed, and replacing current guards with Republican supporters was his prerogative. For that reason, prisons were frequently in a state of turmoil. After a few years of adjusting to the new warden's system, perhaps one that was kindly and less abusive, inmates often faced dramatic changes under strict taskmasters.

That process also had a deeply negative impact on the theory that prisons should be operated as businesses, and that inmate labor was critical for both reforming convicts and paying for prison operations. Replacing management every two or four years was no way to run a business, something that seemed lost on the state legislature. It's no surprise that profits from inmate labor rarely met expectations. The deck was already heavily stacked against success.

The inmate labor program was also a frequent source of violence. When prison industries failed to support the facilities, inmate labor was hired out to the highest bidder. For alert and unscrupulous capitalists, this was a golden opportunity to cut costs and increase profits. At Clinton, Ransom Cook's projections of covering prison expenses through profits from iron mining failed to materialize. In order to compete with Auburn and Sing Sing, Clinton's inmates were advertised in major newspapers as ready and available. Private companies soon employed hundreds of inmates at Dannemora, producing commercial products like shoes, shirts, and hats.

To operate efficiently, inmate labor was closely monitored by the companies. This had an effect on prison discipline in two respects. Severe physical punishment was unacceptable if it prevented an employee from completing assigned daily tasks—for instance, producing two dozen hats or shirts per day. In that regard, company oversight reduced some of the most violent and disabling punishments.

But there was also a strong downside to companies managing

inmate labor. Failure to produce up to daily expectations led to a system of ongoing punishments that were terrifying and painful, but not disabling. Inmates who under-produced were frequently flogged or beaten and sent to their cells for the night, along with shirt or hat materials to work on until they met daily quotas. Through this system of hiring cheap inmate labor and abusing the workforce, companies reaped enormous profits, even as their products competed with those of citizen taxpayers who were funding the prison labor force. For inmates, it was just another evil element of incarceration.

The modification of punishments to accommodate business partners led to a decrease in the use of yoking, the iron collar (a heavy contraption worn around the neck), and the ball and chain, all of which caused missed hours of work. The shower bath remained in heavy use, anywhere from fifty to nearly two hundred times a year, while options like bucking surged significantly at this time.

As described by the Prison Association of New York, bucking consisted of

> ... tying the wrists together, then bringing the hands thus bound down in front of the knees, passing a stout stick between the legs and arms in such a way as to double up and bind the body, as it were, together, and suspending it by placing the ends of the stick upon two chairs. The body is thus brought into a horizontal position, and the head will either hang down or must be held up by the sole force of the muscles of the neck. This is, to say the least of it, a very severe punishment, and if protracted for any great length of time, can scarcely be regarded as otherwise than cruel.

Despite the warnings about its dangers, bucking became very popular with guards at Clinton Prison in the late 1850s, when it was used thirty to seventy times a year under Warden Horace Beach.

Since lengthy punishments in solitary or the dungeon reduced the workforce, Clinton gravitated to a combination of methods that caused pain and humiliation, but left inmates capable of returning to work the next day. Preferred methods at Dannemora were a shower bath followed by one other punishment selected from several options: bucking, shaving half the head, reduced rations, or the iron cap, an uncomfortable hat that was humiliating and very uncomfortable (variations ranged from partial head coverings to full masks). Industrial partners favored such practices that generally kept their low-cost workforce intact.

No matter how wardens, guards, or businessmen characterized the various disciplinary techniques, they were euphemisms that avoided

Bucking (*Harper's Mag.*, 1858)

a simple, one-word description: torture. The Prison Association of New York acknowledged as much in its annual report for 1868:

> The reports of the Prison Association of former years, especially in the earlier periods of its history, abound in relations of deaths, insanity, incurable imbecility, and life-long decrepitude resulting from these tortures.

And yet the same methods persisted in the name of physical abuse and labor production.

In 1869, a new law addressed punishments that had come into use following the restrictions imposed in 1847. Pressured by public opinion following dramatic newspaper reports, the state legislature banned bucking, the crucifix (yoking), and the shower bath. But the same thing that occurred in the wake of 1847's law happened again in 1869: prison guards ignored the restrictions and/or developed new punishments.

At Clinton, use of the dungeon, considered the most destructive of all punishments, increased dramatically after the new law was passed. The dungeon drove many inmates to insanity, which meant transfer to Auburn, where they languished in the asylum section.

Reintroduced at Clinton at this time were the pulleys, the source of horrible agonies—and a favorite tool of certain sadistic guards. The pulleys had first appeared under Warden James Cundall in 1858, and were used by his successor, Benjamin Squire, in 1859. John Parkhurst ran the prison during the 1860s and employed myriad combinations of punishments. The most common element among them was the water bath, applied under his administration approximately 1100

The Pulleys (*Harper's Mag.*, 1858)

times, including 239 times in one year. But the pulleys were a non-factor under Parkhurst.

It was shortly after Warden William Rhodes took the reins at Clinton in early 1869 that the yoke, shower bath, and bucking were declared illegal. Rhodes turned to the pulleys, which he used thirty-six times that year. The process was quick, simple, and brutal. The inmate's wrists were tied individually or bound together with a rope about a quarter inch in diameter, small enough to dig well into the skin when pressure was applied. The rope was connected to overhead pulleys, and the subject was hoisted from the ground, with his full weight bearing on the ropes. Pain was instantaneous, and worsened with every struggle, which by nature was involuntary. The hands turned purple and blue, swelling grotesquely until bursting seemed a certainty. A foot might be strung up to heighten suffering.

Many convicts fainted within two minutes, but to guards at Clinton who had seen others last longer, those men were fakers. With no regard for the outcome, prison men left inmates hanging for fifteen minutes, a half-hour, and in one case, fifty-five minutes. Although it was confirmed that lasting damage almost certainly occurred from any suspension beyond ten minutes, guards at Clinton applied the pulleys on a trial-and-error basis, learning from experience how much suffering an inmate could endure. The same learning curve was applied to other tortures as well—and as it is famously said of doctors, Clinton's guards buried their mistakes.

DANNEMORA BECOMES A DUMPING GROUND

It was by no accident that after opening in 1845, Clinton quickly became New York State's most violent and most feared prison. Initially it was no different from Auburn and Sing Sing, but annual reports of financial losses from Clinton's iron mines prompted moves at the local and state levels to abandon Dannemora as a boondoggle. During the battle for self-preservation, Clinton management countered by offering its inmates to capitalists. Some jumped at the chance for cheap labor, but most found the cost of transporting materials to the prison, and finished goods to market, was simply too high because of the prison's remote location.

At the time, state policy dictated that no inmates could be transferred except when they "may be more profitably employed," which was a major loophole soon to be exploited by New York's other prisons. Auburn and Sing Sing were performing much better than Clinton in terms of industrial output and becoming self-supporting. To bolster and solidify their successful operations, both prisons began requesting transferees from Clinton under logic that was easy to defend: prospects at Auburn and Sing Sing would find the inmates "more profitably employed."

As transfers arrived, overcrowding resulted, while Clinton was reduced to only seventy percent capacity. The solution was a plan that improved business operations at both Sing Sing and Auburn, while ensuring Clinton had little to no chance of ever competing in the labor market. After receiving qualified but idle workers from Clinton, the state's other two prisons began sending transfers north— their sickest, most dangerous, most disruptive inmates, along with the worst escape risks.

This exchange of inmates continued to the benefit of other wardens, while Clinton was saddled with a sorry work force and

Clinton Prison at Dannemora (1869)

Clinton's main gate (1871)

the most desperate, difficult-to-care-for inmates in the state. The prison's remote location also defeated most escape attempts in the early years, adding to Clinton's reputation as the best place to send troublesome prisoners. Those two situations combined to establish New York's northernmost prison as a terror unto itself. Thus developed Dannemora's roots as home to the worst of the worst.

Those same factors help make Clinton the unhealthiest place in the system. Many contagious diseases were brought north among the transferees, whose health worsened because of poorly ventilated buildings, extreme cold, and the prison's barbaric punishments. Days spent in a dark cell, breathing in the toxic fumes of the slop bucket, had an even worse effect on inmates who were already sick. And many were. In 1870, among the maladies treated at Clinton were asthma, bronchitis, chancres, cholera, diarrhea, dyspepsia, dysentery, epilepsy, gonorrhea, hepatitis, pneumonia, retinitis, scabies, scrofula, scurvy, and syphilis. The only prisoners whose health seemed to improve up north were those suffering from tuberculosis.

As time went on, Dannemora became the de facto dumping ground for inmates considered unfit for the prison labor force, a concept the wardens at Sing Sing and Auburn embraced wholeheartedly. In 1877, Sing Sing managed to transfer a number of inmates to Auburn, where they were deemed less than capable employees and not at all helpful to the prison's burgeoning industries. Warden Leonard Welles offered a direct suggestion regarding the misfits, but couched his words as complimentary:

> I would respectfully suggest that such men be transferred to Clinton prison, where, if idle, they could easily be cared for, and where the advantages for the restoration of health are so much better than at Auburn. We have but 1,286 cells, and are

now lodging over 100 men in one room, most of whom are broken down in health.

Welles received support from Auburn's Physician, James Button, who suggested a solution to the needs of

> ... 200 inmates suffering from a range of ailments: lung diseases, crippled, imbeciles mentally or physically, scrofula, urinary afflictions, epileptics, eye diseases, defective vision, heart disease, hernia amounting to disability to labor, aged and generally debilitated, syphilitic, and various forms of diseases.... I think that if this class of invalids could be transferred to the more healthy locality of Clinton prison, their chances of improvement would be greatly increased, and the interests of the State advanced thereby, and I would respectfully recommend that such a transfer be made.

But Dannemora's "healthful" status was questionable, referring mainly to the wonderful effect northern climes had on easing the symptoms of tuberculosis, the world's number one killer. Otherwise, there was little in the way of healthy living at Dannemora. In the words of prison physician Arthur Wolff, Clinton's "want of the facilities for general bathing," was critical, especially considering the excess of dirty work performed daily by the convicts.

> It is inconceivable that a varnish of ... filth is observable on their whole body, not only disgusting to the sight and demonstrably obstructive to exhalation from the skin, but highly dangerous to health. I have no hesitation in averring that the want of general bathing facilities is a fertile source inducing the most favorable condition for the development of disease.

Further exacerbating widespread illness at Clinton, according to Wolff, was the method of laundry and clothing distribution. Poor washing methods left some clothes

> ... saturated with foul and unwholesome emanations. In that state they are distributed without reference as to whom was the previous wearer.... They may have been worn by men who are afflicted with all kinds of transmittable skin diseases.

All those conditions, warned the doctor, were conducive to a health disaster. It was also known by administrators that such unhealthy practices further aggravated an already angry and dangerous lot of criminals, adding peril to the job of controlling them. Rebellious actions, often resulting in injuries to both guards and convicts, were common.

But Clinton, set apart from the state's other prisons by location and the nature of its clientele, was largely left to its own devices. The brutality of life at Dannemora was known locally, but was treated publicly as a political football. Changes, usually minor, came mostly from reformers or investigators who periodically raised questions about violence, abuse, or mismanagement at the prison, which operated in secrecy.

EXPANDING THE PUNISHMENT REPERTOIRE

Such an effort reached newspapers statewide in 1875, with horror stories about the illegal cruelties foisted upon Clinton's inmates by abusive guards. The yoke had been prohibited six years earlier, but creative guards at Dannemora had reduced it from thirty-plus pounds to fourteen, and added several prongs that curled upward for an odd, humiliating look that was imposed upon inmates for days at a time. The alterations resulted in a device that was not specifically prohibited by law, making it a legal punishment that was administered often.

The dungeon remained in frequent use as well, much to the disgust of citizens who read chilling reports that detailed the process. A typical description appeared in the *New York Sun*:

> When a man is confined in the dark cell he is allowed but a gill of water and two ounces of bread per diem, nothing else.... For the first two days he will suffer with hunger and thirst. Then his bowels cease to work. He becomes almost torpid, physically, and is in a great degree unconscious of the process of starvation which is going on. He may endure agony from thirst, for mental conditions may supervene to bring on an intense fever, but he is no longer hungry. The damp, penetrating cold of his stone coffin chills the very marrow in his bones. His whole frame aches from contact with the

unyielding stones, for he has no other bed or seat than the floor. His lungs are poisoned and his stomach sickened by the foul air.

Worst of all to endure are the deathly silence and oppressive darkness. To him it seems as if he were alone in a world immersed in eternal night, and often superstition or a too-vivid imagination peoples thickly with phantom terrors the impenetrable gloom. Again and again prisoners in these hideous dungeons, upon being allowed once more to come forth, have been seen to fall on their knees, weeping with joy at sight of the light.

The cat o'nine tails, a punishing whip and the method of discipline preferred by many past wardens, had long ago been banned. It its place, Clinton now had paddling, a punishment that generated the same wide-eyed fear among inmates as the cat once did, and was credited with driving many men to insanity.

The paddle was a leather-covered board about thirty inches long, with perforations that each raised a blister or angry welt with every blow. The convict was normally stripped naked, his feet strapped down to iron stirrups, and his hands tied with a cord that ran over a pulley. He was stretched to the utmost, which in itself was quite a punishment, but the real torture followed. Completely at the mercy of the keeper, he was spanked across the bare buttocks until submission, but often much further. Punishment was administered in the guard room, which only muffled the screams that still reached the ears of other inmates.

Paddling was guaranteed to break any prisoner: all that was necessary was to keep spanking. Auburn's asylum held many Clinton transferees who had been paddled to near death, destroying their minds and causing terrible injuries, sometimes including profuse bleeding.

In the 1870s, even as the results of investigations into abuse were pending, Clinton guards altered the paddling procedure, causing many convicts to fear the dreaded "black horse." Instead of

Paddling on the Black Horse

stretching inmates with the pulleys, guards lay them stomach-down across a barrel (the so-called black horse), securing their ankles to the floor and their wrists to within a foot of the floor on the opposite side. The guard in charge of punishment slammed the paddle against the inmate's buttocks unmercifully, delivering anywhere from a few blows to more than a hundred. It became one of the most feared and deleterious punishments ever inflicted on Clinton inmates.

The sustained level of violence during its first thirty years firmly established Clinton as the worst of New York's prisons, a status that convict George Appo wouldn't contest. Appo became one of America's most famous criminals, beginning as a teenage pickpocket and developing into a notably versatile crook educated in the prisons of New York. After a stint at Sing Sing, he served time at Dannemora in the late 1870s when he was just eighteen years old. Hardly an impressive physical specimen, Appo stood five feet five inches tall and weighed just 112 pounds, the very definition of frailty. But his youthful, boyish appearance was no guarantee of merciful treatment.

> I was put to work in the laundry at Sing Sing and was subjected to a series of abuses more horrible than any I had ever imagined. From the time I first learned to speak up, to that time, I had said my prayers every day. Prayers were soon abandoned under the treatment I received in prison. It seemed that the more I said them, the worse I was treated. The paddle figured principally in my punishment.
>
> But the treatment I received in Sing Sing was not in it with the torture I got in Clinton prison two years later. On one occasion there, although I was suffering from a gunshot wound in the abdomen, I was beaten until I became unconscious, received a scalp wound, a broken arm, and had four teeth knocked out because I would not do work in the hat shop which was utterly impossible for me to do. After the beating I was thrown into a dungeon. I had offered to do any light work my wound would allow me to perform.... I can name unfortunates who were killed and others who were driven insane by brutal keepers.

By most accounts, Appo's harrowing experience was not out of the ordinary. Although many prisoners reported such treatment, repeated investigations into Clinton's operations rarely yielded results. At times the situation was inexplicable. Official annual reports listing punishments administered at Dannemora featured several methods long banned by law. But the cruelties continued unabated, with discipline resulting from all sorts of infractions. Guards had no tolerance for rule breaking by convicts—but a decidedly high tolerance for themselves breaking the rules of incarceration under which they were employed. Then again, state law as written was one thing: the law as practiced under individual wardens was quite another. The lack of outside oversight led to the emergence of ruthless guards who helped make Clinton legendary for brutality.

PRINCIPAL KEEPER JAMES MOON

At the end of the 1870s, Dannemora had a new warden for three consecutive years. The one constant during that time was the Principal Keeper, James Moon, a man with many years experience in the prison. Keepers controlled different buildings and had guards working under them. As Principal Keeper, Moon ruled over the entire facility's security workers. It was a powerful position with immense responsibility, and set the tone for the prison's guards and other keepers. Under Moon, discipline was harsh, but the complaints of inmate abuse had gone largely unanswered for several years.

The latest investigation into cruelties at Clinton was spawned by an expose published in the *New York Herald* in late 1879. The state's prisons, they said, were guilty of many atrocities, but Dannemora was in a category all its own.

> Sing Sing and Auburn prisons are said to be difficult places for man to reform in, but convicts who have served sentences in the three great criminal retreats of the state say that Clinton Prison is the one place where the unfortunate prisoner leaves all hope behind. Its name is pronounced with a shudder.

The meat of the story came from a recently released Clinton convict who chose to remain anonymous, for good reason—should he ever return there, he might never leave.

> Superintendent Pillsbury does not believe in giving a man a chance to live. His system is silence and hard work. His

policy is to traffic in the labor of the prisoners for the benefit of contractors…. The prisoner is worked like a machine until he sinks from exhaustion or disease; then he is paddled or sent to the dark cell to starve. The New York Tombs or a Tenth Avenue tenement house is a cheerful home compared to that place. It is better to live in a sewer than in Clinton Prison.

He went on to describe rebellious inmates who certainly deserved punishment, but perhaps not to the extent that it was given. Among them was a man named Feeney, serving twenty years for robbery. Using a pipe, he attacked a keeper and was sentenced to an additional ten years—chained to the floor of his cell indefinitely.

Another was Jim Flaherty, who frequently screamed in his cell due to intense pain. Inmates speaking or making noise was forbidden, with no exceptions. After repeated orders for him to stop went unheeded, a guard entered the cell and choked him into silence. Twenty minutes later, the guard returned and found Flaherty had indeed been silenced—permanently. The doctor who had ignored the inmate's complaints performed an autopsy, discovering that Flaherty's screams were due to pain from advanced stomach cancer. For convenience when faced with such incidents, a prison cemetery was located in a swampy section just east of the wall.

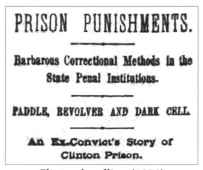

PRISON PUNISHMENTS.

Barbarous Correctional Methods in the State Penal Institutions.

PADDLE, REVOLVER AND DARK CELL.

An Ex-Convict's Story of Clinton Prison.

Clinton headline (1879)

There were more accusations of abuse, but leaders at the state level repeatedly denied all charges. In the *Annual Report of the Superintendent of State Prisons* (published in 1880), Superintendent Louis Pilsbury reiterated that "cruel and unnecessary punishment is forbidden." In the following year's report, Pilsbury added,

During the past year, statements have been widely published, alleging that inhuman punishments were inflicted upon prisoners under my charge. These statements had no higher authority than the assertions of discharged convicts, and were without foundation. Respectable newspapers thoughtlessly gave publicity to these charges which, in spite of constant vigilance, find their way back to the convicts, thus fostering a spirit of insubordination, and adding to the difficulty of maintaining the discipline of the prisons.

The gist of his displeasure was that publishing the inmates' false complaints gave their stories credence, along with the incentive to stir up more trouble. But in reality, the stories had credence because most, if not all, were true, later corroborated by testimony from guards who were present for many inmate beatings and deaths.

Among those to testify before the New York Assembly Committee on Prisons was Elihu Campbell, a former Sing Sing employee who served two years as a keeper at Clinton Prison. His statements provided detailed descriptions of punishment and abuse at Dannemora that left lawmakers shocked and horrified. Everything he reported on the stand, said Campbell, was in the records kept at Clinton Prison, which he had "copied in the dead of night."

There was inmate John Gibbons, who, when faced with paddling, dropped to his knees and begged to be shot instead. He was then shackled into the apparatus and "paddled until the blood came."

The spanking of an inmate named "Hoggy Welch" continued nonstop past the bleeding stage, effectively skinning his buttocks. Welch was then confined in a dungeon, where he set himself on fire and died from his injuries.

Michael Lawless, serving a sentence of twenty-five years, attempted to escape, which at Clinton was dealt with severely. Lawless was paddled and then sent to the dungeon, where he was chained to the floor, emerging ten months later "as a raving lunatic," according to Campbell. The only remaining option was transfer to Auburn's Lunatic Asylum, as it was then known.

The dungeon—stone floors,

Typical cell (*Harper's Mag.*, 1858)

no bed, no bedding, no light, a slop bucket for urine and excrement, no human contact, a slice of bread and a half-cup of water per day—was a medieval torture that Dannemora had mastered. A few days in the dungeon was considered sufficient in most cases, while anything beyond two weeks was excessive. The ten months imposed on Lawless, with disastrous results, was exceeded in the case of William Creswell, another inmate who tried to escape. Creswell, chained to the dungeon floor, was found dead after eleven months of suffering.

When Matthew O'Neil resisted punishment, he was shot in the shoulder and stuffed into a screen cell, even though seven keepers who were present could have easily subdued him without using any weapons. Screen cells were almost identical to the dungeon, except with nail-sized holes in the sides to allow a bit of air and light in.

Thomas Hicks was also lodged in a screen cell, where he was chained to the floor for eight months.

Because Clinton's screen cells allowed small amounts of light to enter, they were considered less harsh than dungeons. Although the difference was slight, screen cells were sometimes used for extended periods, but with dreadful outcomes. Campbell had seen only two inmates survive the punishment intact, and cited another eight convicts who were sent to the lunatic asylum by the screen cell: Joseph Baccari, George Gasser, Peter Guy, John Sinister, George Webster, John Wells, Warren Wood, and Joseph Wright.

GUARD MIKE HAGERTY

Despite so many stories of torture, suffering, and death at the hands of Clinton's guards, the most attention-grabbing story was that of inmate Arthur Hessler, who had suffered near-fatal injuries a decade earlier when the steamboat *Westfield II* exploded near Staten Island. Sixty-six victims died immediately, and another fifty-nine of the injured succumbed later. Hessler required a shoulder brace and a cane to compensate for his disabilities. During a stint at Sing Sing, his confinement papers mentioned Hessler's "high forehead, large nose, and broken back." As a physically deformed inmate, he was unable to perform most of the average work duties.

Following a practice that had become routine, Sing Sing officials sent him to Clinton, where Hessler's introduction to keeper Michael

Hagerty made his past troubles seem like a picnic in comparison.

Hagerty was one of the meanest guards ever to walk the halls of Dannemora's cellblocks. His treatment of Hessler was abysmal by any standard, beginning with depriving him of his brace and cane, without which he could barely stand. When Hessler shook hands with a prison visitor, which was forbidden, he was punished with the yoke, that long-banned contraption that placed heavy weight on the necks of inmates, causing even the strong and fit to struggle. His long-term back and neck injuries made supporting the yoke impossible, and when Hessler collapsed, he was kicked repeatedly by Hagerty. It was just the first of several punishments imposed on him at Clinton, all by the same guard. He was paddled, given the shower bath, and confined to the dungeon. When Hagerty wanted to discipline him further, two other convicts were ordered to drag him from the cell by the heels, his head continuously bouncing off the stone floor as they made their way to the guard room, where punishments were administered. In the dungeon, Hessler was starved into delirium. When he begged desperately for food, Hagerty beat him. Later, for entertainment, he sent a live rat into Hessler's cell and watched him devour it. He was also accused of eating an apple outside of the cell while taunting the nearly starved inmate. Other witnesses said Hagerty made him eat rats and mice on several occasions.

Hessler not only survived the ghastly ordeal, but took the witness stand himself to relate the long list of appalling abuses endured at the hand of Hagerty.

But there was no shame expressed and few denials made by spokesmen for Clinton's team of guards and keepers. Principal Keeper James Moon confirmed that punishments under his leadership included the crown (a heavy, pronged device encircling the neck), dungeons, paddling, and screen cells. Dismissing claims of inmates paddled into insanity, he said none had ever been incapacitated in any way. He had also not chained cell-bound inmates to the floor for any longer than "two or three weeks."

Michael Hagerty himself took the stand, admitting to much of what had been said about him, but without elaborating. Yes, he said, Hessler was dragged by his heels to the guard house; the yoke was used on him despite his infirmities; he was put in a dark cell and starved on bread and water; Hagerty ate an apple near the cell,

The Crown (Harper's Mag., 1858)

but not to aggravate the starving inmate; he told another inmate he might put a rat in Hessler's cell; he saw Hessler eat a rat; and on it went. All the charges—abuses, tortures, excessive use of legal punishments, routine use of prohibited punishments—were confirmed by inmate and guard witnesses, but the state was left wondering how to react.

Opposite the charges were longstanding facts: Clinton housed about five hundred of the sickest, meanest, most dangerous, and escape-hungry criminals in the country, placed under the watchful eye of just forty prison guards. The inmates were forced to work long hours. They lived in tiny, four-by-seven-foot cells. They were forced to maintain silence. They were seldom bathed, lived in filth and vermin, and the food was often terrible. And they suffered horrendous, painful consequences for such violations as raising their eyes to a keeper, making eye contact with other inmates, or speaking. It seemed a wonder there weren't major rebellions every week.

But uprisings led to deaths, injuries, and more punishments. In the deceitful, conniving minds of inmates, there were preferred methods of escaping the violent, depressing atmosphere that permeated Clinton. Nearly every Dannemora inmate had done time elsewhere, providing an awareness that life in Auburn was distinctly better than up north. And within Auburn's walls, the state asylum for insane inmates represented an opportunity. Convict insanity was sometimes attributed to heredity, drunkenness, illness, and head injuries. But the insanity of more than eighty percent of all asylum residents was blamed on prison confinement and masturbation.

Prison confinement was a common reason for transfer from Clinton, particularly those inmates who spent extended periods in screen cells or the dungeon. Paddling also resulted in a number of transfers to the asylum. In those instances, hospital administrators at Auburn faced the task of separating truly insane convicts from the fakers. Oscar-worthy performances by desperate Clinton inmates often foiled their efforts.

The science of the times regarded chronic or excessive masturbation as a sure sign of mental illness, and was deemed common among criminals. For those exhibiting the symptoms, this represented a way out of Dannemora. During a seven-year period, seventeen percent of Auburn's insane male convicts were transferred there due to masturbation. But at Clinton, it remained true that there was no easy way out. Chronic masturbators first received multiple punishments to discourage the activity. An inmate might endure many shower baths, paddlings, and dungeon confinements before a declaration of insanity due to masturbation was issued.

In 1886, two years after the riveting testimony of Hagerty and others, inmates complained publicly that paddling, an illegal method of discipline, continued unabated at Clinton. The principal example cited was inmate John Coffey, who attacked a guard and slashed his face. As punishment, Coffey was taken to the guard room, stripped, shackled to the "black horse," and paddled on the buttocks 152 times. The prison physician then confined him to the hospital for a lengthy recovery period, after which he was sent to a dungeon. The story was expected to incite reformers, but hardly caused a ripple.

In the late 1880s, in fact, punishments at Clinton became more diverse, due in part to major changes in prison labor regulations. With restrictions placed on what items could be produced, and how many convicts could work on certain products, many inmates were left idle. At Clinton, where the population had grown to 775 of the state's most difficult prisoners, as few as a hundred were employed, mostly in the manufacture of shirts, pants, and hats. It was common knowledge among corrections professionals that idleness for nearly seven hundred convicts meant more trouble, more rules violations, and more disciplinary action.

New Methods of Inflicting Pain

Clinton's guards were once again up to the task of devising new methods of punishment not specifically prohibited by law. The Prison Association protested against such abuses, prompting yet another investigation into goings-on at Dannemora.

A state-appointed commission arrived at findings that shocked the public, but hardly caused a stir at Clinton. In the *Annual Report of Clinton Prison* for 1890, it was admitted that pulleys were used for punishment, and the dungeon only as a last resort. The report also said the punishments didn't work for two main reasons:

> Inmates make all sorts of promises of reform, without the slightest intention of adhering to them, whilst the high-tempered and stubborn man will, rather than submit, remain confined until it proves injurious to his health.

But at Clinton, failure was unacceptable. Despite conceding that punishments had not achieved the desired effect, they didn't

Tying up

stop trying. Some guards employed prohibited procedures, while others were innovators, taking a cue from torture aficionados of the Middle Ages. A new favorite at Clinton was named the "tying up" process, which saw widespread use by keepers and guards, even in the warden's presence. Through a trial-and-error period, much to the detriment of those being punished, many variations of "tying up" were developed. The key was adjusting the pain level from intense for short-term, on-the-spot discipline, to slightly lower levels that could be endured for an entire day.

For the guards, the process was quick and simple: a rope attached to an overhead fixture was tied to one wrist of the inmate (handcuffs were optional). Tension was then applied, depending mainly on the operator's whim. The inmate's arm was hoisted overhead as he remained in a standing position, anywhere from flat-footed to on tiptoes. The results—swelling, agony, and fainting—were controlled by the guards for maximum effect. If agony was the goal, fainting was prevented by monitoring the victim and adjusting the rope's tension.

The investigating commission also found that paddling was still used, but with the addition of straps around the convict's thighs and back to hold them more firmly in place. This prevented wriggling that might lessen the paddle's impact. The average number of blows delivered was thirty, but ranged to as high as a hundred in a session and two hundred in a single day. The number prescribed by the state was five to ten. One inmate experienced five paddling sessions within ten days.

But paddling had been largely supplanted at Clinton by the pulleys, which allowed greater control of the pain inflicted. The screen cells and dungeons, otherwise referred to as solitary, also remained in constant use.

The state commission recommended that Clinton's four principal modes of punishment—paddling, pulleys, solitary, and tying up—

> ... should be administered under the most definite restrictions as to severity and admissibility, and should be reserved, on account of their moral effect, for grave offenses and rare occurrences.

At Dannemora, said the state report, they were used several times a week, along with a range of lesser punishments. And despite the law banning guards from striking inmates except during rebellion or escape, the principal keeper had given his men "the power to cuff up prisoners."

The principal keeper at the time was the aforementioned James Moon. In the wake of a state investigation, the *New York Advertiser* published lengthy reports on the exploits of a newspaperman who reportedly was hired as a Clinton Prison guard, working undercover to get the inside story. His subsequent description of Moon was less than laudatory:

> Mr. Moon is the personification of brutality, the worst product of a lumber camp—intemperate, profane, swaggering, and ignorant of any of the amenities of civilization. Barbarous atrocities, which have resulted in physical disability and insanity of the victim, have been charged against him. To many of the shocking crimes committed within the prison

walls, your correspondent, daring one month's service as an inside "guard," has been an eyewitness.

Under Deputy Moon's administration, convicts have been hung by the wrists in shackles for periods of twelve, twenty-four, and thirty consecutive hours; roasted against a laundry heater; frozen, almost naked, in the prison yard; driven to work when scarcely able to walk; worked from daybreak until bedtime; deprived of food and water for four, five, and six consecutive days; beaten in the face with fists and over the head with clubs by keepers while hanging defenseless in the shackles; confined in dungeons for weeks on a daily allowance of one ounce of bread and a gill of water; shackled backward to cell doors for long periods; placed in positions of torture daily for weeks; hung by the wrists with a slender cord of waxed thread until their terrible agonies end in unconsciousness; and subjected to other brutalities and overworked until, as Officer James McGraw remarked, "Two thirds of the loafers are half crazy."

During his one-month stint at Clinton, the reporter came to know Mike Hagerty, the sadistic keeper whose evil deeds were exposed during an investigation at Clinton a decade earlier. It was Hagerty who tormented Arthur Hessler, even watching with bemusement as the starved inmate consumed a live rat released into his cell by Hagerty.

HAGERTY'S CHRISTMAS TREE

Like Moon, Hagerty hadn't lost a step during the past ten years, despite multiple investigations into cruelties at Clinton. It comes as no surprise that Hagerty himself devised the new torture referred to as "tying up," but the original enjoyed a much more colorful name: Hagerty's Christmas Tree, which consisted of a large steam pipe fourteen feet above the floor. Shackles at the end of ropes hanging from the pipe were attached to an inmate's right wrist while he stood on a barrel. When everything was ready, the barrel was kicked away, dropping the victim's feet tantalizingly close to the floor. The pain was described as excruciating, causing unconsciousness usually within two minutes. Hagerty believed many were faking, so he often left them hanging longer, even hours longer, sometimes causing permanent injuries. Victims ranged from teenagers to a fifty-seven-year old who was beaten on the head with Hagerty's cane as he dangled and suffered for thirty-one hours. Those hung from Hagerty's Christmas Tree learned that begging for mercy invariably led to further abuse. But the tree was just one tool in a very diverse toolbox. He was known to beat inmates with his cane and stuff it violently into their mouths. He used his fists on them, and his feet as well.

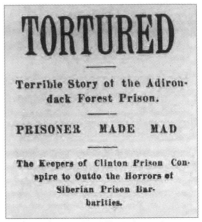

TORTURED

Terrible Story of the Adirondack Forest Prison.

PRISONER MADE MAD

The Keepers of Clinton Prison Conspire to Outdo the Horrors of Siberian Prison Barbarities.

Clinton headline (1891)

But Hagerty was hardly the only abusive guard at Clinton who went to extremes. The undercover reporter also cited Edward Lewis as a brutal keeper. Lewis tested the limits of human endurance in mistreating inmate Arthur Green, who was recovering from serious illness after a long stay in the dungeon—which he had earned by digging a hole through his cell to the roof in an escape attempt. Lewis showed no mercy when Green returned to the laundry work floor, forcing him to stand atop a soapbox "from morning until night," earning him the nickname "Statue of Liberty."

On the fifty-fifth day of punishment, Lewis moved the soapbox closer to the furnace, the sides of which were nearly red-hot, and nailed it to the floor. When the heat grew unbearable, Green tried to move the barrel away from the furnace, but couldn't. Lewis ordered him back onto the soapbox, which the inmate complied with until his clothing began to smoke.

Upon stepping from the box and tearing it from the floor, Green was beaten by Lewis. Principal Keeper Moon then ordered him strung up on Hagerty's Christmas Tree. The reporter described Green's condition twenty-three hours later.

> The scene at the "Tree" presented an awful spectacle. The victim hung to one side, his right arm high above his head, his left arm and shoulder drooping low, the weight of his body straining heavily on his manacled wrist, his face perfectly

76

colorless, his under jaw hanging, his eyes half closed, and the whites rolled upward. His limbs, unable to support him longer, had bent beneath him. His only support was his shackled wrist, and the swollen hand above it was as black as the hand of a negro. He was still conscious; his livid face, distorted with agony, was an indescribable picture of hopeless suffering, and his whole attitude betokened the despair that welcomes death.

Twelve officers, clothed with authority by the great state of New York, were seated near the Tree, eating their dinners with the unconcerned air of men who saw nothing unusual. A guard, to whom such scenes were new, entered the hall to join the mess, and, casting a startled glance at Green, uttered a cry of horror. "What do you think of that, young feller," jeeringly inquired Green's keeper, Edward Lewis, who is the bully of the town and the terror of the prison. On the next day it was rumored that he [Green] had gone mad.

Officer James McGraw admitted depriving inmate James Martin of water for five days for breaking a cup. Two other convicts, Patrick McDonald and Joseph Talent, received the same punishment for trying to escape.

James Gallup, for not meeting the day's work quota, was hung by his wrists until guards believed he had died.

William Thompson, beaten nearly to death by Hagerty's cane, was saved only by two other guards who intervened.

Inmates claimed that several guards were frequently drunk on the job. The violence at Clinton was so extreme that things like being punched, kicked, clubbed, and thrown down stairs were too minor to report. It was, after all, the major punishments that were maiming and killing the inmates.

THE TRAPEZE

Finally, the writer offered a description of the "trapeze" (formerly called the pulleys), taken from inmate accounts and his own experiment of being briefly suspended.

The "trapeze" hangs from the center of the guardroom ceiling, and is the only instrument of torture sanctioned by law for the punishment of convicts. It is a hoisting apparatus, with ropes, pulleys, and hook. On the hook hangs the terrible wax cord. Convicts, when condemned to this torture, stand before the hangman with their hands clasped together until the cord, which is endless, encircles their wrists in a smooth, running noose. The hook is then inserted in the loose end, and the convict is jerked from his feet and hoisted up. The rope is then fastened, and the victim left hanging at the discretion of the deputy or warden.

The Trapeze, used for hanging from thumbs or bound wrists

According to description and personal experience, the scenes at these hangings are awful. Some victims, crazed with pain, struggle frantically, tearing the flesh of their wrists in a shocking manner; some scream, curse, rave, and beg to be killed outright; while others, made insane, perform horrible contortions, and, throwing their bodies high in the air, come down with full force, trying to break the cord, and almost tear their hands off. Their struggles meanwhile cause the cord to cut deeper and deeper, and many suffer in this frightful manner until sheer physical agony renders them unconscious.

The trapeze is one of Mr. Moon's tests in cases of insanity. Convicts who act strangely are brought to the guard room by their keepers as "cranks," and it is on such occasions that Mr. Moon gives that most terrible of orders, "Hang him up; if he ain't crazy we'll make him crazy!"

Supporting the reporter's statements was an additional piece in the *New York Advertiser* in 1891, this one featuring an interview with former Clinton physician Dr. James H. Smith, who had resigned from the state prison system two years earlier. Among the duties of prison physicians was to closely monitor all punishments to ensure the safety of prisoners, who were entrusted to the care of prisons by state law. Smith, a respected surgeon, told of an incident involving the notorious James Moon and Michael Hagerty.

Among the cases of which Dr. Smith gave accounts is that of Henry Lester, who had been punished several times without Dr. Smith's knowledge. The first punishment that was inflicted to the knowledge of the physician was on July 21, 1886. Then he was hung up by the wrists, by means of a waxed cord, for 30 minutes.

While Lester was hanging, Keeper Hagerty taunted him. After he had been suspended for five minutes, Deputy Moon asked him how he enjoyed it. "Oh, he is all right. I will bet the cigars he can hang 30 minutes more without squealing," spoke up Haggerty. "I'll bet the cigars, then, that he hasn't the nerve," spoke up a keeper named Edward Parkhurst.

After this conversation, Lester remained 25 minutes hanging without speaking. In the meantime, the physician had advised Moon to let the man down. Then he insisted upon it.

"You are not going to let the fellow beat us that way, doctor?" asked Moon, who had been enjoying the scene immensely. The doctor simply insisted that the man be put in the cell, and that if on the next day he didn't behave, they might paddle him.

"Oh, we will just paddle him now," said Moon, and Lester was taken down and given 67 blows. For a small offence he was again paddled on August 22. It was discovered from records copied from a book in the warden's office that on July 22 previous to this, Lester had been hung up nine and one-half minutes with waxed cord during the absence of Dr. Smith. During the latter part of August, Lester was confined in a dark cell and kept there until December 11, his condition becoming horrible. He was more like a hog than a human being. It soon became evident that his mind was shattered, and the physician made out papers so that he could be sent to the asylum. The transfer, however, was not made for weeks.

On January 8, Superintendent Baker visited the prison, but before he came, Lester was washed and put in as good condition as possible and placed in one of the ordinary cells. After Baker went away, Lester was put back in one of the dark cells and kept there until the physician threatened to make trouble for Fuller and Moon.

On February 12, Lester was sent to the asylum. A month later, Dr. McDonald, who had charge of the insane convicts, wrote to say that Lester's was a genuine case of insanity. He was also suffering from a deaf ear, which must have been produced by a blow which was given to him while in Clinton prison. Certainly no one will dispute that in the face of such charges, something more will be required to exonerate the prison officials than an "investigation" conducted by Gen. Lathrop, Superintendent of Prisons, on his own hook and after his own methods.

Faced with powerful evidence reported widely in the media, General Austin Lathrop, Superintendent of Prisons in New York State, ordered a full investigation. In the media and among citizens, feelings of déjà vu and great skepticism followed. Clinton Prison, after all, had faced nearly constant investigations during the past twenty-five years for the same issues of brutality. There was nothing to suggest the results this time would be any different.

Committee members appointed to handle the investigation were Secretary Lewis Balch of the State Board of Health; William F. Round of the State Prison Association, and Oscar Craig, President of the Board of Charities. They began probing Clinton's operations, and for several inmates there was at least some relief: fifteen who testified were transferred to Auburn for their own safety, leaving the hellhole of Dannemora behind.

The commission reviewed the past twelve years, taking testimony from current and former Clinton officials, thirty-five

SIBERIA OUTDONE

DANNEMORA A DEN OF HORRORS

Alleged Hideous Brutality of Officials Toward Convicts in the Adirondack Forest Prison.

Clinton headline (1891)

private citizens, thirty-five guards, twenty-three keepers, and forty-six inmates. The results were announced in February 1892:

> The agent and Warden has violated the directions and provisions of the Revised Statues in neglecting to keep a record of entries of complaints, or to provide a means for convicts to make complaint, or to teach the prisoners or direct the labor of the prison.... He has also violated express injunctions and directions of the Revised Statutes in permitting, and in some cases personally ordering punishments of solitary confinement on short allowance, subject to the daily inspection and direction of the prison physician, and in consenting to the direction or continuance of any punishments by inferior officers. He claims on his construction of the statute that these punishments have not been in violation of the law.

The commission then turned its attention to Principal Keeper James Moon and his staff of keepers and guards:

> The principal keeper has violated the law in giving general powers to keepers to stretch and to "cuff-up" prisoners. The punishments have often been severe, sometimes bordering on the line of excessive severity, and in a few cases in evidence crossing such line into cruelty.
>
> Most of the offenses for which severe punishments have been inflicted have been directly or indirectly caused by superior officers in failing to employ competent and properly qualified keepers, perhaps under the pressure of political conditions, and in failing to properly direct the labor of the prisoners, and in failing to provide individual or personal government or treatment of the convicts. Most of the severe punishments appear to have retributive rather than remedial.

The key word was retributive—rather than imposing punishments with the goal of correcting bad behavior, many of Clinton's guards were loose cannons, operating on personal whims, punishing and torturing inmates without any oversight.

After providing explicit descriptions of the corporal punishments meted out at Dannemora, the committee suggested changes that included several firings.

81

> The commission recommends that the following officers should be discharged: Guards Cassidy and McGraw and Keepers McGowan and Conway for having been intoxicated; and Guard Feehan for violation of the rules of the prison and of the provisions of the Penal Code. Keeper Lewis should be reprimanded for excessive profanity and rough conduct. The three modes of punishment should be abolished by the Warden and prohibited by the Superintendent.

Solitary confinement was henceforth to be the primary method of punishment, monitored daily by the prison doctor. Paddling, the pulleys, and tying up—including Hagerty's Christmas Tree—were ended. Notably, though, Michael Hagerty somehow escaped specific mention in the commission's final report.

Change came quickly at Dannemora. Barely a month later, the thirty-five-year-old wooden factory, long deemed a deadly hazard by the inmates, was condemned, and $25,000 was appropriated for a new factory to be built with convict labor. The governor signed a bill providing another $114,000 for adding new workshops and steel cells, and for repairing buildings.

Many of the reforms suggested by the commission were put into practice. For the first time, inmates were allowed to voice complaints personally to the warden. As for future rules violations, each instance was to be reported to the warden, who would hear evidence from both parties. Clinton's chaplain, fully aware of the terrible conditions but declining to rock the boat by speaking up, was replaced. The prison chaplain and physician were two important factors in protecting the safety of inmates while in the care of the state, which was required by law.

By early March 1894, two years after the commission's findings were issued, Dannemora had seen many improvements, including the recent addition of a night school to help combat the low literacy rate among inmates. Could it be that the state's most reviled prison had finally been tamed into something lawful and safe for both the guards and convicts?

Based on Clinton's fifty-year history, the chances of that were slim. And then, with the death of inmate Thomas Lillis on the morning of April 12, the harsh realities of life at Dannemora were driven home once more. Lillis had a terrible record: incarcerated once at Blackwell's Island in New York City, once at Auburn, twice at Sing Sing, and then given five years at Clinton. He had recently been confined to his cell for threatening the life of a fellow inmate, and had attacked Keeper Mike Hagerty with a knife, only to be subdued at gunpoint. An assault on Principal Keeper Ed McKenna would be his last rebellious act. McKenna repelled the attack and used his stick, or cane, to beat Lillis into submission. His wounds were dressed at the prison hospital, where he remained overnight with the expectation of recovery. But in the morning he went downhill fast and died.

An autopsy by Drs. Frank Madden of Plattsburgh and Sydney Mitchell of Saranac found Lillis's heart so diseased that any excitement, like a struggle with the prison guard, would have caused it to fail. None of the blows from McKenna's stick could have caused the death, so the officer was fully exonerated by the doctors' findings, which were considered final.

Six months later, an unrelated incident—in fact, seemingly unrelated to the prison at all—would again shine a light on scandalous behavior at Clinton. It happened at Cadyville, less than five miles east of the prison. On the night of October 5, two men purchased a bottle of whiskey from the hotel operated by George Storrs. A few hours later, Storrs was roused from sleep by loud knocks on his door, but realizing it was the same men looking for more drink, he declined to answer. Loud noises suggested they were stealing his liquor stock, but by the time he reached the whiskey stash, the thieves were gone, along with seven bottles of booze.

The men were wearing regular clothing, but Storrs, a former Clinton employee, recognized their prison-issued underclothing. The next morning he took the train to Dannemora, confronted Deputy Warden McKenna, and identified two men as the culprits. One was the warden's personal driver, and both were part of what was known as the "stable gang." McKenna promised that Warden Walter Thayer would make it right when he returned, and asked Storrs to keep the story quiet.

Details of the incident appeared in local newspapers, with no significance attached to the crime. However, the *New York Herald* followed up with its own secret investigation at Dannemora. The results, published in March 1895, contained claims so spectacular as to seem outrageous and implausible. If only.

STUNNING CHANGE: FROM STRINGENT TO NEGLIGENT

The prison that was so often criticized for excessively strict discipline was now accused of rampant laxity. Inmates, said the newspaper, were allowed to roam freely about the countryside—even with guns in hand! The *Herald*, with remarkable insight, explained why Dannemora's citizens remained mum about what was going on. Group silence is a hard thing to come by, but Dannemora maintained it, and the *Herald* posited why.

"But how about the villagers?" the reader might ask. "Have they not eyes and ears and tongues with which to tell what they see and hear?"

Well, they are neither deaf nor blind nor dumb in a physical sense, but morally they are all three. The reason they are so is this: The village of Dannemora belongs to the prison, it was created by the prison, it lives by it and draws its sustenance from it. There are no manufactures, and the soil is not well adapted for farming, and hence the farming is poor and the farmers are few. All eyes are turned toward the stone walls in hope or in abject submission.

The prison warden is monarch of all he surveys. His word is law. His nod is a command, not only inside, but outside the institution devoted to the so-called "reformation" of criminals. There is scarcely a male in the village who has not been a guard or a keeper or employed in some other capacity, or who does not cherish the ambition to "draw pay" for something or other in connection with the prison.

The smart prison uniform of blue and brass buttons is the great attraction, and nearly every man, hopes to wear it some day. In other villages people talk of church fairs, sociables, and the like; there, the one topic is the prison and its affairs. This has been the case from the very beginning, it is intensely so now, and may be for a long time to come.

Therefore, when anything goes wrong, when there are misdemeanors, corruption, and outrages, these things are religiously kept secret. There is not a man, woman, or child who would breathe them to a stranger. They feel that self-interest demands silence. Walter N. Thayer, the prison warden and agent, has been quoted as saying to the voter: "You must vote for your bread and butter." That is the politics of it.

The charges laid by the *Herald* seemed farfetched, if not outright inconceivable. Inmates dressed in stripes roamed the streets of Dannemora without a keeper in sight. They entered houses to work for private citizens, lounged about the railroad depot, picked up and delivered packages, drove teams of fine horses, and went on hunting and fishing trips, sometimes for several days. Some roamed the streets even at night, and one inmate played piano as entertainment at the fire-company house.

But there was still more. The previous warden, Isaiah Fuller, made do with six or eight horses at his disposal. Warden Thayer had twenty or more fine steeds, housed in stables outside the prison walls. Fifteen to twenty long-term convicts who tended to the horses slept there at night and became widely known as "the stable gang." Their wild escapades were common knowledge in the area, but were protected by the dome of silence maintained in Dannemora village.

Boldness finally led to their undoing, for it was the stable gang that robbed George Storrs' hotel. Despite assurances from the deputy warden, Storrs had not been compensated by the prison for his losses. Frustrated, he spoke freely to *Herald* reporters, as did other citizens who had long been irritated by the relaxed atmosphere surrounding the prison, home to hundreds of convicted felons. Charges were aired that inmates were seen drinking, carousing with women, and sometimes escaped the prison with impunity, perhaps aided by lackluster efforts to pursue them.

The shocking permissiveness was the product of loose administration operating on a stool-pigeon system—inmate informants supplied guards with inside information on drug use, escape plans, hidden weapons, and convicts faking injuries so they wouldn't have to work. In exchange, stoolies received special privileges that in time led to designation as trusties, some of whom were treated essentially as free men, if not family. Reports filtered in of inmates carrying rifles while hunting with boys who were sons of prison employees. Others used prison transportation to consort with prostitutes located a few miles from Dannemora.

It all seemed so outrageous that many chose not to believe. But between the time of Tom Lillis's death in April and the hotel robbery in October, state investigators were already at Dannemora to examine the inmate labor program and determine whether or not punishment reforms from the prior investigation had taken hold.

Accusations from inmates that Lillis had been murdered, and from citizens that dangerous convicts wandered around unhindered, led to a full-blown investigation lasting nearly two years. The closing stages of testimony in early 1896 were particularly revealing. From the witness stand, more than a dozen former guards and dozens of area citizens related their own experiences with unescorted inmates and corrupt practices at the prison.

George Storrs told about the robbery of his hotel by convicts, and of seeing inmates as far away as West Chazy, accompanied only by the warden's son. Several local residents bore witness to inmates on hunting trips, fishing excursions, and berry picking. A former guard said one inmate had a key to the prison armory, where he often slept. Several teenagers told of delivering whisky to convicts, going hunting and fishing with them, and playing baseball with them outside of prison walls. Many witnesses reported the spectacle of inmates tobogganing on snow-covered hills around the village. Several told of prisoners in street clothes, shopping in local stores. Dannemora's chaplain confirmed that convicts routinely worked at the homes of several prison administrators and guards, including Michael Hagerty. Several witnesses spoke of wheelbarrows, picks, and shovels taken from the prison several miles to the Chazy Lake Hotel, which was partially owned by Warden Thayer and John Powers, the prison's purchasing agent. Convicts, sometimes twenty

Clinton Prison in 1892, a few years after completion of the new wall

at a time, were seen at the same hotel, some reportedly staying there for up to two weeks. Local businessmen testified that inmates were selling prison supplies for profit.

Investigators, aware that inmates had provided truthful information that was confirmed through citizen testimony, pursued accusations of a cover-up in the death of convict Tom Lillis, buried more than two years earlier. Dr. Frank Madden had led the autopsy on Lillis, assisted by Dr. Sydney Mitchell of Saranac and Prison Physician Julius Ransom, both of whom concurred with Madden's findings that Lillis had some slight scalp wounds, no fractures, severe disease of the heart, and "his internal organs were in such a condition that excitement would cause death."

Prosecutors called Dr. Madden to the stand and elicited from him testimony that, despite his attempts to be elusive, confirmed that a cover-up had taken place, and that Lillis had been beaten to death by guard Ed McKenna.

> ATTORNEY WHEELER: Were you not told that Lillis had been struck over the head several times with a billy?
> DR. MADDEN: Yes. I was told that he had an altercation with a keeper and had been struck over the head with a short billy. I was told that the wounds were recent, having been received the day before.
> ATTORNEY WHEELER: Have you not known men to live for years with a heart in worse condition than Lillis?
> DR. MADDEN: Oh, yes.
> ATTORNEY WHEELER: You are not able to swear positively that he died from heart disease?
> DR. MADDEN: No, sir.
> ATTORNEY WHEELER: Then you cannot say that he did not die from the blows up in the head?
> DR. MADDEN: Without the blows he would not have died.
> COMMISSIONER BROWN: The question is not what he might have died from, but of what he did die from.
> ATTORNEY WHEELER: Did Mr. Mitchell and yourself come to the conclusion that Lillis died of heart disease?[Objected to.]
> ATTORNEY WHEELER: In your judgment, what was the cause of death?
> DR. MADDEN: It was induced by the violent altercation and assault.

At issue following the lengthy investigation were charges that a lack of oversight by Austin Lathrop, superintendent of New York State prisons, had allowed abominations at Clinton to occur. In other words, he hadn't done his job.

The special senate committee handling the inquiry ruled that Lillis was clubbed to death by McKenna, and that the coroner's verdict of justifiable homicide was not justified; that prison inmates had been allowed unwarranted and dangerous freedoms; that the absence of discipline enabled escapes, burglaries, and other negative results; that prison officials had purchased supplies at excessive prices and pocketed profits; and that officials had used state property for private gain. It was recommended that Superintendent Lathrop be removed from his position. The findings were sent to the governor, who was expected to announce his decision within a couple of months.

Warden Thayer denied everything. No prison supplies were sold, he said, and the only inmate allowed outside at night was one who monitored the wall lights.

> When I came here, the prison was demoralized owing to the charges of cruelty against the management. I changed all that…. It was necessary to punish the disobedient, and the punishments ran from five to ten a day—dark cells and bread and water…. Now I am getting thirty-three percent more work than was ever got before, and have no punishments.

But critics pointed out that most inmates at Clinton worked seven hours a day at sewing clothing or making toys—nothing remotely resembling the hard-labor sentence imposed on felons.

Two weeks after the investigation wrapped up, another headline-grabbing incident took place at Dannemora. Private citizen Peter Keenan, accompanying a friend seeking treatment at the prison hospital, had an altercation with the warden's private secretary, Edward Coughlin, and Principal Keeper McKenna. Keenan was badly beaten, handed over to keeper Mike Hagerty, and later taken to court on charges of disorderly conduct, which were dismissed.

But public outcry and media attention caused Lathrop to order another investigation. Having little faith in the outcome, the *Plattsburgh Daily Press* commented, "Prison 'whitewashing' investigations are so common and so well known that nothing else is to be expected of this case."

Ten days after the assault, the warden accepted the resignations of both McKenna and Coughlin. Five days later, Powers, the prison's purchasing agent, also resigned. He wasn't involved in the Keenan incident, but faced possible discipline related to the larger investigation, including questionable purchases on behalf of the prison, and issues at the Chazy Lake Hotel.

His departure spawned speculation that Powers was being made the scapegoat to atone for widespread misdeeds at the prison, and that certainly seemed to be the case. In October, Governor Levi Morton absolved Lathrop of guilt and dismissed the charges. In a reversal of "the buck stops here" policy, the irregularities at Clinton were blamed on underlings acting without the knowledge of prison officials. Reforms were suggested, but all the testimony about laws and rules broken was for naught. No one else was disciplined.

Less than two years later, in January 1898, Dannemora lost two long-timers infamous for the extreme punishments they dished out for decades. Deputy Warden Jim Moon retired after more than twenty-two years, and keeper Mike Hagerty died of pneumonia after twenty-nine years at the prison. They both lasted just long enough to see the shift from seven years of lax administration back to the more familiar system of strict discipline. Once again, Clinton's guards were running the prison.

CLINTON: OFFICIAL HOME TO THE WORST OF THE WORST

In the late 1890s, New York's prison system was modified by two important new laws. One stipulated that products from inmate labor could only be distributed to state institutions like asylums, normal schools, penitentiary hospitals, and other prisons. Output at Dannemora included boots, clothing, cotton yarn and cloth, knit goods, mats, shoes, tinware, and woodenware.

The second law further cemented Clinton's status as home to the worst criminals in the state. A tiered system was devised for classifying convicts: Class A was convicts serving time for their first felony; Class B was for two-time felons; Class C was for three or more felony convictions; and Class D was for incorrigibles. The plan was to house Class A criminals at Sing Sing, Class B at Auburn, and Class C and D—the worst of all offenders—at Clinton, which would also handle insane prisoners and tuberculosis sufferers. Prison capacities prevented the perfect separation of classes, but the new plan reduced the mixing of first-time offenders with hardened felons and lifers. It also placed more dangerous criminals at Clinton than any other prison in the country.

There were plenty of tough men at Dannemora, but the unusual inmate mix presented control problems. The prison's population fluctuated between eight hundred fifty and eleven hundred. Thirty-nine inmates were in for life, and ninety-five others were long-termers, serving sentences from fifteen to sixty-five years. At the opposite end of the spectrum were more than a hundred teenagers. Keepers knew the mix of young and old could lead to trouble, but no one foresaw the issue that was about to explode.

THE OPIUM SCANDAL

Illegal substances were an issue in most prisons, and alcohol was often the drug of choice. But in 1903, scandal hit Clinton again with an epidemic of opium abuse. The problem had been present for several years, operating under a scheme of suppliers, dealers, and users, many of them younger inmates.

The extensive trafficking system worked efficiently until it was uncovered, quite by accident. As a trusty, inmate "Buck" Blake was allowed to roam about inside the prison, his main employment being to care for the warden's garden in summer and greenhouse in winter. He was noticed going from cell to cell, giving the appearance of peddling something, which was strictly forbidden at Clinton. As punishment, a guard sent him to the dungeon, where he might have spent a few days—but within hours Blake was writhing in apparent agony. When guards approached, he begged for opium, and in desperation tried to work a deal, telling them where to find his stashes. They discovered several pounds of the drug hidden in the prison barn—and more of it buried in the warden's conservatory!

Blake was taken to the prison hospital for treatment, which guards assumed would bring the case to a close. But within hours, several more inmates joined Blake with identical symptoms. The pace continued, and within days the prison hospital had taken on the appearance of an asylum. Questioned further, Blake admitted he was a dealer of opium as well as a user, and the ill inmates were his addicted customers.

Even as Clinton scandals went, this was a big one. State Superintendent of Prisons Cornelius Collins revealed that large quantities of the drug had been smuggled into the prison, creating an inmate population of opium fiends. Guards, keepers, and hospital attendants dealing with problem were overwhelmed.

A deeper investigation uncovered four distinct webs of opium distribution within the prison. Hundreds of inmates were involved, and likely some Dannemora personnel as well. There were agents and subagents reselling among the convicts, and supplies were sometimes withheld as punishment, sending users into the torment of withdrawal. Investigators also uncovered outside sources of money that was funneled inside to the prisoners, a sort of loan program catering to drug buyers.

One of the opium suppliers, hospital attendant Charles Kane, admitted smuggling large quantities to an inmate who packed it into pill form before selling it to other prisoners. Kane was fired, and when the investigation ended, Superintendent Collins visited Dannemora to deliver punishments. Unlike past Clinton scandals involving excessive violence, this one had real consequences. One keeper was suspended indefinitely, a guard and keeper were fired, and a guard, keeper, and storekeeper were allowed to resign. Among those resigning was Edward Lewis, known for delivering punishments equal to those of his old friend, Mike Hagerty.

No one could dispute the disciplinary action, for Collins had gone to unusual lengths to obtain the facts. Pinkerton detectives had been brought into Clinton, posing as inmates to learn about dope dealings from the inside. The results from their undercover work were incontestable and led to a major cleanup at Dannemora.

Changing Times, but Old Habits Die Hard

In early 1910, the state announced that the dungeon, a perennial favorite of guards and keepers at Clinton, would be eliminated. Similar accommodations at Auburn and Clinton would remain in use until blocks of new isolation cells were built. Instead of "the cooler," as Clinton inmates called it—total darkness in a four-by-seven cell, no furnishings other than a slop bucket, limited rations of bread and water, and no human contact—the new cellblocks featured accommodations measuring seven by eight feet, an attached exercise yard the same size, plus work available inside the cell and a garden in the exercise yard. It didn't sound like much, but was a spectacular improvement over the dreaded dungeon, considered by many the worst punishment of all.

Clinton, now sixty-five years old, and by design and law the state's most violent and dangerous facility, had seen many improvements over the earlier days of unchecked tortures. In 1910, the Prison Department of the State of New York issued *Handbook of Information*, which included punishments and humiliations that had recently been banned. Gone by law were punching, kicking, caning, the shower bath, the crown, bucking, the crucifix, paddling, the pulleys, tying up, the hooks, the ball and chain, and innovations like Hagerty's Christmas Tree. Shaved heads and striped clothing were no longer allowed. Indiscriminate distribution of clothing had been abandoned in favored of numbered apparel. The despised lockstep (hand on the shoulder of the inmate in front, foot close behind the same inmate's foot, and all heads turned in the direction of the opposite shoulder and foot) had been replaced by military-style marching. Compared to the days of old, Clinton was beginning to seem bearable. At least it looked that way on the outside.

But state and local officials knew and accepted that Clinton was different on the inside. Disciplinarians at Dannemora were allowed latitude because of unique circumstances. Housed within were rapists, murderers, and lifers, just like any other prison. But what Clinton also had were all three- and four-time felons, plus the worst disciplinary problems that Sing Sing and Auburn couldn't handle.

State policy was to let Clinton men run the prison, and to investigate when complaints were made—but it didn't mean big changes were on the horizon. During the prison's first sixty-five years, investigations were frequent but the results were limited. Those in charge of oversight often agreed that the situation was lamentable, but no one had solutions to incorrigibles other than doing whatever it took to induce submission. There are documented cases where

Clinton inmates in the long-despised lockstep formation (1874)

nothing worked, and punishments continued for years, but men refused to submit.

In 1913, violence at Clinton again dominated the headlines with a story that in some disturbing ways paralleled that of Tom Lillis, who was clubbed to death by a guard nineteen years earlier, only to be passed off as a death from heart trouble. The victim this time was John Heffernan, whose record in the prison was clean enough to earn him trusty status and a clerk position in the prison offices.

It started innocently enough when an informant told Heffernan that inmate Emil Schiff had spread stories about him. Heffernan argued with Schiff, but refused to tell guards the identity of the informant, and was confined to his cell. A guard arrived later, taking him to see Principal Keeper Thomas Coultry.

What happened next varied in the retelling by the two survivors who were in the room: Heffernan hit Coultry, who then struck him with a cane; or Heffernan hit Coultry, and the other guard threw Heffernan to the floor. The differing stories created uncertainty that provided legal protection for the guards, because Heffernan was afterward confined to a dungeon (banned by the state several years earlier), where two days later he was found dead. If he expired from injuries suffered during the confrontation, state investigators couldn't determine fault because there was no consensus between the two surviving witnesses. Each said the other was to blame.

That point became moot when a prison physician, Walter Thayer Jr., ruled that death was achieved by hanging.

The story might have been swept under the rug, but Governor Sulzer's own inspector at Clinton said the coroner's inquest seemed lackluster, and a number of inmates insisted Heffernan was beaten to death with a cane. The governor ordered all information turned over to the county district attorney for a thorough investigation, which included exhumation of the body.

But there was one major problem: Heffernan had been found dead in his cell ten months earlier, which caused a stir only because the discovery was made during a visit by the previous governor, John Dix. The investigation nearly a year later was left with no physical evidence at the death site, and was guided only by the prison's internal documents. The prison physician had recorded Heffernan's injuries as self-inflicted, and ruled his death a suicide by hanging. The DA concurred—despite written reports that blood was found on a plank in Heffernan's cell and spattered on the wall, which suggested a violent beating had occurred.

> I am of the opinion that Heffernan died by hanging. The history of the case shows that the injuries to the vertebrae were caused in this way: that the contusion of the scalp was due to the fact that he beat his head against the wall of his cell.

For good measure, the DA went a step further and said that inmate lies had caused an unnecessary uproar over the prisoner's death.

> There is absolutely no motive shown for the commission of any criminal assault on Heffernan—all of the evidence is to the contrary. It appears to me that it is probable that some witnesses testifying before Mr. Commissioner Blake committed perjury, which, in my opinion, should be investigated at the fall term of the Supreme Court in this county.

Just two years later, Clinton was again the subject of a very public investigation for violent and excessive punishments that were said to be causing insanity. The charges originated with a recently release convict who said frequent suicides resulted from horrible treatment, and that even speaking led to severe punishment.

Coincidental with the inmate's claims was the "Golden Rule" method of reform instituted by Warden Thomas Osborne of Sing Sing, based on the theory that kindness, rewards, and privileges were the key to successful prisons. Warden John Trombly of Clinton countered that strict rules, meaningful punishments, and head-to-head dominance over inmates was the best method of keeping them in line.

In June 1915, State Superintendent John Riley and a team of investigators met with Trombly at Clinton, addressing the charges of cruelty to inmates and urging that he consider changing to the Golden Rule system. During the meeting, an inmate scuffle near the office window erupted into a brief melee as one convict attacked another, slamming an iron bucket into his head before stabbing him. He then turned towards guards and other inmates, daring them to approach. More than a half-dozen men took the man down and beat him into submission. As reported in the *New York Herald*, Commissioner Riley commented,

> That, gentlemen, is what we have to contend with in Dannemora. Maybe the Golden Rule brotherhood will do in Sing Sing, but please don't give it to us.

For seven hours the commissioners questioned Clinton officials over supposed bookkeeping issues and the brutal treatment of inmates. The accusing ex-convict, Alexander Fischer, testified to Clinton's "chamber of horrors" in what he called the "dreadful solitaries." He described a fight between inmates that resulted in guards kicking and beating the instigator to insanity. He spoke of inmates Forsbrey, Dutch, and Soapbox Hardy, held for months and even years in dungeons, which had supposedly been abolished by law eighteen months earlier.

The commission listened wide-eyed to the damning evidence before calling Warden Trombly, Principal Keeper Tom Coultry, and Clinton Physician Julius Ransom to task over the disgraceful treatment of inmates placed in their care. A barrage of questions followed, but the answers they received were not at all what the commission expected.

Dr. Ransom was asked if the dungeon (the solitary dark cell) weren't enough punishment without the inmate receiving minimal rations of bread and water.

> COMMISSIONER WADE: I regard hunger and thirst as elements of human torture.
> DR. RANSOM: This is not torture. People need less water than you think.
> COMMISSIONER WADE: Maybe this isn't torture, but isn't it barbarous?
> DR. RANSOM: I don't say I believe in it, but the law says that prisoners undergoing punishment should be on short rations.
> COMMISSIONER WADE: Isn't this suffering?
> DR. RANSOM: I wouldn't say so. It is privation. I don't like the word suffering.
> COMMISSIONER WADE: Well, isn't isolation, with a bed, sufficient punishment without keeping a prisoner on starvation rations and without what water he wants to drink?
> DR. RANSOM: If you don't deprive some of these prisoners, you can never cure them. Dark cells are not worse torture than anything else.
> COMMISSIONER WADE: I think this is a survival of the tortures of medieval days.

Commission members were further shocked to learn that since the new isolation cells were added two years prior, some inmates had been permanent residents there. The cells had been intended only for special punishments.

> WARDEN TROMBLY: One man has been there two years, ever since they were built, and will probably always remain there.
> COMMISSIONER WEINSTOCK: Who is this man who has always been in the isolation cell?
> WARDEN TROMBLY: He is known as Dutch. He is a bad man all through, and we wouldn't think of keeping him anywhere else. He can get out of any cell that was ever built.
> COMMISSIONER WEINSTOCK: Do you mean he could get out of the isolation cell?
> WARDEN TROMBLY: The cell was never made that he couldn't get out of. No one knows how he does it, but he does. Leave him unwatched overnight and he isn't there. Either the bars

are taken off or the door unhinged, or something.... It was only a short time ago that we discovered he had a scheme all hatched out and ready to put into execution that day to hold up all the keepers and let out the whole prison. The golden rule would be no medicine for him. He'll stay in the isolation cells as long as I have anything to do with it.

The commission said they would personally visit Dutch the next day, to which Trombly replied, "We will show you some other prisoners that the people know little of." They met Dutch, Forsbrey, and others, besides interviewing dozens of inmates who attested to beatings, deprivation, tortures, and unwarranted deaths. About the only positive mentioned during the investigation was that the prison was kept remarkably clean.

But in the end, the commission declined to suggest that Clinton adopt Osborne's "Golden Brotherhood" method of operating:

We find that a considerable proportion of the inmates of Clinton Prison are transferred from Sing Sing, Auburn, and Great Meadow prisons for misconduct, and that Clinton Prison is the disciplinary institution of the prison system, and possibly the same degree of privileges cannot be accorded to the inmates as in the other prisons.

Their recommendations included more yard recreation time, talking allowed during meals, more bread and two quarts of water daily in the isolation cells, and a padded cell for violent inmates.

John Trombly remained adamant that the incorrigibles sent to Dannemora (ironically, some of them shipped there by reformer Osborne) were best controlled and managed by uncompromising discipline. It's no wonder he was known in the system as "Iron Fist."

A year later, Osborne retired from Sing Sing and resumed his attacks on the brutalities of daily life at Clinton, offering his own Osborne System as a much better alternative. He cited two inmates, Marquis Curtis and Robert Minfield, as examples of convicts who, in violation of both state law and morals, had been abused terribly at Clinton and confined in isolation cells indefinitely.

What Osborne failed to mention was that Sing Sing had been unable to control either man before sending them to Dannemora. At

Clinton, both men had attempted several escapes involving knives, guns, and dynamite. During those attempts, several guards were shot and one was maimed for life. Another was struck in the head with a hammer. These were the most dangerous of men, and Warden Trombly made no apologies for how they were treated.

Other wardens came to Trombly's defense, stating emphatically that they could not manage their own facilities without Clinton as the "control prison" of the state, a potential punishment used to threaten inmates and modify their behavior. "Straighten up or you'll go to Dannemora" was a widely used and effective deterrent.

In the words of Great Meadow Warden William Homer:

> When I call a man into my office at Great Meadow and say, "If you do that again you'll go to Clinton," it does more to control not only him but others to whom the word is passed, than anything else I can do. Five years' experience has taught me the necessity of Clinton.

Reformers had to concede that Dannemora's dungeons, with stone floors as beds, had been replaced by isolation cells with a board and a blanket for sleeping. Screen cells had been modified to allow in plenty of light but still ensure that no contact was allowed between prisoners. Tough conditions, yes, but distinct improvements over past accommodations.

Still, meaningful reform seemed to be the wave of the future. Tom Osborne's methods were widely used, including his Mutual Welfare League, a system in which inmates were self-governed. Critics dismissed the idea of convicts overseeing daily prison life as a potential disaster. Still, it worked well to varying degrees, notably at Auburn.

But in 1920, the disagreement between Trombly and Osborne about how to run prisons was settled in most minds with the murder of an Auburn inmate. Under the Mutual Welfare League for the past seven years, Auburn's inmates had enjoyed unprecedented freedoms, even electing representatives. But the more privileges they gained, the more they wanted. The relaxed atmosphere led to boldness, intimidation, arguments, and fights among inmates.

Alarmed leaders warned them not to "cut their own throats,"

which is almost literally what happened. Hours after his involvement in a fight, inmate Philip Nissman was attacked in his cell, where he died from stab wounds to the heart and stomach. Warden Edward Jennings and State Superintendent Charles Rattigan agreed to immediately suspend the league's activities, returning full control of the facility to prison officials. Some of Osborne's other reforms were later implemented in New York's prisons, but the Mutual Welfare League wasn't one of them.

Clinton Prison continued with business as usual, but with one noticeable change: its population continued to rise, surpassing that of the state's other prisons and exceeding its own capacity by the mid-1920s. A crime wave in combination with new restrictive laws on sentencing led to major issues at all of New York's prisons. At Clinton, the level of violence increased as more prisoners rebelled, started fights, and attempted to escape. Even harsh punishments couldn't overcome the issues.

Finally, in 1929, the situation exploded into a huge riot and a defining moment in Clinton Prison's history. Terrible punishments followed in the aftermath, and from the early 1930s forward, Clinton became and remained the strictest, toughest prison in the state, with no escapes from inside the high wall—until 2015.

CLINTON PRISON: VIOLENCE IN THE MODERN ERA

With the era of state-sanctioned tortures long gone, Clinton's guards conducted business with the only tools left at their disposal: intimidation through speech, taking away privileges, and punishment with fists and feet, generally delivered by three or more guards to ensure dominance was maintained. The prison was always an "us or them" arrangement where the guards needed to rule. Without the threat of paddling, the water bath, and other extreme punishments, an aggressive, near-zero-tolerance stance was the only safe way to operate the prison. Given the chance, inmates would overrun the place. When they refused or resisted an order, there was often hell to pay.

For decades after the riot of 1929, most complaints about guard brutality were handled internally, rarely going beyond the warden. Newsworthy items emanating from the prison mostly involved trusties walking away from road crews, precipitating headlines and usually brief manhunts that invariably ended in recapture. Other stories of interest addressed smuggling contraband into the prison, or inmates selling goods for profit. Prison visitors often sneaked in contraband, transferring drugs or other items subtly through shoe-to-shoe contact, or during hugs or kisses. There were instances of guards making extra money selling alcohol, girlie magazines, cigarettes, and prescription drugs to inmates. But in the decades

Clinton's new main entrance (1937)

following the riot, Clinton experienced no major scandals.

In the 1960s, societal changes affected the prison population's racial makeup. A century earlier, Clinton's inmates were overwhelmingly white, but during the Civil Rights era, a shift began as the incarceration rate for minorities accelerated for decades. White-on-black violence that became a staple of nightly news shows in the 1960s was reflected inside Dannemora's walls. Prisoners' rights was also an issue of the times, again linked to racism. More and more, the abuse of inmates took on a racial component, adding an additional layer of ugliness to Clinton's disciplinary system.

The battle over prison reforms encouraged inmates to speak out about mistreatment. Clinton was frequently a target, and for the same complaint that led to so many investigations in the past: brutality. The stories confirmed how little had changed at Clinton in a hundred years. Methods had been revised, but humiliation and physical abuse remained.

In 1968, Clinton inmate testimony in Albany's New York District Court told of beatings with sticks and rubber hoses, of inmates' arms pinned to their sides by officers while others beat them, of being forced to crawl nude on the floor while barking like a dog, and of prolonged punishments in solitary confinement.

For the inmates, it was horrible and demeaning. For many of the guards, it was domination, maintaining an edge in a dangerous place. For outside observers, it was all of the above, tainted with sadism and/or racism.

Following the Attica riot in 1971, which left more than forty dead, including ten prison employees, angry Clinton guards spoke (with anonymity) to the *Press-Republican*'s Forrest Cleland about prisoners gaining more power and rights:

> They can spit at us, assault us, throw urine or feces at us, and we're supposed to smile and try to rehabilitate 'em. I say we ought to use a little "manual rehabilitation." That would be a helluva lot better.

Other veteran guards said the problem was the rise of Black Muslims and the Black Panthers. Staff at Clinton were preparing for trouble, with one officer speaking for all in the event hostages were taken:

> Either kill me or get me the hell out of here. [Said another]: We have no control anymore. They can assault us, call us pigs, and we can't do a damn thing about it.

Clinton's worse section at the time was "the hole," officially known as Unit 14, a 48-cell section occupied by sixteen inmates that Superintendent Edwin LaVallee called "the bitterest men I've ever seen." All were either blacks or Puerto Ricans who expressed revolutionary ideology, a common theme of the times. Their isolation cells were stark, most of them lacking toilets, beds, and running water, which prison men said the inmates once had, but destroyed them in protest of a beating by guards. After that, they had only a mattress and a slop bucket. For all the improvements in facilities over the past hundred years, most of the problems and complaints remained relatively intact.

Less-than-glowing was the kindest way to describe Clinton's reputation. In a front-page article in 1972, David Rotherberg, executive director of a prison watchdog group, said after touring Unit 14, "I have never been so depressed in my life," and called the cells "sickening." Inmates told of beatings, mace and tear gas used against them, and the constant smell of "sweat and excrement."

In 1975, national newspaper columnist Jack Anderson, a Pulitzer Prize-winning investigative journalist, sent reporter Terry Repak to Dannemora for an inside look. She had visited many other prisons for the same purpose, but came away saying that Clinton was "the most depressing and degrading place she had ever visited." She referred to beatings, humiliations, hosings, psychological and physical brutality, and long terms in isolation cells. It sounded like a report straight out of the 1800s.

Anderson added a description of the average cell at Clinton:

> Within the massive gray walls, more than 2,000 sullen inmates are crowded in dank, musty cellblocks. They sleep with roaches in their bedsprings, bed bugs in their mattresses, and an open toilet two feet from their heads.

In 1976, Bob Harsh wrote in the *Lake Placid News* about twenty-seven-year corrections veteran Ray Casey, who worked at Clinton and spoke positively about some modern reforms.

> Mr. Casey grew up with the old system, giving and taking of its violence. He recalled the beating of inmates and his own broken shoulder, both the result of the hard line that separated inmates and guards into hostile camps. Locked into a tight seniority system, Mr. Casey found innovation nearly impossible as both prisoners and guards did their time brutalizing each other within an unresponsive bureaucratic maze.

In 1977, fifteen inmates filed suit against the state commissioner, Clinton's superintendent, and thirty guards, citing punches, kicks, and beatings they suffered in Unit 14 over a period of seven months. Unlike the days of old, such lawsuits had become commonplace. During the six months previous, 168 suits had been filed against Clinton—twenty-eight a month, an increase of eighty-seven percent compared to the same period a year earlier. The state made plans to hire attorneys for the purpose of handling Clinton's legal needs, as Prisoners' Legal Services and other pro-inmate groups used a strategy of bogging down the system. Some of the suits lasted nearly

Clinton Prison's modern wall (circa 1940)

a decade. Brutality was the most common claim, and Unit 14 was frequently the target.

Whispered about was Dannemora's "Goon Squad," groups of guards who were corrections vigilantes, dispensing justice—physical beatings—as they saw fit to uncooperative or disrespectful inmates. Anything that might be interpreted as weakness, like guards being subjected to taunts or threats, was dealt with swiftly and decisively. If inmates gained an edge or acted boldly, the results could be fatal for officers.

LABOR ISSUES: A DIVISIVE STRIKE

One of the most prominent legal issues of that era involved crimes and threats of extreme violence, none of it having to do with Clinton's inmates—this time, it was officer versus officer. In 1979, as contract negotiations between the union and state faltered, a deep division developed between Clinton employees who wanted to strike and those who didn't. The principal issues were seniority rules, wages, and workmen's compensation, the usual complaints of labor against management. Playing a role in the negotiations was New York's Taylor Law, which banned strikes by public employees. Violations carried a penalty of two day's pay lost for every day of work missed.

For an organization seeking recognition of its members as part of the law enforcement community, the idea of breaking the law by striking seemed counterintuitive. But a statewide walkout commenced on August 19, and at Clinton, it got ugly fast. Some union members remained on the job, while others picketed outside. Arguments between co-workers led to shattered friendships, and ultimately to the darkest time at Dannemora since the riot of 1929. Some carried resentment with them for years.

Those who kept working reported watching strikers vandalize a car by slashing the tires, breaking the windows, and urinating in it. By day five, state police revealed publicly that wives and children of men who remained on the job had received menacing phone calls that included death threats. A bomb threat was called in to the home of a deputy superintendent. As in any walkout, it could have been a few bad apples making the phone calls, but that didn't mitigate the terror among Dannemora's citizens.

State police manned the towers, and the National Guard ran the prisons until the strike was settled after sixteen days. The bitterness and division at Clinton Prison lasted much longer. Those who crossed the picket line were outcasts, shunned by former friends and colleagues. As union local vice-president Mike Kelly told the *Press Republican*, "I don't think it will ever blow over entirely. We have to work together, but it will never be the close-knit group it was."

CLINTON BRUTALITY BECOMES A COURTROOM ISSUE

Otherwise, life gradually returned to normal, which meant more violence inside the prison and more inmate lawsuits. In 1981, a Clinton brutality case played out prominently in the media. The issue again was Unit 14, but this story had a new twist: there was videotape evidence of the attack by guards Leonard Welch, a long-term employee, and Stephen Pageau, president of the union that included corrections officers. The incident had taken place fifteen months earlier. They were indicted by a federal grand jury in September for violating the constitutional rights of inmate John Eng "not to be deprived of liberty without due process, and not be subjected to cruel and unusual punishment."

The two men pleaded innocent, and a court battle centered on

Dannemora State Hospital, which later became the Annex

the admissibility of the prison's videotape of the incident, which the judge ultimately allowed.

For most of the nearly thirty-minute recording, the camera was partially obstructed, but still provided evidence that to the average viewer appeared damning. Eng is first seen lying face down with his right side protected against a wall, with Pageau standing over him, delivering about a dozen blows to the head and body. Shortly after, Welch kicks him several times, and Pageau then strikes him a few more times with a baton. In Plattsburgh, Eng was later treated for a broken left hand, plus abrasions and contusions to the left shoulder, arm, elbow, thigh, leg, and foot. Stitches were required for both a scalp and thigh wound. All of his injuries were testified to in court, suggesting excessive violence.

The tape included audio as well, revealing several disturbing exchanges that took place during the incident. "Go ahead, kill me, kill me," Eng shouted repeatedly. "I will, I will, I'd love nothing better. Give me an excuse," a responding voice said over and over.

Two days before the trial began, a vicious incident took place at Clinton, one that might have substantially strengthened the guards' case, but was inadmissible as evidence. Much like Eng had done, an inmate became unruly and attacked two guards, one of whom died from his injuries. Had the jury been privy to the details, they might well have decided no level of violence used to maintain order was "cruel and unusual punishment."

In the case of Welch and Pageau, there were issues with the videotape. Missing were the first few minutes of the confrontation, when the guards said Eng attacked Welch and resisted their efforts to handcuff him. Surprisingly, Eng took the stand and admitted attacking Welch, but said the extended beating by the two guards was far more than necessary to subdue him.

When deliberations lasted longer than the actual trial, a hung jury was expected, but before that could happen, a juror fell ill, resulting in a mistrial. At that point they were still evenly divided on the question of guilt or innocence.

A second trial ended four months later without input from Eng, who failed to show up. Rather than risk a year in jail, the two guards opted to plea bargain for in-house punishment, resulting in a thirty-day suspension and a year of alternate prison employment without inmate contact.

The fight for prisoners' rights and the onslaught of lawsuits continued to erode corrections officers' position of dominance and increase their exposure to danger. Unarmed guards mixed directly with dangerous felons, including inmates with no future and nothing to lose. Stiff punishment would follow if they lashed out, but that didn't stop the incorrigibles. Sudden attacks on officers could cause plenty of damage before armed guards stationed above restored order by gunfire. With assaults came the possibility of death or permanent injury. Clinton, home to the state's largest prison population and the greatest number of violent offenders, carried the highest risk.

Seemingly minor altercations sometimes ballooned into dangerous uprisings, with the possibility of an all-out riot. In 1983, a prisoner suffered a head wound when several officers subdued him for a rules violation. The day seemed otherwise to progress as normal, but shortly before nine o'clock that night, more than nine hundred inmates protested the incident by remaining in the yard. Following a meeting with several convict spokesmen, the order was again given to clear the yard. Inmate fights broke out, and officers became involved. Bursts from automatic weapons fired from two guard towers briefly restored order. Another ruckus an hour later required more warning shots. Thirty minor injuries were reported, fifteen of which were suffered by guards. It was the type of thing that could happen without warning on any Dannemora workday.

Three years later, as officers broke up a fight involving an inmate with a knife, other prisoners in the yard began throwing rocks at them. Tower guards fired nine warning shots to end the attack, after which the prison went on lockdown to ferret out any other hidden weapons. The fight and rock throwing caused injuries to eleven guards and five inmates. Seven officers and one convict were tended to at the hospital in Plattsburgh, fifteen miles away.

Dannemora's dungeons that were widely used during the prison's first half-century of existence featured dehumanizing conditions blamed for many an inmate's insanity. The modern equivalent—solitary confinement, Isolation Cells, Unit 14, Observation Units, whatever the latest appellation might be—served much the same purpose and was the source of many inmate court cases. During the period spanning roughly 1984 to 1994, inmate lawsuits handled by Prisoners' Legal Services won twenty-two settlements against Clinton totaling about $209,000, and attorneys' fees of $97,000. Each of the suits was for brutality and/or excessive force by Clinton officers. On several occasions, a half-dozen or more guards were named as defendants in a single suit. Many officers were named in more than one filing.

During Clinton's first one hundred years of operations, lawsuits were less common and seldom successful, but times had changed. Charges of brutality in 1990 were behind a suit that lasted the entire decade, ending with a financial award of $50,000 to former Clinton inmate Anthony Perri by U.S. District Court Judge Neal P. McCurn. The suit hinged on

> ... cruel and unusual punishment through their deficient treatment of his mental illness, and by brutal conditions under which he was held at the Clinton Correctional Facility from March 22, 1990, to October 6, 1990.

That treatment, said McCurn, violated the Eighth Amendment. Court papers at times read like the description of a medieval dungeon—or a Clinton dungeon from the 1800s.

> In March 1990, plaintiff was transferred to the Clinton Correctional Facility where he was placed in the Special Housing Unit ("SHU"). Thereafter, plaintiff was sent to the

prison's Observation Unit ("OBS") on three separate occasions. OBS is a separate inpatient unit at Clinton which is staffed by both OMH (Office of Mental Health) care professionals and DOCS officers. Plaintiff's transfer to OBS came about as a result of behavioral incidents.

In one incident, plaintiff slashed his arm in a suicide attempt. In another, he climbed the wall in the SHU exercise yard and placed the razor wire atop the wall around his neck and wrists. The prison staff talked him down, but he was removed to OBS when he became disruptive. Plaintiff spent a total of 108 days in OBS confinement consisting of 5, 32, and 71-day segments.

Plaintiff alleges that his conditions of confinement in OBS were inhuman and degrading. His cell contained only a sink, toilet, and a brightly glaring light that shone twenty-four hours a day. A small window in the solid metal door was the only means of seeing into or out of the cell except for an outside window that could be opened or closed from outside the cell by a correction officer. When later the window was opened, plaintiff's complaints of being cold were ignored for hours. He was held in this cell without clothes or a blanket for two months, and he developed body sores from having to sleep naked on the cold floor.

He had no personal possessions and no basic necessities such as soap or a toothbrush in his cell. He had no writing materials and was denied all legal work, his address book, and mail. There was no opportunity for personal contacts between inmates in OBS because there was no programming, exercise, recreation, or group therapy. Inmates were only permitted to leave their cells for a five-minute shower twice a week or to go to the visiting room.

On May 21, 1990, plaintiff smeared feces and urine all over himself and his cell and began to refuse solid foods. No attempt was made to clean that cell by prison authorities, and plaintiff was confined therein until May 31, 1990, when he was removed to another cell at OBS, where he was confined under the same conditions.

On June 19, 1990, while supposedly under constant suicide observation, plaintiff severed an artery and inflicted other injuries to his body. On June 22, 1990, he was sent to Central New York Psychiatric Center ("CNYPC"). On July

31, 1990, although still displaying signs of mental illness, he was returned to Clinton because the CNYPC staff believed it was not equipped to treat him. Upon his return to Clinton, plaintiff was again placed in the prior harsh cell conditions without clothing or a mattress.

On September 19, 1990, plaintiff again reacted to alleged harassment by correction officers by destroying the sink and toilet in his cell over a two-hour period without intervention by correction officers. When an officer finally entered his cell, he was cuffed, shackled, and thrown face down on a cot where he was kicked in the rectum, causing severe pain.

On September 24, 1990, and October 7, 1990, plaintiff attempted to hang himself. On both occasions, no one endeavored to cut him down until he had lost consciousness.

On October 11, 1990, he was again sent to CNYPC, where he remained until discharged from CNYPC to Sing Sing Correctional Facility on December 6, 1990. Plaintiff maintains that he received inadequate medical care at CNYPC because it lacked the capacity to treat patients like himself who needed long term intensive care, and that he was compelled to go through the inhumanity of cell life in OBS because Clinton also lacked the capability to provide the required mental health services needed by individuals afflicted with mental illness as serious as his.

One doctor testified that Perri had a "biological temperament disorder" as a result of background deficits—abandoned at age ten by his mother, his father a heroin addict, and Perri forced into foster care. As a result, the diagnosis was Attention Deficit Hyperactivity Disorder. Another doctor reviewed Perri's record and saw no "major mental illness, but, rather, a personality disorder founded in his childhood which was extremely hard to change and very difficult to deal with."

Nine years after Perri's case was filed, the court ruled that through the fault of the state, the "plaintiff sustained physical and mental suffering," which would be compensated for by $50,000 plus court-related costs.

Years later, Perri became a courtroom regular. In a 2012 ruling of the United States District Court, Eastern District of New York, a judge noted, "The plaintiff is a frequent litigant in this court," and followed with a number of case titles—four against President Barack Obama, two against Mayor Michael Bloomberg, one against U.S. Attorney General Eric Holder, and others against several state and federal officials. The suits were dismissed for one reason or another, and were mostly related to perceived local, national, and international conspiracies against him.

Three years before Perri's case was finally settled, another brutality suit against Clinton officers earned inmate Charles Allaway a settlement of $40,000, plus $20,000 for Prisoners' Legal Services. The Correctional Association reported that seventeen inmates claiming brutality by Clinton guards won or settled lawsuits during the 1990s. Many corrections officers viewed those cases from a different perspective: winning inmate lawsuits and boosting convicts' rights weakened the role of officers, and weaker officers were more vulnerable to inmate aggression.

But legal filings could work the other way as well. By the early 1990s, two of every three New York inmate deaths were due to AIDS. Myths and ignorance surrounding the disease led to hysteria, which only began giving way late in the decade to science and practicality. Inmate fatalities were reduced by research, but guards remained at risk in a violent environment where the spilling of bodily fluids was common. Explosive, dangerous inmates who were infected with the AIDS virus sometimes used their illness in despicable ways. At Clinton in 1996, inmate Geraldo Malave pleaded guilty to two counts of attempted murder for threatening guards Robert Ayotte and Gary Brushnefski with intentional infection during a 1995 incident. The attack involved Malave smashing his face on a table and spitting blood at them, an effort that increased his sentence by four and a half to nine years.

For their own safety, front-line prison employees had to set aside the effects of lawsuits and public criticisms to remain focused. Clinton guards regularly dealt with difficult inmates, the threat of murderous outbursts at any moment, drug trafficking, gangs, and a host of other issues. People in the North Country have said offhandedly that corrections officers—with good pay, great benefits, and flexible work arrangements—have it made. And like police officers and the military, there's often easy time during many workdays. But it's also a given with all three occupations that violent confrontations are likely to occur, and at times like those, you couldn't pay most folks enough to even consider taking their place. If the average clerk or mechanic job came with the premise that just one day a year, a certain issue would come up—the need to forcibly subdue a dangerous person, fend off a sudden and violent attack, or have urine and feces thrown in your face—one might consider putting the application aside. Corrections officers risk all those things and more on a daily basis.

In 2006 it was announced that inmate assaults statewide were at their lowest level in nearly twenty-five years. At Clinton, the exciting news was that only twenty-eight assaults had occurred during the past year. Not many occupations would cite that as a positive statistic, but with a history like Clinton's, it was heady stuff.

The actual attacks were one thing, but the detrimental effects of ongoing risk and anxiety were quite another. Heart trouble, depression, and other maladies have been proven more prevalent among corrections officers. Union and prison officials have suggested hobbies, part-time employment, and other purposeful pastimes as valuable distractions that can help counter the effects of the corrections workday.

But fights, stabbings, gang attacks, prisoners ranting in solitary, excrement and urine thrown, and threats from convicted killers are things many people never witness in a lifetime. How does one deal with it as a normal part of the day?

Maintaining control amid the mess has always been considered critical, and at Clinton, the methods known to have worked in the past were intimidation, strict enforcement of the rules, and physical force when necessary. There's no denying the physical component has played a prominent role. It's been an ongoing theme at Dannemora for more than a hundred fifty years.

In October 2014, the Correctional Association of New York delivered its latest report on Clinton, providing a blunt assessment of the past three years, which read much like previous appraisals.

> Clinton Correctional Facility has an infamous history of staff violence, brutality, dehumanization, and racist attitudes that are an affront to any sense of humanity.
> ... Our investigation revealed that these longstanding abuses at Clinton remain pervasive. The CA's review of

conditions at the prison found frequent infliction of solitary confinement for months and years, inadequate medical care, a high incidence of suicides and self-harm, and a dearth of meaningful programs.... Overall, the level of physical violence and staff abuse and intimidation, the pervasive environment of oppression, the lack of proximity to any urban center, and the tensions derived from vast racial and cultural disparities between staff and incarcerated persons at Clinton epitomize the worst aspects of mass incarceration in New York State. New York must reverse the downward spiral of excessive punishment, isolation, warehousing, violence, and abuse at Clinton and across DOCCS....

A suggested first step was "by ending the brutality of prisons like Clinton."

At one time, "foreigners" (immigrants) in Clinton were the equivalent of today's non-whites. Otherwise, the 2014 report could just as well have been written in 1914, or even 1860. That's how much, or little, has changed.

Clinton Prison Riots

Only twice in Clinton's history have riots occurred. The first took place at the hospital, and the second involved the prison proper.

The Utica Lunatic Asylum was built in 1843, and the State Lunatic Asylum for Insane Convicts was added at Auburn Prison in 1859. To meet increased needs, a new, 550-bed facility was opened in 1892 at Matteawan, east of the Hudson River, replacing Auburn's asylum. Just seven years later, the Dannemora State Hospital opened its doors, serving inmates who were declared insane at any point after conviction, while Matteawan continued to serve inmates declared insane prior to conviction.

Today, Clinton Correctional Facility has two main parts: the large, walled section known as Clinton Main, and the former Dannemora State Hospital, today known as the Annex, which is rated as a maximum-security facility, but has dorms and rooms instead of cells.

THE HOSPITAL RIOT, 1907

Dannemora's hospital riot took place on August 22, 1907. Prison officials were perplexed at how the men had organized the revolt, but after lining up and preparing to take to their beds for the night, 320 inmates suddenly flooded into two large dormitory sections and barricaded the doors with furniture, preventing guards from getting inside. They then went furiously to work on the barred windows, apparently hoping to break free and escape.

Prison guards with guns were dispatched outside and ordered to shoot at any windows where inmates were seen trying to escape.

Dannemora State Hospital

A fire hose was aimed at the windows, but the convicts inside used mattresses to block the heavy flow, while continuing to work at the window bars with iron bedposts and a sledgehammer and chisel.

The yelling of the inmates and repeated gunfire brought townspeople to the scene, where they worked as reinforcements to help contain the convicts. While many shots were fired outside, men inside continued efforts to break through the barricaded doors, finally succeeding two hours after the riot started.

Walls and windows were damaged, and the two dormitories were wrecked. Several inmates were injured during the riot, and one, Isaac Dubois, was shot dead by one of the guards.

The Riot of 1929

As early as 1922, Clinton housed fifteen hundred inmates, while Auburn had thirteen hundred and Sing Sing twelve hundred. The upsurge in population was attributed to increased criminal activity, much of it linked to the effects of Prohibition. With the added effect of drastic mandatory sentences imposed by the Baumes Laws, which were passed in 1926, Clinton was hurtling towards the greatest disaster in Dannemora's history. The terrible truth is that state commissions, inspectors, and prison officials saw it coming and warned of pending tragedy, but no one stepped in to prevent it.

Overcrowding was one of the first indicators that trouble was brewing. By 1925, Clinton had more than a hundred inmates sleeping in corridors. The state suggested minor adjustments that did nothing to address the actual overcrowding—adding officers in order to lengthen the inmates' workday, and increasing supervisory pay to match employees at other prisons, thus incentivizing Clinton staff to remain on the job despite worsening conditions.

America was in the midst of a crime wave, with tens of thousands of Prohibition violators cramming the nation's courts and crowding the jails and prisons. Nowhere was the effect worse than in New York, where only a few small sections of the state were *not* considered hotbeds of illegal activities. As the situation worsened, New York State threw the proverbial pail (perhaps barrel better describes it) of gasoline on the fire by passing a law imposing draconian punishments on criminals.

It was a case of political pandering, taking advantage of public sentiment with solutions that on the surface appeared fair, but carried potentially terrible repercussions that should have been studied thoroughly. Prison officials warned of almost certain riots, but legislators forged ahead in 1926, passing the Baumes Law, named after the chair of the state's crime commission, Senator Caleb Baumes.

Without delving into the ripple effects predicted by prison administrators, lawmakers opted for radical changes that imposed harsh sentences for even minor offenses, and restricted the abilities of judges to consider extenuating circumstances during sentencing.

The principal damage was contained in a few simple but stringent clauses: longer sentences were imposed on first-time offenders; a fourth felony conviction required life imprisonment without parole; no parole was allowed for convicts who used guns while committing crimes; and no good-behavior credits could begin accumulating until the minimum sentence was served.

The effects on New York's overcrowded prisons were immediate. Limited good-behavior credits and the restriction or elimination of parole meant more prisoners were serving longer sentences, which in turn meant more prisoners were forced to sleep in hallways outside of cells, or inmates had to double bunk in cells considered small for even one occupant.

Worst of all was life imprisonment for a fourth felony. While it

Clinton Prison (1929)

sounded sensible to the average law-abiding citizen, it ignored the realities of prison life, where hope was the key to keeping order. The law also failed to redefine felonies. Classified with murder, rape, and bank robberies were the stealing of small amounts of money—and chicken theft. For a fourth offense of stealing perhaps fifty dollars or a few chickens, New York State sent several violators to Clinton Prison for life.

Dannemora was the state's designated home for three- and four-time felons. The Baumes Law added significantly to that segment of the prison's population—men who had no future, no hope of ever leaving Clinton, and thus no incentive to behave. As predicted, the inmate population became increasingly unruly. Some focused on escaping, which for lifers was the only option left, albeit an unlikely path to success based on Clinton's reputation. Others became disruptive in a variety of ways, breaking facility rules, refusing to work, and fighting with other inmates.

In 1927, reorganizing the state's Prison Department resulted in the creation of the Department of Correction. Among the issues faced early on were conditions at Dannemora as assessed by the Sub-Commission on Penal Institutions:

> The situation at Clinton prison is a most difficult one. On account of the lack of sufficient cell room elsewhere and for disciplinary reasons, Clinton Prison receives many long-

term convicts, violent men, robbers, burglars, murderers, and because of their records of crimes, desperate characters without substantial hope of release for many years. There are men quite sane and only criminal by their own desires.

Others are dangerous psychopaths, the men who are subject to disorder or rebellion at any moment, and who would stab, shoot, or kill at any opportunity, or join gladly in a prison break…. The safety of the prison is threatened because of the insufficiency of personnel for guarding a collection of dangerous men whose cynical criminality and murderous tendencies are probably not equaled in any other prison.

Recently Warden Kaiser intercepted packages containing twelve large-caliber revolvers and 400 rounds of ammunition for the pistols. He had information that an entry was sought for a quantity of dynamite. The armament, had it reached the vicious criminals for whom it was intended, would under certain circumstances have been sufficient to effect a prison delivery [breakout] of hundreds of desperadoes with possible serious loss of life.

Disciplinary and housing reasons compel the incarceration of these men at Clinton Prison. Planning and scheming for release and breaks to freedom are going on continually among them. The prison's safety is always menaced. Apparently the situation is well in hand under Warden Kaiser's continual watchfulness, but that is strained always because of the lack of personnel for supervision and guarding. In view of the apparent danger, it is strongly recommended that the warden's request for sufficient personnel to guard properly the prison and its inmates be heeded. It is a case where proper towers on the prison wall should be provided, and that these be armed with sufficient repeating rifles and machine guns to quell any outburst that may happen.

There are desperate criminals confined at Dannemora whose loot from robberies, hidden outside, according to prison officers, is sufficient to finance attempts by bribery to break down the poorly paid guard system and furnish arms for rebellion and means to carry out general prison escapes.

If that weren't prophetic enough, the following confirmed that prison officials knew the repercussions of those shortcomings far better than lawmakers did:

> In that prison [Clinton], the disciplinary question is a serious one. Idleness among the dangerous characters imprisoned there promotes lawlessness. A successful rebellion or prison break would be most costly in life and property. Every precaution must be taken against such a horror.

By 1927, Clinton's fifteen hundred inmates included nearly a hundred twenty lifers and four hundred men with sentences of twenty years or more. The facility was already three hundred beyond official capacity, but the madness continued until the predicted horror arrived on July 22, 1929.

As approximately thirteen hundred inmates were leaving the mess hall, they failed to organize into designated groups in the yard. Guards tried to pick out the leaders in hopes of maintaining order, but the officers (unarmed, as always, so that no weapons could fall into the hands of the convicts) were badly outnumbered. Within seconds the situation escalated from unruly to completely out of control. The whistle that ordered inmates to their cells was ignored.

Officer Ernest Bressette was struck with stones and a mallet, while in the tailor shop, Officer Arthur Murphy was assaulted. Both men suffered head injuries, but managed to reach safety, with Murphy escaping in dramatic fashion. A knife-wielding convict chased him to the prison wall, but was shot as he closed in for the kill. Murphy then climbed out on a rope thrown to him from officers above.

Inmates set fire to several buildings and took a civilian powerhouse employee, Peter Dame, hostage. A team of armed troopers and guards approached the scene and trained their weapons on two hundred inmates, who released Dame to safety. The convicts then demolished the dynamo that provided lights and power to both the prison and Dannemora village.

As heavy smoke filled the yard, some convicts recognized an escape opportunity and began climbing the walls by forming human ladders. Armed guards atop the twenty-foot-high wall opened fire with shotguns and machine guns, the latter weapon being a new addition due to the prison unrest of recent years.

The prison siren, which like the cannon of old delivered the news of an escape, brought villagers rushing to the aid of guards. Weapons were carried from home, while other locals emptied the gun and ammunition supplies of two hardware stores.

Calls went out to the state police barracks in Malone, and in less than two hours, nearly fifty troopers arrived from a dozen villages ranging from Champlain on the Canadian border to Tupper Lake, deep in the Adirondacks. From Plattsburgh, two companies of the 26th Infantry arrived with rifles and tear gas, ready to help but unable to act without direct orders from Washington. A half-dozen U.S. Border Patrol officers and several conservation men joined the effort to suppress the riot.

The carpenter, weaving, and tailor shops, plus a storehouse, dry kiln, and a huge pile of lumber were all burning, adding to the general mayhem. Unable to enter the prison, firefighters from Dannemora, Lyon Mountain, Morrisonville, Peru, Plattsburgh, and the 26th Infantry aimed their hoses over the walls at burning targets.

The inmates were armed with clubs, knives, picks, shovels, and any other usable objects, but gunfire from the walls forced them to take cover inside several buildings. With all prison personnel safe, and a battalion of armed lawmen and civilians surrounding the prison, officials had the upper hand. A phone call from the inmates

Clinton Prison riot (1929)

to Principal Keeper Asael (Asa) Granger made no specific demands other than for the shooting to cease. This was agreed to, but with the exception that any convicts approaching the prison wall would be fired upon with deadly intent.

Three hours after the riot began, Granger led three guards and eight state troopers into the prison yard and gave the inmates two options: come out of the buildings peaceably, or be forced out. One by one they complied, until all that remained was one resistant group of convicts. But with no weapons to counter rifles, shotguns, and machine guns, they too surrendered.

Granger was later cited for thinking on his feet during the standoff. When planes were seen overhead—not a common sight in 1929—he warned that they were deployed by the military to bomb the inmates if they didn't give up the fight. The planes actually carried newspaper reporters and photographers.

Even after order was restored, the inmates remained defiant, destroying items in their cells, rattling the bars loudly, and shouting threats at inmates and civilians alike. By midnight, after ammonia guns were used in the cellblocks, things had quieted, but a tense, anxious atmosphere remained.

The aftermath revealed that three inmates had been shot dead, two of whom were at Clinton courtesy of the Baumes Law. One of

Smoke rises above Clinton Prison during the riot (1929)

them, Harold Brunner, was felled while chasing Officer Murphy. The other two fatalities were Clyde Shackelford and Herman Reese. Twenty inmates were injured, including six by gunfire.

Electricity and water service were restored at Dannemora within a day, the village reservoir having been drained in order to quench the fires. Selected inmates were released from their cells the day after the riot to clean up the mess and begin restoring order. Buildings that were partially burned or destroyed were mainly old wooden structures that would be replaced by modern fireproof buildings. The overall cost of repairs was assessed at $173,000 (equal to $4.2 million in 2015).

The prison's internal investigation revealed that the planned uprising had been delayed by a day for an unusual reason: respect for sporting competitors. The nearby community of Lyon Mountain, about eight miles due west of Dannemora, was home to the highest-grade iron ore in the world. It was mined there for a century by men considered the toughest in the region—men who also developed the best baseball team in the north. Likewise, Clinton Prison originated for the purpose of mining iron ore. Mining was no longer done there, but the prison with the hardest, toughest criminals in the state developed a similarly superb baseball team that dominated most opponents during the 1920s, with excellent pitching and hitters who were considered unstoppable. In the region, there was no better matchup than the Lyon Mountain Miners versus the Clinton Stars.

On Sunday, July 21, the Miners visited the prison and defeated the Stars, 8–3, behind the stellar pitching of Clifford "Lefty" Martin, who stifled his opponents that day on seven hits, one walk, and twelve strikeouts. While handing the convict squad their first defeat of the season, the much-admired Martin retired the hard-hitting Stars 1–2–3 in every inning except the first and fourth.

The plan that day was for the Stars' first baseman to toss his glove in the air as a signal to begin taking hostages and attempt a mass escape. In attendance inside the prison was a large contingent of fans from Lyon Mountain, and a very large number of inmate spectators—the perfect opportunity for creating chaos.

But the Stars had such respect for Martin as a competitor, for the superior skills he exhibited that day after falling behind early, and for the Lyon Mountain fans who followed baseball as if it were religion—fans they had become familiar with during a friendly rivalry of several years—that they abandoned the murderous riot plan, putting it off until the next day. It was the last anyone would see of the mighty Clinton Stars. In the wake of the riot, prison officials canceled the baseball program.

The riot may well have been a mild substitute for what nearly occurred at Clinton less than a year earlier, when two shipments of pistols, rifles, guns, and dynamite were intercepted before reaching a gang inside the prison. With such an arsenal behind a mass escape attempt, the loss of life could have been far greater than what resulted from the riot.

Prison management attributed the disturbance to several lifers who, on multiple occasions, had planned escapes with the help of old cohorts still on the outside, some of them from New York City. A week after the rebellion at Clinton, a riot occurred at Auburn Prison, resulting in two convicts killed, four guards shot, and eight convicts successfully escaping. State Commissioner of Correction Raymond Kieb said he had no doubt the two riots were connected, for Arthur Barry, who escaped during Auburn's riot, was a member of the same gang involved in the Clinton uprising.

At Dannemora, stiff punishments were in order. It was announced that fifty ringleaders of the revolt had been identified and placed in solitary confinement on a diet of bread and water. The number of men in solitary was either understated at the time, or expanded in the coming months, for accusations of brutality were later leveled against Clinton regarding 191 inmates who were locked in the infamous dungeons, a punishment that had reportedly been discontinued decades earlier. Nothing came of the charges, perhaps because the explanation seemed logical: space was limited after rioters destroyed parts of the prison. Former Sing Sing Warden Thomas Osborne, long a critic of Clinton, said he believed the charges of abuse were true. A state investigation, compiling four hundred pages of testimony from six hearings that included eighteen inmates, thirty-three guards, and two prison officials, found otherwise.

In December 1929, Auburn endured another riot, this one resulting in the death of the principal keeper and eight inmates. In the aftermath of any major prison event, inmate witnesses were quickly moved to other facilities, where they could be questioned by investigators without fear of retribution from guards or other prisoners. A large number of unfortunates at Auburn were transferred to Clinton, a move that soon generated claims of extreme abuse. Inmates told of disgusting cell accommodations, feedings that were intermittent at best, and food that was unpalatable—mash potatoes, for instance, that included unidentified foreign matter and crawling worms. They also reported being removed from confinement periodically for severe beatings, and then dumped back into their cells without medical care. An investigation found no supporting evidence other than the testimony of inmates, which was deemed untrustworthy. They were, after all, not only criminals, but participants in a deadly uprising at Auburn. Finding sympathy among state officials was unlikely.

Two years after the riot at Dannemora, investigators cited several possible causes. There were too many incorrigibles at Clinton Prison; disruptive inmates should be spread throughout the system; security was lax; more guards were needed; the inmate workload was too light, leaving many convicts idle for extended periods; the food was bad; and prison conditions were horrible.

But those long familiar with the workings of prisons, from wardens down to guards, cited overcrowding and hopelessness, both of which were caused by Baumes Law, which put more people into prisons for longer terms and created many new lifers. Defenders of the law countered with a convoluted argument: if the men behind the riots were Baumes offenders, the law worked because it put them right where they belonged.

No one was denying they belonged in prison. The debate was over how long they should be held, and prison experts stood against permanent incarceration except for the very worst crimes and criminals. Baumes was a failure because it replaced hope with desperation. A return to the parole system and open-ended sentencing concluded the experiment.

In the aftermath, reforms were instituted at Dannemora, new cellblocks were added, and the outer wall was rebuilt to a more imposing height of thirty feet. Most significant of all was that the 1929 riot marked the end of an era, and the beginning of a new, more secure Clinton from which no one escaped for the next eighty-five years.

Officers Under Attack

Unarmed corrections officers mingle with murderers, rapists and other violent offenders, but are required to be in command at all times. Physical assaults by inmates, with weapons or bare hands, are the worst offenses and must be dealt with decisively. But any challenge to authority, any boldness that isn't firmly shut down, can encourage minor escalations that lead to physical action.

Injuries to guards are far more common than the general public realizes. The assault reports on the New York State Correctional Officers & Police Benevolent Association, Inc. (NYSCOPBA) website make for interesting—and often frightening—reading. Entries like "Inmate elbowed and punched CO during pat frisk, rupturing his ear drum and dislocating his shoulder," and, "Inmate assaulted CO in mess hall, resulting in bruising/swelling to right orbital, right shoulder, and right side of neck," are surprisingly frequent.

A closer look reveals that such events are statistically less common at Clinton Prison, but not because the inmates are better behaved. Many physical attacks have occurred at Clinton, but in a facility where guards maintain dominance, the repercussions are quick, forceful, and decisive. What might appear as excessive force to the average citizen is sometimes lifesaving, preventing an escalation of further violence or future attacks. In those instances, weakness, or the appearance of weakness, can have lethal consequences down the road.

"That's not how it should be" is a reaction common not only among reformers, but average citizens as well. And it's not that way in most prisons. In places like Clinton, however, where the population is dominated by violent felons, that's the reality that has existed historically. Officer Leonard Welch, who retired after thirty-four years (1963–1997) as a corrections officer, was a veteran of many physical confrontations. As he put it, "They aren't here because they missed Sunday school."

To remain safe, corrections officers must be alert at all times, but even then, stuff—often very bad stuff—happens, as illustrated by a brief look at some frightful incidents from Clinton's past.

NON-FATAL ATTACKS ON OFFICERS

1863–ANSEL WOOD: As he was being transferred to a different cell, convict John Gillin attacked guard Ansel Wood, slashing him with a knife. Guards carried firearms at that time, and several shots were fired, one of them striking Gillin in the face and killing him.

1873–ANDREW MORHOUSE: Keeper Andrew Morhouse was struck from behind and knocked unconscious for several minutes, leaving a wound that exposed the skull.

1874–ABNER ROBERTS: Keeper Abner Roberts was assaulted by a convict using a heavy iron bar, causing serious shoulder injuries. Another inmate helped foiled the attack, which ended the prison career of Roberts in 1875 after fifteen years of service. By a special act of the legislature three years later, he was awarded $1000 (about $25,000 in 2015).

1878–EDWARD GAY: In the prison's hat-making department, an inmate struck guard Edward Gay over the head with a piece of gas tubing, grabbed the officer's revolver, and ran out the door. There he encountered guard Henry Wittie, who fired a shot that passed between the convict's arm and body. A third officer fired at the inmate, and a fourth, Michael Hagerty, disabled him with a shot to the leg.

1886–JOHN McGOWAN: Inmate John Coffey attacked keeper John McGowan and slashed him four times, but the guard overcame his attacker without suffering serious injuries. Coffey was beaten in the guardroom, strapped down securely, given 152 lashes with the cat, sent to the hospital to ensure he survived, and then placed in a dark punishment cell.

1890–WILLIAM MEAD: Keeper William Mead of the laundry department was attacked by William Taylor, the inmate who supplied split wood for the furnaces. Taylor swung the blunt edge of his axe at Mead, who avoided the brunt of the blow but was knocked unconscious. The inmate reached for Mead's gun, but other convicts prevented him from doing any further harm. A week later, the five inmates who intervened and were credited with saving Mead's life—Van Rensselaer Clark, Clarence Davenport, William Kelley, A. Ramsay, and William Seabrook—were issued pardons. The attacker, Taylor, was ordered confined to his cell for ten years, after which another twenty years of sentence time awaited. He was later transferred to Auburn Prison, where he killed a fellow inmate in late 1892, slashing his throat from ear to ear. For that crime he was put to death in Auburn's electric chair in August of the following year. Officer Mead later filed a claim with the state for $5,000, but was denied on the basis that assault by convicts was a routine risk of the keeper and guard jobs.

1892–MERRILL WEED: Kitchen Keeper Merrill Weed was stabbed in the back with scissors by inmate William Smith, who later said he believed Weed was poisoning his food. Further damage was thwarted by another inmate, George Long, who took the scissors from Smith as he prepared to strike again. Smith was locked in solitary, but was also declared insane, requiring transfer to the asylum at Matteawan. Weed survived his injuries.

1893–MULTIPLE GUARDS: An elaborate plot to kill several guards and escape the prison was foiled by information received from a snitch, who passed a note to the principal keeper as inmates filed by in lockstep. Warden Walter Thayer quietly investigated the details provided in the note and found them to be correct. Several inmates admitted to the plot, leading to a full facility search that uncovered a number of weapons and tools. Among the items found were files, saws, drills, pieces of iron, a chisel, and a crowbar. Thayer took the story to the governor, who pardoned the snitch.

1904–AMOS LAFORD: In the Dannemora State Hospital, attendant Amos Laford was attacked by convict Patrick Riley, who had been declared insane. Riley fashioned a weapon from the metal cover of a floor drain and slammed it into the back of Laford's head, fracturing his skull. The attendant survived his injuries.

1907–MULTIPLE GUARDS: Inmate Edward Russell, declared incurably insane, filed his sixth writ of habeas corpus, seeking release from prison. He summoned to Dannemora the governor, three justices of New York's Supreme Court, and several other officials, claiming they had joined with President Theodore Roosevelt in a conspiracy against him. He was taken to Albany and present his case before some of those men, but lost. On the return trip to Dannemora, he leaped from the train in an escape attempt, but was recaptured. Later, at Clinton, he used stones and a sock to make a slingshot and attempted to strike an officer's head. He also gave razors to a pair of insane inmates and urged them to attack the prison guards.

1910–JOHN HEALEY: During an escape attempt, Officer John Healey faced off against two inmates wielding handmade guns. He refused an order to open a door and instead moved forward to effect their capture. One of the inmates discharged his weapon, hitting Healey in the hand and chest. The escape was unsuccessful, but Healey spent weeks in Plattsburgh's Champlain Valley Hospital recovering. Ten years later, Healey advanced to the position of principal keeper.

1917–MULTIPLE GUARDS: Occupying Clinton's isolation cells were inmates who had stabbed a guard in the back, kicked an officer in the groin, knocked a guard out with a brick, and put a guard in the hospital for ten days with injuries suffered while stopping an escape.

1921–THOMAS KELLY: Officer Thomas Kelly was checking on a group of inmates when one of them, William Walters, struck him on the head with a piece of rubber hose filled with lead. Kelly went down, but remained clearheaded enough to summon other guards, who stopped the escape attempt. He recovered after a short time away from work.

1930–LEO GILROY: Hospital guard Leo Gilroy suffered multiple stab wounds to the face and back during an attack by inmate Joseph Fink. There was no apparent reason for the assault other than possible insanity. The officer recovered.

CLINTON CORRECTIONAL OFFICER FATALITIES

AUGUSTUS WRIGHT, 1861

Augustus Tyrannus Wright of Watertown was Clinton's and New York State's first prison guard killed in the line of duty. While overseeing inmates in the iron-rolling mill, Wright was struck in the head with an iron bar wielded by James Sewall, who took Wright's gold watch and revolver before leading the escape of fellow convicts Daniel Baker, Patrick Brady, William Judd, Alexander Paquette, and George Pettit. A seventh inmate was caught outside before he could clear the picket wall surrounding the prison. The prison warning bell was rung, and the cannon was fired to broadcast widely that an escape had occurred. All the convicts were recaptured within three days. It was determined that the plotters of the breakout were Sewall, Brady, and Hall, and that Wright had died instantly from the heavy blow to the head.

The trials of the escapees began in October. Sewall's lasted just a day, resulting in a guilty verdict. He was sentenced to hang after one year of solitary confinement, as provided in New York's Hartung Law. His cohorts opted for separate trials, four of which were held in February 1862. Representing each defendant charged with murder was George Clark and the redoubtable Smith Weed. George Pettit was found not guilty, while William Judd's case ended with a hung jury. Both men were characterized as followers in the breakout. Patrick Brady and Marion Hall were each found guilty, after which they presented lengthy statements to the court. Hall's ended with a comment about sentencing.

> Your honor, I am not pleading for my life because I do not want it unless I can enjoy it, and I cannot enjoy it at Clinton Prison. Death in its most aggravated form is a welcome messenger, and one that is wooed by me, as a friend that will e're long relieve me of my earthly misery....

The judge obliged, sentencing both men to hang. The Hartung Law still applied, so they faced execution after a year of solitary.

But a series of legal changes affected New York State's death penalty during the 1860s. Wright's killers were ordered held until the sitting governor ordered their execution. No one did so, and in 1872, Governor John Hoffman commuted the sentences of Sewall, Brady, and Hall to life.

Sewall died in Clinton Prison on Thanksgiving Day 1881. Brady and Hall were pardoned in September 1889 after more than thirty years at Clinton (including time served prior to the escape).

In 1869, the state awarded a benefit of $2,500 ($45,000 in 2015) to Louisa Wright for the loss of her husband.

Dr. Charles North, 1917

In 1904, Dr. Charles H. North, who had previously served as prison physician at Matteawan and at Clinton for the past two years, was named superintendent of the Dannemora State Hospital. Among the inmates to arrive there during his tenure was Chris Reichart, a 1909 transfer from Sing Sing, where he was doing time for second-degree murder. At Dannemora, he remained in the insane asylum, behaving well enough to earn trusty status in the carpenter shop, located in the basement.

In 1919, Dr. North visited Reichart's cabinet shop, away from the main carpenter shop, and watched him work on furniture as they talked. Attendants in nearby rooms heard them conversing normally, but a sudden yell brought them running. Dr. North lay dead on the floor, a spear-like instrument thrust almost completely through his chest, penetrating the heart and lungs. Reichart had planned the murder by sharpening a long chisel, attaching it to a handle about three feet long, and hiding it for use against the doctor. There were no witnesses, and the testimony of an insane person was inadmissible as evidence. Reichart would only say that the doctor wouldn't let him return to the main prison body.

Charles J. Gunter, 1919

The murder of Charles Gunter, a guard in the tuberculosis hospital, was nearly a double homicide. It appeared his attackers planned to escape at the beginning of the evening shift, a departure that might go unnoticed for some time if they killed or disabled the guard. But Gunter's six-o'clock replacement, Daniel Cummings, arrived a half-hour early when the convicts were preparing for the breakout. While exiting a room, Cummings was ambushed by inmate Walter Levandowski, who had cut off a piece of fire hose with the nozzle attached to use as a weapon. Whipping the nozzle against Cummings' forehead rendered him temporarily unconscious. He awakened only to see Levandowski returning with a knife aimed at Cummings' throat.

But the officer fought back, minimizing the slash wound and kicking his attacker, who ran off. Cummings then managed to reach a nearby room and summon help. Several officers rushed to the scene and captured Levandowski and a partner, Leo Jankowski, as they were exiting a window. A trail of blood where Charles Gunter had been dragged led to Room No. 8, where he lay on the floor unconscious, with wounds similar to those of Cummings, but more serious. Gunter died the next morning. Cummings, with a serious head injury and a minor throat wound, survived.

Levandowski, serving life for manslaughter, and Jankowski, serving twenty years for assault, were both charged with first-degree murder. First to go on trial was Jankowski, depicted by prosecutors as the mastermind who orchestrated the plan, using Levandowski as a tool and planning to blame him should something to wrong. After less than three and a half hours of deliberating, the jury returned a verdict of guilty. His sentence was electrocution at Sing Sing on January 19, 1920, just thirty-eight days away.

Ten days later, Levandowski's trial ended with the same result, but with execution set for the week of January 26. In both trials, guards testified to overhearing the two defendants talking in the isolation cells about having just killed one guard, and maybe two.

In early February, when the executions were delayed, Levandowski confessed in the presence of three men his attorney, the principal keeper, and the prison chaplain—that he alone had committed the murder of Gunter.

> That at about 5:30 on the afternoon of April 17, 1919, I got out of my bed and called Charles J. Gunter, who was the guard on duty at that time, and asked him to come down toward the last private room in the hall. As he passed this room, I hit him on the back of the head with a hose nozzle and as soon as he fell, I cut his throat two or three times with a knife.

A few minutes later, after rendering Cummings unconscious, he abducted Jankowski and ordered him to cut the bars and protective screens on a ward window. When several guards arrived on the scene, Levandowski attempted to escape through the bars, but couldn't because Jankowski hadn't been able to saw them through. Cornered, with several guns trained on him, Levandowski surrendered.

In the signed confession, he emphasized that Jankowski had no knowledge of the plan or of the attacks on the two guards.

While appeals concerning Jankowski's fate played out in court, both men waited on Sing Sing's death row, and both applied to the governor for clemency.

They received no mercy, and at the end of May, they died in the electric chair on the same day, Levandowski going last to give the governor ten more minutes to pardon Jankowski. He didn't.

DANIEL NICKERSON, 1934

At morning roll call on March 25, inmate Vincent Amerigo, alias Vincent DeLeo, remained in his cell, pleading illness, which required a visit to the prison physician. Officers Fred Beckett and Lewis Hamilton took DeLeo from his cell and ordered him to remove his hands from his pockets. One hand came out with a knife, and a battle ensued. During the struggle, Hamilton was cut four times on the wrist and chest, and Beckett was stabbed twice, including once in the

stomach. Nickerson, responding to the commotion, attempted to club DeLeo, but the inmate stabbed him in the heart. Hamilton finally took the knife away from the convict, and as they fought, Beckett grabbed Nickerson's club and hit DeLeo on the head, disabling him.

The three injured officers and DeLeo were cared for at the prison hospital, after which Beckett and Hamilton were transferred to Champlain Valley Hospital in Plattsburgh. DeLeo had five scalp cuts but no fractures. Nickerson never left the prison, dying from his injuries less than two hours after the attack.

Prison officials said DeLeo disliked guards, but had a particular

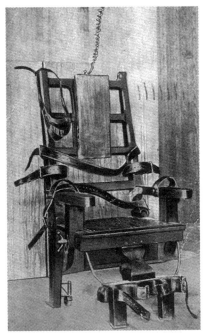

The electric chair in which DeLeo, Levandowski, and Jankowski died at Sing Sing

grudge against Beckett, who was in charge of DeLeo's section. No other reason was given for the attack. During the riot of 1929, thirty-five knives were stolen from the prison's cotton shop, and thirty had since been recovered. DeLeo's made it thirty-one. The riot had taken another victim five years later.

In court, the defense said DeLeo believed he was being removed from his cell for a beating, and his brother testified to DeLeo's insanity. The jury didn't buy any of it, taking less than an hour to deliberate. Just over three months after the stabbing, DeLeo was sentenced to die in the electric chair. An appeal and a clemency hearing bought him a few more months of life, but on the night of February 21, 1935, DeLeo was executed.

CLAUDE CROMIE, 1982

Corrections Officer Claude Cromie was a resident of Bouck Street in Dannemora and a veteran of twenty-one years without any inmate assaults. The fatal incident took place in the Annex, where the much-admired Merle Cooper Program was offered to inmates with special needs. Following a disturbance in the recreation room, Cromie and Sergeant William Badger were removing the unruly inmate, who initially offered no resistance.

But as handcuffs were being applied, he punched Badger in the face and viciously kicked Cromie, who fell to the ground and never regained consciousness. At the hospital in Plattsburgh a half-hour later, he was pronounced dead.

Renowned forensics expert Dr. Michael Baden was flown by helicopter from Albany to Plattsburgh for the autopsy. He determined that Cromie's death resulted from a heart attack caused by the assault and groin kick, but also noted evidence of early-stage coronary arteriosclerosis.

The inmate, Peter Catapano, remained unidentified until well

Claude Cromie

after he was transferred to Comstock. He was charged with first-degree manslaughter and second-degree assault, but the presence of arteriosclerosis in Cromie's system was used as leverage by the defense. Catapano agreed to a plea bargain, admitting guilt to criminally negligent homicide and attempted second-degree assault, both with sentences of two to four years. Adding those to his current sentence meant Catapano would first become eligible for parole in 1998. He was discharged from prison in August 1999 after serving the maximum sentence.

Nice Try: Attempted Escapes from Clinton

In Clinton's early days, the firing of the prison cannon was a call to arms. For every man to break out of prison, the cannon was fired three times, sending two important messages: protect yourselves, and go hunting if you're so inclined. The standard reward, offered many times in newspaper advertisements, was fifty dollars for every escapee captured and returned to the prison. To families surviving by farming, hunting, and fishing, fifty dollars (equal to $1600 in 2015) was a substantial windfall. There are still residents in the region who recall collecting escapee bounties into the 1950s.

But the truth is, the public and even most corrections officers aren't aware of the role escape has played in the history of our older prisons. Escapes from Clinton were less a point of controversy than a fact of life for the prison's first eighty-five years, exactly half the facility's life. There were few guards per prisoner, but unlike in modern times, the keepers were armed, allowing them to supervise large groups. Their guns were to intimidate inmates and keep them in line, but were first and foremost a means of personal protection. Should a group become unruly, it was either shoot early or suffer the consequences. Despite the armed guards, escape attempts were frequent.

As plot lines evolved surrounding the 2015 breakout, Governor Andrew Cuomo repeated the long-held belief that no one had ever escaped from Clinton. Nothing could be further from the truth, but it's important to know that not all escapes are equal.

Clinton's escape history is best divided into three categories. The first covers 1845 through 1888, when the prison's outer wall

NOTICE.

WHENEVER a convict escapes from Clinton Prison, three guns will be fired as a signal to the inhabitants of the surrounding country. If more than one convict escapes at the same time, three guns will be fired for each person.

Citizens should not expect at all times, to find an escaped convict dressed in the striped uniform of the prison. It is supposed that the convict who escaped on the 8th inst., had a citizens overcoat with him, and they will always embrace the first opportunity to steal a suit of citizens clothing.

In all cases of escape a reward of fifty dollars will be paid for each convict apprehended and returned to the prison.   RANSOM COOK, Agent.
Sept. 10th 1845.

Advertisement with instructions on use of prison cannon as escape alarm

consisted of tall wooden pickets in typical stockade formation used to protect forts. The second addresses 1889 through 1929, during which Clinton was bordered by a twenty-foot-high stone-and-concrete wall. The third runs from 1929 to the present, encompassing an era of relative lockdown following the riot. Among the changes made after the riot was raising the outer wall to a height of thirty feet.

Newspaper articles and official reports mention at least sixty escapes involving more than a hundred twenty-five inmates during the decades of the stockade fence. For convicts working around the prison grounds on mining-related jobs, opportunities to flee were plentiful. The biggest problem they faced was there was nowhere to go. Surviving in the northern wilderness had brought many a good man to his knees, and for those unprepared, like inmate escapees, there was scant hope for success. The pressing need for food and water soon drove them to nearby homes and farms. The majority of those men were captured within a few days.

Clinton's very first escape happened while the prison was still being stocked with its first inmates. Warden Ransom Cook picked up the fifty recruits from Sing Sing in June 1845, and forty-four more from Auburn later in the month. While he was on the Auburn trip, two inmates laid a long pole against the fence and climbed over the pickets. Their plan was to head twenty miles north to Canada, but without a compass or any other method of navigation, they fell victim to the natural tendency to circle, and after several hours found themselves in sight of the prison. They then headed east and made it several miles before hunger, fatigue, and biting insects forced them into situations that eventually led to recapture.

Escape attempts of that type were frequent, but with armed guards on the watch, death was sometimes the outcome. In 1854, two convicts made a break for it, and one of them, John Swan, was killed when a buckshot pellet struck him in the head. The officer was absolved of any wrongdoing by a court finding that "said act was faithfully in the discharge of his duty as a guard at said Clinton Prison and in the service of the People of New York State."

Between 1889 and 1929, there were at least a hundred twenty escape attempts involving about a hundred seventy inmates. Compared to the early years, the higher numbers during the presence of Clinton's imposing new wall seem contradictory, but there were mitigating factors. Between 1860 and 1920, the prison's population nearly quadrupled, and in 1900, Dannemora State Hospital was opened on prison grounds, but outside of the high wall and thus in a less secure position.

Inmate work crews of "trusties" were used during this time to build roads and undertake other state-funded projects. Those crews were comprised of men who were adjudged more reliable than most prisoners, and were often short-timers (in the final years of sentence completion), which presumably meant they were low escape risks. But as often as three times a month, such men walked off the job, causing manhunts that usually led to recapture. During this middle period, most escapees fled either the hospital or a work crew.

In the final category, from 1930 to the present, there were sixteen escapes involving twenty inmates, nearly all from the hospital or road crews. Even the trusties sometimes presented great danger. In 1933, Wesley Alger walked off a crew during a snowstorm, robbed a house, and later nearly killed a volunteer member of a posse with a shotgun blast, the brunt of which struck the man's arm.

At times the prison seemed so secure that workers lapsed into complacency instead of recognizing that constant vigilance is what created the tight security in the first place. In 1948, several Clinton guards were suspended after inmate Edward James escaped a cellblock and nearly made it over the wall using a ladder. James was an exception, but he could have killed an innocent citizen had he made it to the outside even for a few minutes.

Still, escape attempts from within the wall were rare events, and those from work crews led to changes in policy. When the state ended the practice of using inmates from maximum-security prisons for outside projects, escape from Dannemora's hospital was the only realistic means left. Fleeing from inside the high wall was believed impossible—until 2015.

People are fascinated with tales of triumph against great odds, a theme epitomized in any escape from maximum-security prisons. The story of Richard Matt and David Sweat captured the public's imagination, but few felt sympathy for them as individuals or hoped they were never captured. While both are now part of the prison's history, they are hardly the most notorious, most dangerous, or most feared inmates to be incarcerated at Clinton. Surely theirs was among the most ingenious plans to exit the prison—of that there's no doubt. But they are not without company, just like *The Shawshank Redemption*'s plot was not without precedent, even at Dannemora.

Aside from the many individuals who walked away from work crews or fled the prison hospital, a number of truly hardened criminals have escaped from Clinton in the past. Several have gone over the wall, some have gone under, and others died trying. Some even "escaped" inside the prison for a month or more, eventually getting beyond the wall to enjoy liberty, albeit briefly. Several of their stories share parallels with that of Matt and Sweat.

1873: Rebellion in the Forge

In 1873 the busiest building in Dannemora was the iron forge, which ran day and night, and was the workplace of reputedly the toughest men in the prison. The graveyard shift consisted of forty men watched by three guards and one keeper, all of them well armed. The iron gates to the building were kept locked, with a fourth man stationed outside the gate.

At about 2 a.m. on June 17, inmate Charles Albertson of Troy, a recent escapee who was bound with restrictive chains, grabbed the keeper and held him while inmate John McLaughlin of Brooklyn slammed an iron bar against the man's skull, knocking him unconscious. Another inmate used the bar to disable a second guard, and a third inmate, Robert Renforth, used a stone hammer on another guard's head. Guns were taken from each of the disabled men, and an all-out rebellion was imminent. But the fourth guard notified the outside man, who went for help.

The convicts, meanwhile, grabbed sledgehammers, iron bars, and a ladder, planning to break through the prison roof. Since the forge was close to the picket wall, they could drop to the ground and escape into the woods.

But the alarms sounded inside and outside the prison, summoning other guards and men of the village. The convicts knew the effort was hopeless, for no matter where they exited, armed guards and civilians would be waiting for them. The injured guards reported that the rebels abandoned the escape attempt, and most of them willingly returned to work.

Albertson's sentence was commuted three years later, but both he and McLaughlin would pay return visits to Clinton.

1908: EMIL OTTO

A snitch derailed the plans of Emil Otto to escape through a tunnel by surfacing inside the prison near the wall and climbing it to freedom. Otto ingeniously used jackscrews to lift one of the heavy stones forming the floor of his cell. Each night after lockup, he raised the stone and worked on the tunnel, packing the dirt into small bags that other prisoners dumped in the back of the hall, an area not frequented by prison guards. With the tunnel near completion, a convict working in the same hall told officials about Otto's plan. He was removed from the cellblock and locked in a dungeon.

1910: EDWARD BROGAN AND FREDERICK SCHULTZ

An informant revealed to prison officials that two revolvers and some dynamite had been smuggled into Clinton, but a cell search revealed nothing. The information proved valid when explosions occurred around 2 a.m. in the cells of Edward Brogan and Frederick Shultz, who used dynamite to blow off their cell doors in an effort to escape. Several officers overpowered the inmates and locked them in chains, after which revolvers were found in the cells of both men. The explosions caused only minor damage to the cellblock. It was believed that the guns were smuggled into Clinton by a trusty, and that the dynamite was left over from a similar attempt a year earlier when explosives were stolen from a road gang's supplies.

"Neddy" Brogan, alias James Haley, alias John Kelly, was a tough character, reportedly a one-time leader of Newburgh's Bridge Gang, responsible for many robberies and murders. He began committing crimes at age fourteen, and was in the Albany Penitentiary at age fifteen. In 1905, during a burglary trial that ended in a life sentence, Brogan was asked to explain why he ran after seeing police on the street. The ridiculous reason—because he was in poor physical condition and suddenly wanted to see a doctor—confirmed that he couldn't think on his feet in the court *or* the street. Brogan also denied the prosecutor's claim that he had been imprisoned in Virginia State Prison as James Haley, and in Pennsylvania's Eastern Penitentiary as John Kelly. He was then forced to expose his tattoos, which matched the descriptions provided by officers from both institutions.

The jury took all of eight minutes to find him guilty. Moments later, he was handed a life sentence at Sing Sing, but as a proven incorrigible, he was sent to Clinton Prison.

The Virginia arrest, it turns out, was for dynamiting a safe, and his sentence had been lengthened after a failed escape attempt—a blueprint for Brogan's actions at Dannemora five years later.

Cell Hall at Clinton Prison

1918: James Doyle

Court appearances required inmates to leave Dannemora, and any trip outside the walls represented an escape opportunity. Inmate James Doyle, serving twenty years for burglary, was returning from a court session in New York City, but remained handcuffed to Officer Edgar Farrington the entire time. Hoping to escape, he made a desperate move at Montcalm Landing in Plattsburgh. A request to get up and stretch was granted, and when the officer stood with him, Doyle smashed his head through the heavy glass window and launched himself through the opening. The officer remained inside, while Doyle dangled outside the moving train. After a brief struggle, his weight pulled Farrington from the train, and the two of them fell twenty feet into Lake Champlain. The officer won the ensuing battle despite a sprained wrist and injured leg. Doyle, badly bruised and suffering from a head wound, was returned to the prison.

1929: Bruno Montorio (alias Nick Mastro)

In 1924, Bruno Montorio of Schenectady was reprimanded for disrupting his seventh-grade classroom. He responded by physically attacking the teacher, who subdued the boy and filed charges of third-degree assault. Montorio was a real tough kid who had been boxing inter-city matches since around the age of ten. He was so well acquainted with the local court system that his attack on the teacher constituted a parole violation, even though Bruno was just sixteen years old at the time.

Despite several corrective measures in the past, he remained a young man out of control. The court sentenced him to sixty weeks at New York City's House of Refuge on Randall's Island, a juvenile delinquent facility that—with cells, strict rules, required schooling, and enforced labor—mimicked prison life.

After his term expired, Bruno joined the army, but on June 5, 1926, within six months of enlisting, he deserted with a friend, Frank Mallock of Hillside, New Jersey. Leaving Fort Slocum on western Long Island, they set out for Buffalo. While stopped at a Binghamton diner, they saw a patron, Anton Roefs Jr., pay for his meal from a wad of cash. They finagled a ride with him, and when Roefs stopped to fix his car near Owego, they took a hammer from the vehicle's back seat, beat him into unconsciousness, and drove away. Passersby saw Roefs crawling on the roadside and came to his aid.

Police pursued the two eighteen-year-olds, who abandoned the car and stole a boat. Relentless pursuit and several warning shots ended in the capture of both boys after a long chase. Bruno gave his name as Nick Mastro, but he was eventually identified correctly.

When the two young men appeared in Tioga County court, a small measure of mercy was bestowed upon Mallock, who expressed remorse. But for Montorio, of whom the *Binghamton Press* said his "only regret appeared to be that he hadn't succeeded in killing Roefs," there was none. Mallock received a total sentence of ten to twenty years, but Bruno's was fifteen to thirty years. Considering his background since childhood, what happened next wasn't surprising.

Accompanied by the sheriff, he was shackled to two other prisoners while en route to Auburn Prison. But he managed to wriggle out of the handcuffs and took off running through the streets of Auburn, with the sheriff and others in hot pursuit. Although several shots were fired, he escaped, albeit temporarily. Hours later, an Auburn police officer captured Bruno and delivered him to the prison. At his court appearance on the escape charges, he pleaded guilty under his new identity of Nick Mastro. The county judge added seven more years to his sentence.

Mastro's first six months in prison were spent at Auburn, making clothes and license plates before a transfer sent him to Clinton at the end of 1926. In July 1929, his name was featured in newspapers across the country in stories covering the major riot that occurred at Clinton Prison, leaving three inmates dead and several injured. Among the latter was Nick Mastro, who was shot in both legs.

But just seventy-four days later, instead of being a small part of a big story, he was the headliner in one of the most dramatic moments Clinton Prison had ever seen. On October 3, during the daily recreation period in the yard, Nick grabbed a light pole near the main wall and started climbing. Reaching the top, he began moving towards a place where he might drop to the ground, twenty feet below, without injury. Manning Post No. 2 atop the wall was Guard Jeremiah Callahan, who carried a billy club as he confronted Mastro. They battled hand to hand, with Callahan being pushed towards the edge of the wall, risking a potentially deadly fall.

Having witnessed the encounter from the principal keeper's office, guard Thomas Brannigan grabbed a revolver and ran to help. As the two men grappled atop the wall, Brannigan feared hitting Callahan with a bullet, but driven by the urgency of the situation, he took aim and fired. Reports differed over the number of shots, but Mastro was struck in the hip, allowing Callahan to break free. Rushing to

> **Dannemora Attempt to Flee and Battle on Wall Fatal to Nick Mastro, 21**
>
> Clinton headline (1929)

the guardhouse, he grabbed his machine gun, and as Mastro came towards him again, Callahan squeezed the trigger, killing him on the spot. The coroner ruled the shooting as justifiable homicide.

1953: JAMES ATTILIO AND CLIFFORD LAWTON

A pair of bizarre incidents occurred at the Dannemora State Hospital in late October 1953. One of the two took place in the hospital yard and was referred as an escape/suicide attempt. Two inmates, James Attilio and Clifford Lawton, took their shoes off and began scaling the side of a hospital building that served as a prison wall, but which had three-foot overhanging eaves that prevented escape. After using window bars to climb to the eaves, they either fell or threw themselves twenty feet to the cement floor below. Both men suffered only minor injuries.

The other incident occurred in a hospital bathroom, where a contractor making repairs to a wall found a cache containing knives, hacksaw blades, and a loaded pistol, items that could have led to a terrible catastrophe. It was at first suspected that the two inmates who climbed the outside wall were somehow related to the hidden items, but when the truth was finally discovered, prison officials were incredulous at a sequence of events beyond all imagination.

A former Franklin County town supervisor, Hyman Weiner, was also a popular, widely known druggist in Saranac Lake for many years. After taking a job in January as pharmacist in the Clinton Prison hospital, he became acquainted with inmate Charles Di Umberto, who had twenty-six years left to serve on his sentence. His record included thirty-seven arrests in the past twenty-two years, with ten other arrest warrants still unserved.

His forte? Di Umberto was a con man, and Weiner was his next dupe. He first talked the pharmacist into bringing him quantities of alcohol, coffee, sugar, and shaving lotion from the outside. Then—as an inmate in a hospital for the criminal insane—he somehow convinced Weiner to take part in an outlandish scheme that began with the purchase of a .38-caliber pistol on New York City's black market. On a visit to relatives, Weiner bought the gun, and upon return, he smuggled it into the prison and gave it to the inmate.

And Di Umberto's plan? Officials were looking for a gun rumored to be hidden somewhere inside the prison. His idea was to hide the .38 and then pretend to discover it. By turning it over to prison authorities as the hidden gun, he might in return be given a retrial, or perhaps receive time off for good behavior. It seemed far too wild to be true, but a two-week investigation confirmed that Di Umberto had indeed conned the pharmacist.

In another plan concocted for the same reasons, Di Umberto organized a phony escape plot with a dozen inmates, and then snitched on them in hopes of being rewarded by prison officials for preventing a breakout.

Weiner's many friends in the Saranac Lake business community and town government vouched for him in court, where most of the nine counts against him were dismissed. But there was no denying he had committed an egregious offense that could have led to innocent deaths. On one count, he was given six months in the county jail.

1956: Frank Flynn

On October 18, in an incident similar to one in October 1953, inmate Frank Flynn climbed one of the building walls that enclosed the hospital yard. With more than three hundred convicts watching, he used window bars to reach the overhanging eaves while ignoring the pleas of hospital employees.

Flynn, either accidentally or intentionally, fell head first, suffering a fractured skull that led to his death three days later. His effort was first believed to be an escape attempt, but in light of two previous incidents involving throat and wrist cuts, it was classified by the coroner as a suicide.

1981: Howard "Buddy" Jacobsen

Millionaire Buddy Jacobsen was named America's leading horse trainer for three consecutive years in the early 1960s, and became president of the Horsemen's Benevolent and Protective Association.

But in 1978 he was arrested for murder in a love-triangle case in New York City, where he shot, stabbed, and bludgeoned a man to death, dumped the victim in a vacant lot, and set the body on fire. During his trial, a sister of Assistant District Attorney William Kelly was murdered, and another sister received a phone call saying only, "You're next." It was suspected to be the work of Jacobsen's associates, but regardless, he was found guilty in the murder case.

In June 1980, while he awaited sentencing, a visitor claiming to be his attorney exchanged clothes with Jacobsen, who then walked out of the Brooklyn House of Detention. He was recaptured forty days later in California.

With a sentence of twenty-five years to life, he was sent north to Dannemora. In May 1981, he was placed in solitary confinement after the discovery of an escape tunnel, said to be the work of his inmate friends. Five months later, a federal judge ordered Jacobsen's release from solitary, after which he was transferred to Auburn. Both actions appeared related to his status as a millionaire, and the numerous political and social connections he had made through the world of horseracing.

Dannemora's Greatest Escapes

1860: Abraham Kingsbury
(Alias Charles F. Whiting, A. M. Kingsland)

In early August 1855, General Robert Halsey's room at Saratoga's spectacular Congress Hotel was robbed. The accused was fifty-six-year-old Abraham Kingsbury, a well-known swindler and con artist who secretly entered Halsey's room, picked the lock on a trunk, and made off with bonds and jewelry valued at about $12,000 [$339,000 in 2015]. In February 1856, he was convicted of burglary and sentenced to nine and a half years in Clinton Prison.

In April 1860, he inconspicuously escaped, walking out of the main gate while clad in civilian clothing, posing as a visitor. Nearly a year later, James F. Whiting was arrested for jewel theft in Philadelphia. He was recognized by police there as a prolific swindler, and one detective recognized something else: Whiting was actually Abraham Kingsbury, an escapee from New York's Clinton Prison. He denied it at first, but finally conceded that Kingsbury was his true identity, and that several swindles since escaping Clinton had earned him $20,000 [$554,000 in 2015]. By the end of January, he was returned to Dannemora for completion of his sentence, which was set to expire in June 1865.

1864: George E. Gordon

Found guilty of first-degree murder in the death of New York cattle buyer Owen Thompson, George Gordon was sentenced to hang on the morning of February 16, 1865. While charging the jury, the judge declared that Gordon's failure to account for his whereabouts at the time of the murder was "of conclusive character," whereby "doubt ripens into certainty" ... meaning that if the jury had doubts, his silence indicated guilt.

That was incorrect according to the law, and because of the error, New York's highest court ordered a new trial, which nearly ended in a hung jury after sixteen hours. Stalled at eleven for conviction and one standing firm for innocent, they were ordered by the judge to try again. After nearly six more hours, a compromise was reached, finding Gordon guilty of second-degree murder. He was sentenced to life in Clinton Prison, where he was assigned to work in the underground iron mines.

In April 1868, a dozen convicts, led by George Gordon and Adam Cole (who had escaped four months earlier but was recaptured, p. 149), staged a rebellion. Six hundred feet below the surface, they disarmed a guard, tied and gagged him, and headed for the surface. Using the first guard's gun to disarm the officer at the mine opening, they escaped over the wall of pickets. The prison cannon was fired to announce the breakout, sending armed citizens and guards in pursuit of the escapees.

The snow-covered ground made for easy tracking, and gunshots were soon heard echoing in the woods. In early afternoon, one prisoner was brought in with a bullet wound to the arm. Shortly after, another convict was returned with a serious gunshot wound to the chest. Five more escapees were brought in by nightfall.

The next morning, two more were captured, including George Gordon, who engaged in a gun battle with pursuers until he ran out of ammunition. The last man, Cole, surrendered two days later following a similar shootout.

Both men suffered harsh punishments for the trouble they caused, but Gordon would eventually prove he was different from the average inmate. The possessor of a creative mind, he developed several inventions while serving as a Clinton inmate. In January 1876, he patented an apparatus to propel a variety of boats using two driving shafts, "the object being to support the hull of the boat above the surface of the water, to avoid the friction heretofore created in forcing the boat through the water, and to increase the speed of the boat."

As described, his design was a forerunner of the modern, powered catamaran. Gordon was offered $25,000 [$583,000 in 2015] for half interest in the idea.

His ingenuity attracted the attention of guards and officials, some of whom urged the governor to pardon a man of such talent who had already served more than a decade at Clinton. Gordon continued inventing while petitioning the governor for clemency, but it wasn't until December 1896 that there was any movement. Governor Levi Morton commuted his sentence from life down to fifty-two years, which meant that with time off for good behavior, he would be released in five months.

On May 8, 1897, the fifty-eight-year-old Gordon was freed after serving thirty-one years in Clinton Prison. Although the woman he married long ago still survived, there was no spouse waiting for him. The law allowed any wife of an inmate serving a life sentence to seek an incontestable divorce, which Mrs. Gordon had done, and had since remarried. George died in 1913.

1867: ADAM COLE

In late March 1867, Adam Cole and two other inmates escaped from Clinton Prison. Cole was a well-known criminal in the Chatham area, about twenty miles southeast of Albany, which is where the law caught up with him nine months later. After five burglaries in two days at Chatham Four Corners, a man was seen running from a local barn. The neighborhood was alerted, and local citizens gave chase, throwing rocks and using clubs while running down and capturing two suspects. One of them admitted to being Clinton Prison escapee Adam Cole. That night, Cole attempted to escape the Hudson jail, but was caught. Clinton's warden arrived the next day and returned him to Dannemora.

In late April 1868, less than five months later, Cole conspired with George Gordon (p. 147) in leading the escape of twelve Clinton inmates from the underground iron mines. After disarming and tying up two guards, they climbed over the picket wall. A springtime storm helped thwart the effort, making tracking easy in the fresh snow. A few days after the mass breakout, Cole engaged in a shootout with pursuers and was the last of the escapees to be captured.

1867: Billy Mulligan

Mulligan, a transferee from Sing Sing, led two other men on a breakout, according to the *Police Gazette*, "by squeezing through the drain, and ran off to Lake Champlain, robbing and plundering all the way down." Mulligan was shot during the recapture of all three escapees at Plattsburgh, and was looked after in the prison hospital.

1867: Bob Magee, Charles Brady, and 12 Others

In the Albany–Saratoga–Troy area in the early 1860s, Bob Magee always seemed to be in trouble with the law. During the Civil War, he was involved in bounty fraud that reduced recruits for the Northern Army but earned him a small fortune. At one point Magee had more than $20,000 [$400,000 in 2015], but lost most of it in a "bounty bubble" and squandered the rest on women and partying.

For various crimes, he did time in the Ballston jail, the Albany Penitentiary, and finally at Clinton Prison, where he was sent in April 1867 for fifteen years on a first-degree burglary conviction.

In early September, he led a group of fourteen convicts from the nail factory to the prison yard, where they placed a ladder against the prison's picket wall and escaped into the woods. Clinton's guards opened fire, and thirteen of the escapees, including Magee, were soon in custody. Still missing was Charles Brady, who made it all the way to Chicago, where he was arrested in May 1868.

A few weeks after the breakout, Magee escaped Clinton again and headed north to Canada. After a month's freedom, he was captured in Kingston, Ontario, 140 miles west of Dannemora, and returned to prison.

Besides outright escape, which had twice failed, Magee tried leveraging some low-level political connections to get a petition started, with the end target being a governor's pardon. Signatures were sought in the Troy area, but nothing came of it, and he was forced to complete his sentence.

As soon as he was free again, Magee resumed criminal activities with his old cronies. For dynamiting the safe at the Copake Iron Works, he was locked up in the Hudson, New York, jail, where he and four other prisoners, including his regular partner in crime, James Frawley, pulled off an incredible escape. Men on the first floor dug to the empty dungeon below, and then dug sideways through the next three dungeons until their group consisted of five convicts. Working together, they tunneled to the outside, angled upwards for six feet, and emerged in the jail's yard.

Magee next surfaced two months later in Toronto, Canada, where he was jailed for burglary. Returning to the U.S., he stayed on the move, showing up in Philadelphia, Cincinnati, and other cities while committing crimes ranging from routine break-ins to dynamiting safes.

But he was also skilled at election fraud, a trait valued highly by unscrupulous politicians, of which there was no shortage. In Albany, Troy, and elsewhere, Magee's services had often been called upon at election time. On short notice, he could provide a small team to dissuade voters, or rustle up three hundred men for a repeater job. Repeaters were men hired to vote more than once, sometimes in a single city ward, and sometimes voting for party candidates in multiple wards. His men were taught how to falsify registration forms, allowing them to vote many times using various assumed names. Magee could also be hired to disrupt elections, either by intimidation or trickery. The political connections he made sometimes helped keep him out of jail or obtain early release, especially when his services were needed.

Magee's next arrest came about simply by chance. While on the lam in 1885, he stopped overnight to visit family members after missing a connector train. Several rewards had been offered for his capture, and when Magee was spotted in Troy, a chase ensued, ending with his arrest on a rooftop. He was confined to the Hudson jail, from which he had tunneled seventeen years earlier. While housed there, he nearly managed another breakout when friends placed a ladder at his window. Several shots fired by a deputy foiled the attempt, and to ensure he remained locked up, jailers chained Magee to the floor for the remainder of his stay.

For assault with intent to kill, he was remanded to Auburn Prison for two and a half years, but was transferred to Dannemora in November 1885. After release in mid-October 1887, Magee continued operating outside the law, often with impunity when it came to election fraud. He was a very busy man, providing repeaters to stuff the ballot boxes, or scaring voters from polling places.

During a long career of crime, Bob Magee committed dozens of major robberies, served time in numerous jails and prisons, made several escapes, and generally terrorized the population from north of Albany to Columbia County. Despite that history, he was granted a pardon by acting Governor Timothy Woodruff in September 1900. The pardon was accompanied by official "Restoration of Citizenship"—which included, ironically, Magee's right to vote.

1868: JAMES AUSTIN AND CHARLES TWEED

James Austin and Charles Tweed escaped Clinton Prison in late 1868, but were quickly recaptured. In March 1869 they did it again, climbing a chimney passage to the roof of a prison building, dropping to the snow-covered ground, and climbing over the pickets. After stealing a horse and cutter from a nearby barn, they headed south into the Saranac Valley, but became lost. Turning back towards the prison, they sighted a search team and ditched the horses, running to the woods. Guards James Christian, Michael Hagerty, and Thomas Harney tracked them down and returned the pair to Clinton.

1868: GEORGE LONG

On February 20, 1868, George Long was found guilty of grand larceny and sentenced to three years and six months in Clinton Prison. On May 14, twenty-three days later, Long escaped and made his way to Northville in Fulton County, where he lived under the name Fred Lee and resumed committing crimes.

In August 1869, after burglaries at Fish House, Batchellerville, Gloversville, and Greenfield, he and a partner were arrested by Sheriff's Deputy Peter Pulver at the Ballston rail station. In their possession was silverware from a Gloversville robbery.

Seizing the first opportunity, Long tried to escape, firing a shot that grazed Pulver's scalp. The deputy returned fire, hitting him twice in the leg. The two men were jailed at Ballston, where the sheriff learned that Long was a Clinton Prison escapee. On August 20, 1869, a guard accompanied him back to Dannemora.

On June 23, 1870, Long escaped Clinton for a second time. Shortly after, he was arrested under the alias James Thompson and sentenced to five years at Sing Sing. After completing that sentence, he committed robberies in Albany, Waterford, and West Troy before fleeing to Philadelphia, where he was captured. Multiple convictions followed, along with a dual sentence. For the Albany County crimes, he was given five years in the Albany Penitentiary, and for the Saratoga County crimes, he was sentenced to twenty years in Clinton.

In late 1878, he was released from Albany and sent north to Dannemora. In August 1880, Long made a third attempt at escaping Clinton, this time through a roof, but was foiled. The effort added to his sentence, and he still owed the prison more than a year of unserved time from escapes in 1868 and 1870. The adjustments resulted in a release date of January 21, 1896.

But as an incorrigible, George continued committing crimes after being set free. In 1901 he was again sentenced to Clinton, and was released in July 1903 at the age of fifty-seven.

1869: PETER CRISS

Peter Criss was known in the late 1860s as a horse thief in the Galway–Glenville area southeast of Saratoga Springs. Following

An early watch tower at Clinton

the theft of horses, wagons, and related gear, he was jailed at Schenectady in 1869, but escaped. After recapture, he was given a term of thirteen years at Clinton Prison.

In mid-January 1871, Criss and John Riley escaped from Clinton by cutting through a building's sheet-iron roof, but were quickly recaptured.

Just over two years later, in March 1873, Criss was at it again. A rebellion by a half-dozen inmates working in the forge was briefly chaotic, but of all the men involved, only Criss made it to the roof. The guard inside had been disarmed, but the one outside opened fire. Criss kept going anyway and managed to escape unscathed.

Three months later, he surfaced about thirty miles west of his old Saratoga stomping grounds, where he stole a buggy from one business and a horse and harnesses from another.

A reward was offered for the unknown thief's arrest, but the trail ran dry in the Catskills. Criss, meanwhile, ended up in Kingston, New York, where he arranged to stable his stolen horse on a farm and work there to build up some capital. The farmer observed that Criss wasn't much of a worker but took a real shine to the ladies, whom he accompanied one Sunday to church. There the farmer saw a Peter Criss wanted poster and had him arrested on the spot.

He confessed the thefts, and the stolen goods were returned to their Fort Plain owners. At the same time, a messenger from the county sheriff's office happened to mention the story while on business at Dannemora. The warden, suspecting their prisoner was his missing escapee, provided identifying information, which led to a confession. Criss was returned to Dannemora to complete his term.

1874: John Filkins

There are more legends surrounding John Filkins than any other man who ever escaped Clinton Prison. The crime that brought him statewide attention was known as the Albany Express Robbery. It's an interesting, multifaceted story, but the shorter version here tells the tale. On January 6, 1871, as the train on the Albany & Boston road was slowly leaving the city, Filkins burst into the express car and pumped three bullets into messenger Thomas Halpine—one in the right side of the neck below the jawline, and then, while standing over him, carefully placing one below the right eye, and another in the right ear, leaving no question of the intent to murder.

He then robbed the express safe of an unknown amount. The number initially given to the press was $1225 [$26,000 in 2015], but it was believed to be far higher, perhaps up to a half-million dollars [$10 million in 2015]. Filkins knew there would be substantial cash on hand, for like Halpine, he had worked many years as a messenger for both American Express and Merchants' Union before becoming a transfer agent. With a partner, he started a new express company, but it failed. He then opened a bakery, but couldn't meet his debts, which spawned the decision to rob the express train.

Five days after the shooting, when the investigation pointed towards Filkins, police attempted an arrest at his home. No one was there, but left on a baker's table was fresh dough for the morning products, a sign that he had skipped out quickly. A $5,000 reward was immediately offered for his capture.

After reading a description of his bearded self, the fugitive shaved his chin whiskers and headed north at a rather slow pace through Ballston and Saratoga, reaching Glens Falls after six days of travel. He then continued north to Lake George, Warrensburgh, and Schroon Lake, where he registered at the Ondawa House under an assumed name.

Suspicions were raised by the stagecoach driver about the man's true identity, but actual proof was needed. Filkins was known for a few physical abnormalities that included a deformed thumb, the result of an accident while coupling trains. Through trickery, the man's odd digit was viewed, and shortly after, he was arrested. While acknowledging he was Filkins, he denied the crime, claiming to have fled north only because police sought to blame him for the robbery.

While in custody, he exuded confidence that vindication would soon come, but there was a catch—the man he shot three times in the head had survived. Filkins was paraded before him at the hospital, and after an arranged conversation between the two in the presence of others, Halpine was certain they had the right man.

The high-profile trial that followed was fascinating, portraying Filkins as a Mason, a member of the Methodist Episcopal Church, a business owner, a thirty-seven-year-old father of two, and a man of character and integrity. But in the end the verdict was guilty of robbery, and the sentence was twenty years in Clinton Prison.

By mid-May 1871 he was at Dannemora, and by mid-November, Filkins already had an escape plan in place. He had somehow obtained certain keys, but the scheme was discovered and he was relegated to Clinton's terrible dungeon.

In mid-April 1872, exactly six months later, Filkins made a second escape attempt. Using a knife, he filed the metal bar holding his cell door shut and went cell to cell, releasing inmates Dennis McGarry, Augustus Noyes, and James Robinson. He then lit some gunpowder "torpedoes" that exploded, creating a smokescreen, providing cover while they sledgehammered the iron bars around a window and escaped. Guards rushed in and fired into the smoke, but no one was hit. The foursome managed to get outside the picket walls, where Filkins was captured.

As punishment, guards shaved half his head and face, shackled him in large, heavy irons, and locked him in a dungeon. Two months later, after returning to the general population, Filkins prepared an escape plan for July 4—line his cell door with gunpowder, ignite a large explosion, and disappear amid the confusion—but his intentions were discovered, preventing the attempt.

He had remained single-minded about escaping since his arrival at Dannemora, but time in the dungeons after each breakout attempt was debilitating, depressing, and unproductive. Guards considered him the worst convict yet confined at Dannemora, and his record made him the most scrutinized inmate as well—not a good thing for a man hoping to escape.

After the latest attempt, Filkins adopted a different approach, blending into the prison system, biding his time, and looking for quality opportunities. A year later, he was still watched closely, but was considered the best employee in the separator, which was part of the iron ore production facilities. Another year passed with no issues—quite the turnaround for a convict who had three escapes planned during his first nine months in prison. The shrewdest, most cunning inmate at Clinton hadn't seen the inside of a dungeon in a long time. And he never would again.

Clinton Prison had a wall of pickets for the first forty-three years (1880)

On the morning of September 15, 1874, John Filkins for all intents and purposes vanished from the face of the earth. Plattsburgh newspapers reported that he exited Clinton's main gate while wearing civilian clothes, and by the time his absence was discovered, Filkins was long gone. That was the explanation offered by prison management because it was the only scenario they could imagine.

The standard reward of fifty dollars for the capture and return of any Clinton escapee didn't apply in the case of Filkins, who was considered a very dangerous man because of the ruthless assault he committed, and dangerously smart as well. A $250 reward was offered by the prison, but less than two weeks later, Governor John Dix added a state reward of $500, which was matched by the American Express Company, bringing the total reward to $1250 [equal to $27,000 in 2015]. Suspicions were that Filkins had stolen nearly a half-million dollars in the express robbery [$10 million in 2015], and had used part of it to bribe Clinton's gatekeeper into letting him walk away. But again, no one had any proof.

Most escapees from Dannemora were found not far from the prison within a few days, but this case was different. Two weeks after he disappeared, Filkins was reportedly sighted seventeen miles north of the prison at Mooers Junction, just three miles from the Canadian border. At nearby line crossings, border agents asked male strangers to remove their shoes and show their feet, for the fugitive was known to have several toes missing. But Filkins remained on the loose.

In mid-November, an express robbery in Toronto heightened speculation that he had indeed gone to Canada and resumed committing crimes. The latest robbery involved five men and no shooting, but otherwise was recognized as a near duplicate of the Albany robbery by Filkins several years earlier. An unconfirmed report later added that a knife originating at Clinton Prison was found in the Toronto rail car.

While the search for Filkins in Canada continued, he was reportedly seen in the streets of Syracuse in late December, but investigators again came up empty.

In July, a widely circulated newspaper story pronounced the mystery solved with the discovery of a skeleton in the main sewer beneath Clinton Prison. As the story was told, during the annual cleaning of the sewer line, a human skeleton was found submerged in the effluent. It was presented as fact that Filkins had planned to escape through pipes linked to the main sewer and then exit some distance from the prison, but had encountered steel bars at the end of the pipe. He then tried to retrace his path, but was unable to return to his cell and thus died amid the filth.

The tale smacked of wishful thinking to help protect the prison's reputation. Claims were made of positive identification of the remains as Filkins, but there was no mention made of the skeleton possessing any of his physical abnormalities: a deformed thumb, a set of small false upper teeth, or three missing toes. Without that information, his own family remained unconvinced.

It was widely reported that Clinton's warden had written to the *Troy Times*, dismissing the story as a hoax. It was also true that a convict *had* been recently found alive in the sewer system, having lifted a stone cover and wedged a board in place, keeping him above the sewage. But that inmate had been captured and was locked up in one of Clinton's dungeons—by some accounts an even worse place to be than the sewer.

There was no stopping the legend that was building around the name Filkins. Even as the death-in-the-sewer story circulated, there were published reports of personal encounters with Filkins in Canada and in Fonda, New York. From time to time, stories surfaced in the news about his supposed activities, often placing him north of the border. He was everywhere, it seemed, and yet nowhere.

Almost exactly a year after Filkins disappeared, a remarkable thing happened: another convict at Clinton seemingly vanished without a trace. It was later learned that Inmate William Creswell (p. 160) had secreted himself underground within the prison for a lengthy period. The story was sensational, and certainly big enough to stand on its own merits, but became more famous for possibly exposing the escape route used by Filkins. Much of the coverage suggested that the blanket and prison suit of Filkins were found in the same underground hideaway, thereby solving once and for all his mysterious disappearance—he had hid underground prior to escaping. But it was all speculation. Nobody knew for sure how Filkins escaped or what had become of him.

The next story in his saga was soon to follow. In October 1875, James Malone of Ontario, Canada, crossed the St. Lawrence River by ferry to Ogdensburg, where he telegrammed Clinton Prison with an important message: he had just captured John Filkins. But while Mr. Malone was sending the telegram, his loosely held captive had disappeared. Prison officials recognized the man's description as an inmate named Manning who had escaped months earlier. Guards were sent to locate him, but inexplicably, Manning showed up at Clinton Prison a few days later and recommitted himself.

And so it went, with the name John Filkins popping up in newspapers every so often, causing his long and unusual story to be reviewed. In 1876 he was mentioned as doing well in Canada, where he was safe from extradition to the United States. In 1878, when Dannemora's shoe shop was being remodeled into a hat-making department, the remains of a body were reportedly found inside a wall, according to the *St. Albans Messenger*. Coins found in the clothing were of recent vintage, leading to the belief that the deceased was Filkins—if there were any truth to the story at all.

Two years later, the *Troy Times* reported that Clinton's principal keeper received a letter stating that the writer knew of Filkins' whereabouts, and inquired about the reward that was offered for his capture. In 1882, newspapers from Albany to the Canadian border revealed that authorities had discovered Filkins' location and were preparing papers to bring him back to New York. In 1888, a former inmate friend of Filkins told the American Express Company he had recently seen the fugitive, who owned a large ranch in Manitoba Territory, Canada. The company sent a detective out west to investigate, but like all the other stories about Filkins that had surfaced over the years, nothing came of it.

Much was said and written about him after he disappeared from Clinton Prison at the age of forty. Census records reveal that just nine months after Filkins escaped, his wife Sarah registered with the state as widowed. She registered in the same way for every census through 1900, and when Sarah died in 1902, she was buried in the Albany Rural Cemetery—in a lot owned by John Filkins, whom she hadn't seen (as far as we know) for thirty years.

There is no burial record for John Filkins, but there are two things we do know about him: he was never returned to Clinton Prison, and the large haul from the Albany Express Robbery was never recovered by the owners.

1875: WILLIAM CRESWELL

Inmate William Creswell pulled off one of the most unusual Clinton escapes ever when, in mid-August 1875, he simply vanished from sight. Dannemora officials conducted a thorough investigation that was repeated several times over, resulting in no evidence of a breakout. The warden stated publicly that Creswell was believed to be within the prison grounds, but for weeks the search continued, to no avail. Extra guards were posted around the prison day and night, but after more than a month, it was conceded that he must have indeed somehow escaped.

About six weeks after Creswell disappeared, he was seen digging potatoes on a farm in Saranac Hollow, just a few miles south of the prison, where he was easily captured.

After returning to the lockup, he revealed the secret behind such a mystifying disappearance. Beneath the prison's ore shed was a crawl space that had been searched, but beneath the crawl space was an area about twenty inches deep, four feet wide, and seven feet long. Debris blocked access to the lower space, where Creswell remained hidden for weeks.

When he was finally comfortable that officials had called off the internal search, he emerged from hiding, dug a hole beneath the picket wall, and escaped. There was little doubt that other inmates helped by providing him with food and other needs while he was underground, but Creswell didn't rat them out.

He suffered terrible punishments in the aftermath, concluding with a term in the dungeon. But if Creswell possessed anything, it was resolve. A little over a year later, he led seven inmates in another escape attempt. Instead of beneath the floor, this one was literally through the roof—of the iron mine. Rather than follow the iron vein, they created a passage to the surface and exited outside the guard posts. None of the men made it very far, however, and all were recaptured on the same day.

But more than any of the other escapees, Creswell paid dearly for his latest adventure. Multiple breakout attempts branded him an incorrigible and led to more of Clinton's tortures. The prison's dungeon, which could drive a man insane within weeks, became Creswell's final home. He died there eleven months later.

1876: JACK WILLIAMS

Jack Williams had two Clinton escapes linked to his name, and both contained unusual components featured in no other Dannemora breakouts.

He was sentenced to Clinton in January 1875, and six months later took part in an escape scheme that was only partially successful. Williams and three others worked the overnight shift in the forge, which was very close to Clinton's wall, with Dannemora's main street just on the other side. They widened the hole where a belt passed outside the building, and through that opening went three men. Williams was quite heavy (newspapers described him as "a stout man") and unable to fit through the hole, forcing him to stay behind. The three men dropped to the street and ran for the woods, but were captured soon after their absence was discovered.

A year later, Williams put his great size to good use in a second attempt, one that involved Clinton's famous cannon—and a candidate for president. The cannon at Clinton was installed when the prison first opened in 1845, and public advertisements defined its purpose: to broadcast for twenty miles in all directions that a breakout had occurred. If one inmate escaped, the cannon sounded once; if more than one escaped, the cannon was fired three times for each escapee. The system had to be followed religiously in order to work, with the end goals of public safety as well as public assistance in capturing dangerous criminals. Most wardens forbade its use for any other reason, even to celebrate the Fourth of July.

But in 1876, political excitement was at a fever pitch for New York Governor Samuel Tilden, who was about to announce his candidacy for president of the United States. Overzealous supporters arranged to have Clinton's cannon carried off to Plattsburgh for a big Fourth of July celebration, highlighted by statewide confirmation that Tilden was running. Jack Williams, serving a second term at Clinton, chose this same time for his departure. While overseeing a crew of three other inmates, Williams grabbed the convict deepest in the mine and tied him up. Working towards the surface, he did the same to the next two men, leaving no one available who could reveal his escape. Utilizing ropes and grappling hooks, he then climbed the picket wall, descended on the outside, and walked away.

When his absence was discovered, the cannon/alarm was at Plattsburgh, fourteen miles away, something Tilden's local political foes gladly shared with the media. Williams, a prolific criminal in the Albany area, was eventually returned to complete his term.

1876: WILLIAM AHEARN

On November 19, Ahearn slipped out of Clinton Prison without notice, aided by his cellmate, who put a dummy in Ahearn's bed and answered for him during morning roll call. With a good head start, he almost left the area by train, but three days later, a prison hat was found on a Plattsburgh street. The escapee was tracked down shortly after and returned to Dannemora.

1877: PETER MCLAIN

Peter McLain was a native of Dobbs Ferry, a rural area along the Hudson River north of New York City, where for many years he led a prolific gang of thieves who terrorized the countryside. For a robbery at Dobbs Ferry in 1875 and several other crimes, he was sentenced in 1876 to fifteen years in Sing Sing.

Like many of New York's hardened criminals, he was transferred to Clinton, where McLain was placed in the corner of a top tier, affording a bit more privacy than other cells. After making preparations to escape, he complained of illness for a few days in March 1877 and was confined to his cell—just what McLain wanted.

By picking away at the stone ceiling and using a jackscrew, he raised a large stone, allowing access to the roof's underside. After cutting a hole, he climbed out onto the roof, located a lightning rod, and slid to the ground. To delay detection of his absence, he left a dummy in his bed and hung a towel to obscure the hole in the ceiling.

After hiking a few miles southeast to the Cadyville area, he stole a horse, but released it before reaching the next toll booth, deciding it was best to hide in the woods for a day. Under cover of darkness, he entered a house, stole some food and three suits of clothes, and left the North Country behind.

In 1883, six and a half years later, a detective for the Hudson River Railroad arrested a man named Patrick Ryan for trying to shoot the brakeman on a passing train. Ryan was convicted and sentenced to a term of two and a half years at Sing Sing, where he was recognized as the notorious Peter McLain. After completing his time at Sing Sing, McLain was sent north to serve out his term at Clinton.

1886: LOUIS PERYEA (OR PERYER)

Louis Peryea didn't escape from inside Clinton, but he caused more than the usual excitement generated by an escapee who simply walked away from a work crew. For stealing a man's pants, watch, and nine dollars in 1885, he was sentenced to two years in Clinton Prison. In July 1886, while working in a hayfield during extremely hot weather, he was allowed by guards to wear different, lighter clothing. Peryea showed his appreciation by running off at the first opportunity. The prison cannon sounded soon after, alerting area residents of a breakout.

While heading for his Ellenburg home, Peryea encountered a fourteen-year-old girl, who was alone picking berries, and sexually assaulted her. That night he sought to rob the familiar store of John Havens, whom he knew slept inside the business. To distract the owner, he set a nearby horse barn on fire. While Havens was fighting the fire, Peryea entered the store, stole three pistols and a few hundred dollars' worth of supplies, and hid in the woods. The burning barn was a total loss, destroying three horses and quantities of hay, straw, and grain.

The following day, Peryea stopped at a farm and asked for food, which he paid for with a watch stolen from the store. After he left, the farmer spread the word, and many of the two hundred men hunting for Peryea, including prison guards, closed in on the area. Several warning shots were fired by pursuers as he ran into the woods. When the large posse surrounded him and threatened to shoot, he finally surrendered after five wild days on the run.

He was delivered to the prison, and at a later court appearance, Peryea admitted to stealing an overcoat, twenty gold rings, eight watches, and other items, all of which were returned to Havens. He also confessed to the sexual assault and burning the barn as a diversionary tactic so he could rob the store. His previous career of burglaries and other crimes reached Canada, Vermont, and several northern New York locations.

Peryea was released from Clinton Prison in June 1887, but was sent to the county jail pending the resolution of other charges. A decade later, he was wanted in nearby Chateaugay for crimes committed a year earlier, including arson, burglary, horse theft, and robbing the post office. By 1896, when he was captured in New Hampshire at age thirty-four, Peryea had spent twelve years of his life behind bars. In November of that same year, he was committed to Clinton for another two-and-a-half-year stint.

1891: HENRY "SOAPBOX" HARDY
(REAL NAME CHARLES O'CONNELL)

In February 1889, prolific criminal Henry Hardy found himself in deep trouble, facing trial for the robbery of two New York City banks on the same day by employing an unusual method: placing a soapbox on the floor, stepping onto it, and relieving the teller of cash.

Some say the legend was just that, and there was no actual soapbox. In a story carried years later by the *Police Gazette*, Hardy is quoted as saying about the soapbox, "...I was fond of it. It had been my friend in many a tough game."

At five feet eight, he didn't appear to need a booster, but true or not, the name stuck. While awaiting his court appearance, Hardy pulled off a feat previously believed impossible—escaping from a locked holding pen at the rear of the courtroom. He somehow worked his way into a nearby compartment, jumped from a second-story window to the street below, and disappeared for six months.

Following his capture, Henry was convicted of both bank robberies and sentenced to eighteen and a half years in prison. Like most dangerous convicts from New York City, he was shipped up the Hudson River to Sing Sing, arriving there in mid-March 1889. But having already been established as an escape risk, he was transferred a week later to Clinton Prison, where security was legendary.

Hardy remained alert for breakout opportunities, but came to appreciate Clinton's reputation as a fortress. Seeking a more nuanced way of leaving Dannemora, he prevailed upon criminal friends from New York City to provide him with more than $500 in cash, but it wasn't enough to bribe his way out. There was little he could do other than behave, follow the rules, and hope to somehow be named a trusty, which might lead to employment outside the prison wall.

But in late 1891, Henry took note of a painting crew hired to work in the warden's residence. Before going home, the men removed their caps and overalls for use the next day, which gave Hardy an idea. If one of the men were absent for illness or some other reason, he might use their work uniform to effect an escape.

A few days later, two of the men didn't report in, and Hardy seized the moment. Donning a painter's cap and overalls, he approached the first gate just as inmates were entering the yard for lunch, using the commotion to his advantage. The gate was opened for him without question, and after passing through the outer portal, he made his way to the woods and began to run, putting as much distance between him and the prison as quickly as possible. Heading southwest, he purchased two guns and various supplies at Cadyville before laying low in the woods for a few days.

He then went to Plattsburgh, and on his fourth day of freedom, sporting a fake mustache, Hardy paid a young boy to purchase for him a train ticket to New York City. But the agent knew the boy and began asking questions. A detective looking for the escapee overheard the conversation and approached the stranger in the mustache, who pulled out a gun and fired. His aim was off target, and the officer returned four shots, the last of which struck Hardy in the knee, disabling him. Found in his possession were $529, a map of Clinton County, and two handguns.

He was returned to Dannemora and placed in the hospital, which, because of ongoing construction, was temporarily housed in the warden's residence on the third floor. His injuries were severe enough that amputation above the knee was proposed, but Hardy wouldn't allow it. After more than two months, he shed the leg cast and began hobbling around the hospital on crutches.

Not only had he retained his leg, but in mid-December, exactly ten weeks after being shot, and only four days after the cast was removed, Soapbox Hardy disappeared from Clinton Prison for a second time. It just didn't seem possible, partly due to his physical condition, and also because a 12:35 a.m. head count verified his presence, but at 12:45 he was gone.

Hardy had torn his bedding into strips to create a makeshift rope, and fashioned a hook from a brace on his cot. Clad in his underclothing, he lowered himself from the window and, bad leg be damned, dropped to the conservatory roof, twelve feet below. Clinging to a water pipe, he made his way to the piazza, stepped onto the prison wall, hooked the rope to the wall railing, and lowered himself to Dannemora's main street.

And just like that, he was free once again. Biographers, reporters, and lawmen differ on whether he went to Albany, New York City, or Montreal. In Canada, authorities claimed with certainty that Hardy hit the Bank of Quebec for $3,000 and the Bank of Montreal for $7,000 more [a total of $268,000 in 2015] before fleeing to Europe. New York State prison officials said Hardy remained hidden in the Plattsburgh area for five weeks, and then went to New York City, where he took a cattle steamer to Europe. Their source of information? A letter, reportedly from Hardy, mailed from Birkenhead, England, to Warden Isaiah Fuller of Clinton Prison, saying that he had to laugh at their efforts to contain him at Dannemora.

Hardy then went to work at what he knew best: crime. Among New York's convicts, he was known for an amazing ability to escape, but also for being somewhat of a gentleman—a nice, well-mannered fellow who never cursed and knew how to be fashionable. He was also a learned man, said to have read encyclopedias during his prison terms, and was fluent in three languages.

And that's the type of persona Hardy presented as debonair Edward Carson, a millionaire American mine owner, whose wealthy lifestyle in Europe was secretly financed by bank robberies in Berlin and Baden-Baden. Living in a luxury apartment in Frankfort, and hobnobbing with a pair of English nobles, Hardy was having the time of his life. But it all came unglued when he was arrested at his hotel on July 21, 1892, for having robbed the Reichsbank in Frankfort of $60,000 [$1.6 million in 2015]. American authorities were notified of his arrest and sought extradition, but German

Henry "Soapbox" Hardy

officials advised they would have to get in line. Hardy, they said, would be paying for his crimes before returning to the states.

After conviction, he spent the next thirteen years in a German prison, employed in a tailor shop, where he began saving small strips of cloth to make a rope for an escape attempt. When the effort failed, his punishment was a whipping—stripped to the waist, he received sixty lashes, with a full minute expiring after each blow.

But Hardy didn't give up, trying twice more to break out, resulting in whippings of thirty lashes. The escape attempts earned him nine years in solitary confinement—shackled to a forty-pound ball and chain, with limited food rations, and only ten minutes exercise a day while wearing a mask to prevent him from seeing the face of any other prisoner.

When Hardy's release was imminent in 1905, he faced extradition to the United States, where Dannemora officials were eager for his return. Clinton Warden George Deyo, accompanied by a state detective from Sing Sing, set sail for Europe in early September to bring Hardy home.

But six weeks later they returned empty-handed due to a glitch caused by the U.S. State Department, delaying his November 7 release. In heavy irons and guarded by two men, he finally arrived in the states on January 13, 1906, under charge of Captain Saumermann of the steamer *Amerika*, and was turned over to New York State authorities. There were no pleasantries awaiting him at Clinton after Hardy's unscheduled absence of fourteen years. He fought with inmates and guards, and was deemed an "arch-agitator and instigator to riot." He tried smuggling letters to outside convict friends, seeking tools and weapons to fulfill an escape plan, which only invited more scrutiny. Considered far too dangerous to mix with other prisoners, Hardy was confined to a screen cell twenty-two hours a day for the next seven years, with the other two hours for daily exercise. The screen mesh prevented physical contact with anyone and precluded the passing of notes.

Hardy had no choice but to do his time, finally gaining release on March 20, 1913. A few months later, he was arrested in Cleveland and sentenced to thirty days in jail. On August 15, five months after he left Clinton, the New York State National Bank in Albany was robbed of $879. On September 1, the Pinkerton Detective Agency in

Chicago telegrammed that they had in custody Charles O'Connell, alias Soapbox Hardy, who had committed the robbery. He was extradited to New York and locked up in the Albany Penitentiary.

On Monday, November 3, Hardy had a female visitor who brought him a half dozen hacksaw blades. His plan was to saw the bars and escape on Tuesday, Election Day, when a smaller staff would be on duty. But the plan was discovered and Hardy was banned from receiving any more visitors.

A month later, he pleaded guilty to first-degree grand larceny in exchange for a sentence of five and a half years at Clinton Prison.

By this time, the forty-nine-year-old convict had spent twenty-three years behind bars, having served his first term at age eighteen. But he hadn't changed, and once again was a disruptive inmate at Dannemora, leading to severe punishments for having a knife in his cell and fighting with other inmates.

Nothing much good ever came from being tossed into Clinton's isolation cells, but Hardy became one of the rare exceptions. The punishments appeared to have driven him insane at the same time an insanity expert was conducting tests at Sing Sing, where reform Warden Thomas Mott Osborne was in charge.

In September 1916, Osborne arranged for Hardy's transfer as part of the clinical study, and for several months Henry enjoyed respectful treatment. But he soon proved the Clinton keepers correct that Hardy was an incorrigible. Among the people working tirelessly to improve conditions for convicts at Sing Sing was a woman reformer. After arranging for another inmate to secretly take a photograph, Hardy maneuvered himself into a position very close to the woman, and then attempted to blackmail her with the picture. She went to prison authorities instead, and in August 1916, just eleven months after his arrival at Sing Sing, Soapbox Hardy was sent back to Clinton.

In late January 1918, his sentence for the Albany bank robbery expired, and Henry Hardy was released. So many years at Clinton had extracted a serious physical toll, leaving him weakened, gaunt, and limping badly. The knee that was seriously injured by a bullet back in 1891 had recently developed complications, and Hardy, now fifty-three, needed crutches to walk. When he left Clinton, the next stop was New York City to have his leg amputated above the knee.

Exactly a year after his release from Dannemora, an elaborate money-order scheme was uncovered on the East Coast. On October 22, 1918, seventy-seven money orders had been stolen in Minneapolis, Minnesota, for resale to other criminals. Twelve of them, made payable to druggist Robert J. Barton, were passed just prior to Christmas at a dozen Boston jewelry stores, netting him the modern equivalent of seventeen thousand dollars. Barton's address was Minneapolis, but he had a room at the Parker House in Boston, which he left ten days later. Postal inspectors and detectives trailed him to Baltimore, where it was found he had purchased rings for forty dollars at several stores, using money orders for one hundred dollars as payment, thus absconding with a ring and sixty dollars in cash from each store. They finally caught up to him in Washington, where he was arrested.

The prisoner, who walked with a cane, had in his possession a box containing one of the rings. Closer examination of the detainee revealed a cork leg, which, when removed, held thirty money orders, many of them filled in and ready for use. Barton's identity was determined to be false, but he refused to divulge any information about himself or the men who sold him the stolen money orders. Pinkerton detectives were consulted, and within a few days, using photographs and criminal records, they named the perpetrator as Charles O'Connell—better known as Soapbox Hardy.

Confronted with the information, he acquiesced. In January 1919, he offered a full confession in court, and related how he earned his unusual moniker. Early in his life of crime, a leather-covered box the size of a suitcase was his favorite prop. He chose a bank, spent time observing the tellers at work, and on the chosen day made his move. Approaching the counter, he used a question or some pretense to send the teller away from the window. Then, placing the box on the floor and stepping onto it, he'd reach in with a hand, cane, or hook and make off with large amounts of cash. He admitted to sometimes departing smoothly with a tip of the hat, and making himself scarce as soon as he hit the street.

On the charges of money-order fraud, he was sentenced to twelve years, but at that point, Hardy knew death was near, so the length of his sentence mattered not at all. He pleaded instead for one act of mercy from the judge—that he serve his time at the Federal

Penitentiary in Atlanta. Henry believed tuberculosis was killing him, and that the southern climate would perhaps add a little extra time to whatever life he had left. Besides, said Hardy, he had heard that federal pens took better care of convicts than did state prisons like Clinton in New York.

Even though the facility was crowded, the judge obliged him, and on February 1, Hardy became an Atlanta inmate. Knowing that the end was near, he made his own funeral arrangements, and days later, just six weeks after arriving at Atlanta, he died. Hardy was buried in his native Brooklyn, in a cemetery overlooking the Hudson River. His final act, posthumously, was on the side of the law, a place he had never visited while alive. In a Minnesota courtroom, two defendants who robbed the Liberty State Bank of Minneapolis were presented with unusual evidence—Liberty bonds taken from the hollow wooden leg of Soapbox Hardy.

1892: THOMAS "BUNCO" O'BRIEN

Thomas was known in legal circles as Bunco O'Brien, the best swindler in the country, and used a slew of aliases to boot. He and an associate, Reed "Kid" Waddell, have each been credited as the inventors of goldbricking—selling gold-coated bricks of metal as solid gold. Whether or not they invented it, they both used the method to earn a small fortune.

Another scam favored by O'Brien was to purchase cattle from a farmer for a few hundred dollars, but leave the animals on the farm for several days until it was convenient to pick them up. Within a day or two, O'Brien's partner showed up at the farm, admired the same cattle, and offered a much higher price than O'Brien had paid. The farmer agreed to the second deal, and when O'Brien showed up for his stock, the farmer bought the cows back for several hundred dollars more than he originally paid so he could resell them to the second buyer. The second buyer, of course, never returned, and the two men, with a profit of usually $300 to $500, moved on to the next victim.

O'Brien gained fame working his way around the country without actually working at all, cheating people out of their money at every opportunity and with every scam imaginable. In 1889, he bilked an elderly Albany man, John M. Peck, out of $10,000 [$265,000 in 2015]. With lawmen eyeing him as a suspect, O'Brien slipped away and escaped detection for more than two years. In late 1891 he was finally arrested, but promptly jumped bail and fled to England. With Scotland Yard on his tail, he left for Belgium, and then Paris, but returned to England, where he was arrested by year's end and extradited at the behest of the U.S. State Department.

In late March 1892, he was convicted of burglary and sentenced to ten years in Clinton Prison, where, by several accounts, he was treated more like a celebrity than an internationally known thief. Most incoming prisoners were shaved about the head and face, but O'Brien was spared the discomfort and embarrassment. He also wasted no time in seeking a way out of Clinton—but for a man of his deceptive talents and charismatic personality, an old-fashioned, over-the-wall escape was out of the question. Deceit was his game, and no one played it like O'Brien, for his stay at Clinton was shorter than that of any other escapee.

It must be said, though, that he escaped as a prisoner, but did not escape from within the prison. With several of his confederates, O'Brien developed a plan that began with a habeas corpus suit, claiming that his extradition to the United States was illegal. This was a government matter, requiring that he appear in federal court in Utica. On April 16, less than three weeks after he arrived at Clinton in handcuffs and irons in the company of six experienced guards, O'Brien departed in the care of but a single officer—recently hired guard James Buck, to whom he was shackled. Buck was given no warning that O'Brien was a particularly slippery character. Their journey of a few days would generate headlines for months and become the source of many court sessions to determine just what transpired.

The short version is that Buck was instructed to remain chained to the prisoner except while taking meals. They traveled south to Albany and then west to Utica, where O'Brien's arraignment ended as expected, with the judge denying his claim. But the trip was not about illegal extradition. It was to employ O'Brien's own skills and those of several cohorts in effecting his escape. He was unshackled and enjoyed the run of the city, having put his keeper at ease, which was a bunco artist's bread and butter. To distract and occupy Buck, there was drinking involved, and a woman, too, all with the goal of gaining O'Brien's freedom.

A few days later, the following exchange of telegrams took place.

BUCK: Mistake has been made. What shall I do?

WARDEN THAYER: What is the nature of the mistake?

BUCK: Prisoner has escaped.

That conversation occurred two days *after* O'Brien vanished. He was tracked to New Orleans, but by then had already left for Europe. Information was wired ahead, precipitating his arrest at Havre, France, where he was held pending the arrival of Scotland Yard detectives. But somehow O'Brien escaped, either by manipulating the police with his charm, or by bribes. But either way, he was free.

O'Brien later showed up in Haiti, where he and a partner sold drugs and served for a short time as soldiers with a group of insurgents. He then sailed to Buenos Aires, but always a big spender, he eventually ran short of cash.

O'Brien and Kid Waddell had worked together many times, but theirs was a love-hate relationship based on Waddell constantly being asked to fund O'Brien's schemes. From Buenos Aires in 1895, he reached out to Waddell in Paris but received no reply. Angry at being snubbed, O'Brien sailed to France, tracked Waddell down, and pumped several bullets into his old friend, ostensibly for refusing to help him financially. Waddell succumbed to his injuries a week later.

O'Brien was convicted of murder and sentenced to life at Devil's Island in French Guinea, where he died in 1905 of peritonitis.

Back in New York, after an embarrassing investigation of O'Brien's escape from Clinton in 1892, the warden and all other parties but one were absolved of any blame—Keeper Buck was found guilty and sentenced to three years at Auburn Prison. Many believed he had accepted bribes, but the judge said he "was not willfully guilty." Buck admitted he had been fooled by O'Brien, making him just one of many who were duped by the great bunco master himself.

1893: MIKE RAFTER AND JOHN KEARNEY

Mike Rafter and John Kearney made their escape in early July 1893 by slipping away from a road crew, something that dozens of other Clinton inmates did—but Kearney made it much farther from the prison than most escapees. Rafter, a well-known area thief who became known as the "Jesse James of Clinton County," avoided capture for three days, but was finally snagged at Clintonville, twenty miles south of the prison.

His partner remained at large, and a month later, the *Burlington Free Press* reported that Kearney, alias Jere Leonard, had joined the Canadian army and was stationed at St. Johns, Quebec, about twenty miles north of Rouses Point on the Canadian border. He was also reportedly seen at Elizabethtown, but a team of searchers sent there found nothing. Six months after the escape, Warden Thayer of Clinton Prison was contacted by the Baltimore, Maryland, chief of police, informing him that John Kearney was in custody. Thayer and Keeper Hagerty escorted him back to Clinton, where he served the remainder of his sentence (just three months), plus a year of good-behavior time he forfeited by escaping.

1898: Charles Crossman

Charles Crossman made two escape attempts from Clinton within the same year, but to differentiate, there were two Charles Crossmans who served time at Dannemora in the late 1800s. One was from Crown Point, about fifty-five miles south of Dannemora, but the one who escaped was a Switzerland native who immigrated to the United States in 1896. It appears he arrived as a criminal, for by early summer of that same year, he had already committed several burglaries in Columbia County and was held for trial. In October he entered a plea of guilty and was sentenced to ten years and six months in Clinton Prison.

On June 27, 1898, after returning from lunch to the basket department, Crossman grabbed the ladder used for oiling the basket machine and, carrying a paper that made it look like he was on official business, went to the end of the building and stepped outside. Laying the ladder against the portico, he climbed to the roof, pulled the ladder up, and placed it against the side of the next story, where it barely reached the eaves. After reaching the building's upper roof, he ascended to the peak and followed it until an oil shed was directly below. Crossman then slid down the roof, landed on the oil shed, jumped fifteen feet to the ground below, and headed for the woods.

Prison employees were unaware of the breakout, but a Dannemora resident witnessed the entire sequence of events and notified officials. Later that afternoon, Crossman was spotted in a field three miles east of the prison, and was caught within a few days. He was clad in the prisoner uniform bearing four stripes, a recent innovation to clearly denote incorrigible and dangerous inmates.

If that designation was meant for anyone, it was Crossman, for just five months later he attempted another escape in spectacular fashion. Both he and a partner, Charles Collins, wore the four stripes and worked in a shop in the northeast part of the yard. At 10 a.m. they went to the corner of the yard, and in under three minutes, a guard noticed their absence.

By that time, Collins had thrown a rope ladder over a light fixture near the prison's outer wall, climbed up, and engaged guard George Olmstead in a hand-to-hand struggle at the top of the wall. As they fought, Crossman climbed up, took the guard's rifle, tossed the rope ladder to the outside of the wall, climbed down, and ran for the woods amid a hail of bullets.

Collins, meanwhile, won his battle against the guard, but with other officers rushing towards the commotion, there was no time to climb the rope ladder. He instead leaped through the guard-room window to the ground some thirty feet below, where he lay stunned from the impact and bleeding from many glass cuts. Officers were quickly upon him, while others pursued Crossman, who several times turned his rifle towards them but didn't shoot. One of the men took a shortcut near the old mining quarry, and Crossman's run was soon over. It turned out he hadn't fired because he didn't know how to operate the rifle.

A month later, both men pleaded guilty to attempted escape and received additional sentences of five years each. They were confined to Clinton's horrible dungeons, with no furnishings other than a slop bucket, no light in the cell, and minimal daily rations of bread and water. After release to a regular cell,

A FIGHT FOR LIBERTY.

BULLETS FLY THICK AND FAST AT DANNEMORA.

Desperate but Unsuccessful Attempt of Two Convicts to Escape From Clinton Prison.

Headline covering the escape of Charles Crossman and Charles Collins (1898)

there were reports that Crossman had become addicted to opium. He planned another escape, but it was discovered shortly before the actual attempt.

He was again sent to the dungeon, but the ever-resourceful Crossman found a way out. The next day, he was found dead in his dark cell, having fashioned the slop-bucket's rope handle into a longer cord, secured it to the cell bars, and strangled himself.

1898: George Bowers and Perry King

Early Monday morning on October 12, Clinton keeper James Clancey began rounding up the convicts of Company No. 18 to begin their workday in the clothing department. But cell No. 22 on the third tier, home to Perry King, had an eight-by-twelve-inch section missing at the bottom. A prison uniform was on the floor, and King was nowhere to be found. Twice recently the warden had been warned that King was about to escape, but a search of his cell had revealed no contraband.

Clancey sounded the alarm, and moments later found the same situation in cell No. 34, home to inmate George Bowers. The warden, after being apprised of the situation, immediately suspended the two officers who had been on duty the previous night. Their job was to continuously patrol opposite sides of the cellblock, and to light up each cell every two hours with a lantern to see skin, confirming each inmate's presence. If no skin was visible, a hook was used to reach through the bars and pull clothing back to reveal skin, an action that would have prevented any escape attempt.

But where were the missing inmates? Their path was traced to the ground floor and the bath-house, which formed part of the prison's outer wall. Using a skeleton key to open the door, they locked themselves in the bath-house, accessed a window eight feet above the floor, and cut through the protective iron bars. Climbing outside, they dropped twelve feet to the ground and made for the woods. As employees of the clothing department, they had prepared inconspicuous civilian clothes and left their prison suits behind.

During the manhunt, seventy-five men were stationed around the area. As expected, the two convicts didn't make it far in the heavily wooded North Country. Late Tuesday afternoon, they were found occupying an abandoned home on the outskirts of Lyon Mountain village, about nine miles west of the prison, and offered no resistance. After further investigation, it was determined that keeper Howard had been asleep the night of the escape, and keeper Mitchell was inexplicably absent. Both were fired. A warning went out to other guards, but a few nights later, another keeper was fired for sleeping on the job.

The escape of Bowers and King bears certain similarities to that of Matt and Sweat in 2015: cell No. 22 on an upper tier was involved; they worked in a prison clothing shop; rectangular holes were cut out of two cells; they counted on guards being asleep and missing important checks; they were dressed in civilian clothing; and they headed into the woods west of the prison rather than east towards populated areas.

1902: James Concannon

Early on the morning of May 12, inmate James Concannon dug through the wall of his cell to a ventilation shaft. Climbing inside, he ascended to the roof, which he followed to the prison's outer wall, dropped to the ground, and disappeared into the forest.

Just before entering the trees, he was spotted by a guard, who sounded the alarm. Search teams immediately began pursuit in Concannon's general direction of travel, which was southeast. At about 10 p.m. he was seen near Cadyville by keepers Edward Gay and Sheridan Phillips, who opened fire when he refused to halt. Concannon vanished into the marshy area along the Saranac River, but unbeknownst to his pursuers, one of the bullets had found its target. He continued another mile and a half, finally arriving at a barn on the property of Mrs. Thomas Harney, where he took refuge in the hayloft and pulled the ladder up.

The following day, Mrs. Harney entered the barn and noticed an inmate uniform apparently hung to dry. She left and returned with two men, and as they talked, Concannon called out that he was hurt. They brought him to the house and contacted prison officials, who took him to the prison hospital. Doctors determined that the bullet had struck him in the back and lodged near the kidneys, but was not life threatening.

1903: Peter James (alias Eddie Jacques)

Peter James made arguably the most amazing escape ever from inside Dannemora's wall. He came to Clinton in the usual manner, by collecting many arrests and committing a serious felony. In August 1896, Peter and three accomplices were robbing the store of Walker Adams at Bedford Station, Westchester County, New York, when they were interrupted by the owner and his son. During the chaos that followed, Mr. Adams was shot dead, but his son killed two of the robbers and injured James, who was arrested and locked up in the White Plains jailhouse. Two months later he escaped, but was later recaptured in Baltimore. For the death of Adams, he was convicted of second-degree murder in October 1897 and sentenced to life at Sing Sing, where he was assigned to the shoe shop.

In early 1898, James was transferred to Clinton. That he was not your run-of-the-mill criminal was evident in how *Police Gazette* magazine portrayed him:

> Peter James belongs to the old school of bank burglars. He is a master mechanic, can make a key out of a stick of wood, figure out a safe combination with a piece of wet tissue paper and the keenness of his ears, and can tunnel his way like a mole into a bank vault and loot it at his leisure.

At Clinton, he looked for opportunities, and eventually secured a job in the tin shop, located just inside the main wall running along Cook Street. An engine in the building's cellar supplied power to the shop, and James eventually became the engine's mechanic. This gave him frequent and often unmonitored access to the basement area. By staying out of trouble and evincing trustworthiness, he found himself alone in the cellar, sometimes for extended periods.

By studying his surroundings, James came up with an unlikely plan of escape, one that would be years in the making. His excellent mechanical skills proved critical for any chance of success, for the idea was to tunnel beneath the outer prison wall, link with the sewage system, and gain access to manhole covers.

Overcoming so many logistical challenges would be inconceivable to most people, but James went to work with persistence and determination. Using hand-made tools fashioned from tin scraps secreted from the shop, and choosing a certain stone in the basement wall as a starting point, he picked at it for only a minute or two at a time so as not to raise suspicions by long absences from the main floor. Not much could be accomplished in a minute or two, but Peter James had a lifetime of minutes to work with.

With the rock finally loosened, he devised a method of removing and replacing it to prevent detection of his work. The poor lighting in the basement area was helpful in that regard, making any disturbance to the wall less noticeable. Bit by bit he developed a system that proved workable. The cellar's dark corners provided options for depositing dirt removed from the tunnel. Stomping it down heavily was effective, inconspicuously raising the floor as the tunnel lengthened. After the first several feet were dug, James somehow procured coveralls so he could work without soiling his prison uniform and raising suspicions.

Other issues arose—bracing the tunnel sides, for instance, so they wouldn't collapse—but he found solutions. Realizing that Dannemora's main road was several feet lower than the land inside the prison, James angled the tunnel straight down to ensure he didn't run smack into the main wall. For whatever job confronted him, he made some sort of tool from scraps sneaked into the cellar. The digging itself was arduous, but with time a non-factor, he just kept plugging away. Even a handful of dirt represented progress. To prevent collapses and ensure the tunnel's integrity, boards were used to shore up the sides and roof.

For more than two years he managed to keep the project hidden from Dannemora's guards, but a few fellow inmates—John Comins, John Elliott, and Edward Kennedy—eventually caught on that something was up. He swore them to secrecy in exchange for allowing them to join the escape plan. By that time the tunnel had reached the prison wall, and James was faced with a real brainteaser: how to remove the rock from the starting point and crawl more than twenty feet to resume digging without a guard visiting the cellar and catching him at work.

He devised a plan, scrounged for materials, and patiently set up an ingenious alarm system. A long piece of twine was somehow threaded from the cellar to the main floor of the tin shop, where his three co-conspirators could subtly access it. At the basement end of the twine James attached a small bell, which he carried with him into the tunnel. Should a guard head for the cellar, a quick tug on the string by someone on the main floor alerted James. There were many close calls and false alarms that led to panicky exits from the underground passage, but the system worked.

The tunnel gradually extended until it met the brick wall housing Dannemora's sewer pipes, running down Cook Street. Breaking through the wall and following the pipe, James was able to locate a manhole cover, but encountered two problems: it was located in the middle of the road, and a gate of iron bars prevented access to it. Over time, he procured an iron bar and bent the gate sufficiently to allow passage. Further exploration along the main pipe led to another manhole in a field across from the prison, where bending the protective gate in the same manner provided access to a much better exit point. And there he breathed fresh, free air before returning to the cellar and devising plans for the big day.

James instructed his accomplices to save bits of food, fabricate tin flasks for carrying water, and create civilian clothing for each man so they could ditch their prison uniforms. Whenever an item was obtained, they were to smuggle it to James, who would add it to their escape cache.

After four years of tunneling more than fifty feet and overcoming so many obstacles, the big day finally arrived. On the afternoon of July 18, 1903, all four men made it to the basement, changed into their new clothes, and began crawling through the tunnel. When they reached the exit, it was raining heavily, reducing the likelihood that any townspeople would be outside and catch a glimpse of them. They accessed the railroad tracks just south of the village and headed east for a few miles before turning north towards their intended goal, Canada, twenty miles away.

About two hours after the convicts departed the manhole, guards discovered that inmates Collins and Elliott were missing. The alarm was sounded, and an internal head count revealed that James and Kennedy were also unaccounted for, prompting a full search of the prison grounds. Four inmate suits were found in the tin-shop cellar, and the tunnel was discovered.

Within a few hours, as many as three hundred men were searching area woods and fields for the escapees. Clinton's warden took the unusual measure of replacing the standard fifty-dollar reward for recaptured convicts with a more ominous offer—$250 for the return of Peter James, dead or alive.

Over the next few days, sightings of the men were reported at Rouses Point, Beekmantown, Ellenburg, and Schuyler Falls, but all proved to be unfounded. However unlikely a successful breakout from Dannemora was, it began to appear they had pulled it off.

But for all the intricate planning, one problem was encountered that Peter James didn't foresee. The food they had collected over time consisted of bread pieces and bits of corned beef. Elliott began suffering severe stomach cramps, presumably from eating spoiled food. The others helped him along until he finally had to be carried, but the burden became too much. Medicine was needed to relieve his suffering so they could move faster.

Meanwhile, a massive manhunt in all directions from the prison had come up empty. Not a single clue was found, and as far as prison officials knew, the four were long gone. But protocol required that the search continue in the prison's general vicinity until solid evidence proved the escapees had left the area.

On day four of the manhunt, the escapees had traveled north about seven miles to the hamlet of Purdy's Mills, where they broke into Purdy's Store and obtained the medicine Elliott needed, along with hats, coats, socks, canned goods, and $14 stolen from a safe. They also destroyed the store's phone so the robbery couldn't be reported, but when the owner discovered the break-in, his home telephone foiled that part of the plan.

The burglary was just what prison officials needed—a strong indication that the escapees were still in the northern woods. Searchers, including men placed on watch, saturated the area, and when Elliott left the forest cover on the following morning, he took a bullet to the hip. But with the help of his comrades, all four escapees avoided capture, fleeing

HAS ANYONE SEEN PETER JAMES OF CLINTON?

There's a Reward for Him, Whether Dead or Alive.

He's a Desperate Man, Says the Sheriff, and He Is Wanted in Jail Again.

Headline (1903)

west for a few hours until they encountered the Great Chazy River near the settlement of Alder Bend. There Elliott and Kennedy were finally caught.

"Great" Chazy referred only to the river's size in contrast with the Little Chazy, for the Great Chazy was in some places less than twenty feet across. But the heavy rain that accompanied their escape from prison also left the river badly swollen and very dangerous. James and Collins followed the torrent north for several miles, with searchers hot on their trail.

Trying to cross the river nearly killed both of them, but Collins helped James, who was a non-swimmer, and together they made it to the opposite bank. Continuing north to the Altona area, they jumped a freight train, finally catching a breather. But just when it appeared they had made it, armed men boarded the rail car and ended the manhunt.

Three of the men were sentenced to additional time, but Peter James, the brains and brawn behind possibly the greatest escape ever from Clinton Prison, was already a lifer.

Accessing the village's underground piping wasn't the only similarity between his plan in 1903 and that of David Sweat in 2015. James and Sweat initially checked out the manhole covers alone, prior to their breakouts, and both men were slowed by partners after escaping. Had either man opted for a solo exit, their chances for success, admittedly slim, would have been much better.

1904: James Roberts and John Stewart

Roberts and Stewart were trusties employed in the boiler house. On the night of Sunday, January 10, they used a rope ladder to scale the prison wall and escape, carrying with them small quantities of food. After walking to Plattsburgh under cover of darkness, they took refuge in a barn at the fairgrounds on Boynton Avenue. Hiding out in a loft during the daytime, they ventured out at night with a pail to get water from a nearby well. After losing the pail in the well, they ate snow, but by the end of the fourth day, both men were desperate for food and water.

Leaving the barn in the evening, they visited the home of David Lagoy on the corner of Bailey Avenue and Champlain Street. Lagoy provided them with food and drink, but notified authorities after they left. The pair headed north of the city, following the lakeshore onto Cumberland Head, apparently planning to cross the lake to Vermont. But prison officers were tailing them, and wisps of smoke rising from the cedars in Martin's Swamp were a dead giveaway. The two escapees were arrested there while trying to warm themselves by a fire.

They couldn't have known that their breakout had led to the death of a prison guard. On Monday afternoon, Dennis O'Brien, a fifteen-year employee at Clinton, was posted at the Bluff Point rail station to ensure the escapees didn't catch a ride heading south. When a train pulled onto a siding to let another pass, O'Brien stepped onto the tracks, unaware of the second train's presence. He took a direct hit and was killed by the impact.

No charges were filed against the two convicts in relation to O'Brien's death, but both were tried and found guilty of escape. In a surprise twist, Stewart provided an alibi for his partner by claiming to have planned everything, and then threatening Roberts with an iron pipe if he didn't join in the escape. Prison guards countered Stewart's testimony, characterizing him as a more cowardly man, and Roberts as the dangerous one, having nearly killed a Montgomery County jailer in the past.

Roberts, already a prison veteran at age twenty-one, was released from Clinton in January 1906, but was returned in October on a grand larceny conviction. Stewart, who had already served at least three previous prison terms, would also return to Dannemora.

1908: DARWIN HINCKLEY

Darwin Hinckley of Kingston, New York, was sentenced to Clinton Prison in 1895 on forgery charges, and was paroled in 1899. In 1907, he was again convicted of forgery, and in January 1908 was returned to Dannemora, where he earned the position of trusty and was assigned to the night shift in the boiler house.

On June 22nd, at age fifty-eight, Hinckley became Clinton's oldest escapee when he scaled the prison wall using a ladder, pulled it up behind him, and descended on the outside.

The ensuing manhunt at first focused on the Peru area, but

three days later, a fisherman near Cadyville saw Hinckley run to the woods, leaving behind a sock and a shoe. On his fifth day of freedom, he was captured while walking on railroad tracks at night in the vicinity of Cadyville's Catholic church. He might have made it much farther from the prison, but on the drop from the ladder to the ground, Hinckley had sprained his ankle, which had swollen to where a shoe wouldn't fit.

He was returned to Dannemora to finish his sentence, but shortly after release, Hinckley was again arrested for passing forged checks in the Kingston area.

Before those cases were resolved, three sticks of dynamite exploded in the bedroom where his wife and two daughters slept. One girl was unhurt, but his wife and other daughter were badly burned. Darwin Hinckley was charged with the crime, and in late 1914, he was sentenced to fourteen years for a second felony assault conviction. Dannemora again became his home until June 1915, when Hinckley, 66, was transferred to Sing Sing.

1909: James Kelly and Frank Burrows

Kelly and Burrows, a pair of trusties working the graveyard shift in the boiler house, collaborated on an escape on March 29 at 4 a.m. Their method was the same as Darwin Hinckley's nine months earlier, using a ladder to climb the wall, and then pulling it up to climb down on the outside. Rushing to the prison barn, they took the warden's horse and cutter and headed over Dannemora Mountain.

Within minutes of their departure, a guard noticed they were missing and called the keeper, who notified officers at the lumber camp near Chazy Lake. About four miles from the prison, and nearly two miles before reaching the lumber camp, the escapees attempted a ninety-degree turn at Ledger's Corners. The sleigh flipped on its side and was damaged, so they began walking, but were captured by searchers within minutes. Both men received sentences of one year and nine months added to their terms.

WENT OVER PRISON WALL

TWO CONVICTS MAKE BREAK
FROM CLINTON PRISON.

Kelly and Burrows headline

1911: Leonard Lockwood

Leonard Lockwood arrived at Dannemora in January 1910 after making the rounds of several United States prisons and one in Australia. In mid-January 1911, during a morning exercise period, Lockwood climbed the board section of the prison's north wall and escaped into the woods. But winter breakouts in the deep snows around Dannemora bear scant hope for success, and when Lockwood's absence was noticed, guards on snowshoes quickly picked up his tracks. He made it about six and a half miles east to a reservoir in the West Plattsburgh area, where he was recaptured in exhausted condition. Besides the time added to his term at Clinton for escaping, Lockwood still owed a New Jersey prison nine years.

1911: Charles Edwards

On the night of his escape, trusty Charles Edwards was repairing a pump in the powerhouse. A guard discovered he was missing, and it was deduced Edwards had scaled the prison's east wall. His whereabouts remained unknown until about twenty-four hours later, when a call came from a Peru store, inquiring about the escapee's description. Information provided by the prison matched that of a stranger who had visited the store, so men were immediately dispatched to Peru.

Edwards was nowhere to be found, but on the following evening, three Peru men—William Bosley, Elizor Lapoint, and Silas Trombly—located him about two miles from Peru on the railroad tracks to Ausable Forks. Edwards surrendered without resisting.

1914: Thomas Hannon
(alias Louis Rushford, F. J. O'Connell)

Prisoner No. C–11030, Thomas Hannon, didn't escape from inside Clinton, but he's notable as one of the few escapees who were never recaptured. He also wasn't dangerous on the level of most Clinton inmates. Hannon had a lengthy arrest record for robbery and assault in Massachusetts, where he served time in six jails and one prison. In late 1913, he was arrested as a pickpocket in Albany, New York, but the wallet contained enough cash to merit a grand larceny charge that sent him to Clinton Prison for one year.

Short-timers were routinely assigned to road crews, and with such a brief sentence, Hannon was considered a short-timer by mid-1914. He was put to work in Ellenburg, about ten miles north of the prison, and walked away from the camp late one night. Heading west on foot, he stole a horse for speedier travel, and then abandoned it to again travel on foot. At that point the trail dried up. Since Hannon was an experienced railroad man, it was theorized that he jumped a train going west to Malone and then north into Canada.

The usual search crew was dispatched from Clinton, but a week later the hunt for Hannon was abandoned, in part because his sentence was almost finished when he left.

The normal method of pursuit in such cases was to stay on top of law enforcement in the areas where the escapee lived and where his crimes were committed. In nearly all instances, the convict was eventually captured and returned to prison.

But Hannon was never caught, and his fate remains a mystery. Still on Dannemora's books in the 1950s, forty years later, was the uncollected fifty-dollar reward offered for his capture.

1914: George Vogan

George Vogan got off to a rough start in life. At age ten, he was the subject of a newspaper story with an uncomplimentary headline in the respected *New York Sun*: Little Boy's Hard Luck Tale: Just the Invention of a Ready Liar. It seemed a harsh portrayal of a poor lad who came to New York City to find his family and spend Christmas with them.

But it was discovered that his parents and six siblings lived in Manhattan, and George had been such trouble at home that he was finally committed to the Catholic Protectory, from which he had recently escaped. The protectory had rules of admission, and a child of George's young age was only accepted if they were "truant, vicious, or homeless." Homeless wasn't an issue, and vicious didn't apply, but truancy seemed a good fit.

George was trouble wherever he went, leading to escalating punishments. From the protectory, he was sent at age thirteen to the House of Refuge on Randall's Island, a reform school. At age sixteen, he was sentenced to Elmira on a grand larceny conviction. At twenty-one, he was in the New York Penitentiary for attempted grand larceny. At age twenty-three, George finally hit the big time with a sentence of four years at Sing Sing for stealing a milk wagon, with horse attached.

He was transferred to Clinton, where an unblemished record earned him trusty status and the maximum time off for good behavior. Nearing the end of his term, George was assigned to a road crew, where a rules infraction triggered a threat from the keeper to write him up, which would add four months to Vogan's sentence. With revenge as his motive, George decided to escape, figuring the keeper would not only be blamed, but would also be assessed the fifty-dollar reward money paid for captured escapees. Vogan was well aware of Clinton's reputation as inescapable, so he didn't expect to get far, but would give it his best try.

When George slipped away from the crew, his absence was noticed almost immediately, and the chase began. He later claimed to have climbed a tree, and that guards passed directly below his perch. After the search was called off, he began a pattern of walking at night, stealing whatever food he could find, and hiding in trees during the daytime.

Following several days covering an estimated forty-five miles in a roundabout path, he reached Saranac Lake, where the theft of a farmer's overalls and other clothes allowed Vogan to ditch his prison suit. He next jumped a freight train to Buffalo, where he hired on as a fireman on a boat headed to New York City. From there he took a job on the S. S. *Philadelphia*, which left the pier just three minutes before detectives arrived in hopes of arresting Vogan.

The ship landed in Liverpool, England, and George, despite believing it was unwise to return, did so anyway, taking a job as fireman on the *St. Louis*,

ESCAPED

$ 50.00   REWARD

George Vogan - - - "C" 10218

|362237|

George Vogan

which was heading back to New York City. Several weeks after he left Europe, detectives began searching for him on every incoming ship, and on the *St. Louis* they hit paydirt.

The *Washington Post* reported that Vogan, an outgoing, garrulous sort, asked for the smallest opportunity:

> I'll catch it hot when I get back to Dannemora. I ain't anxious to go. Gimme three seconds' start—just three seconds—on this cop. He can use his gun and do anything else to get me back, but gimme that much of a chance for a getaway and I'll stand the consequence without a squeal.

The commissioner declined, and George was released to Clinton officials three months after his escape.

1919: MICHAEL GAFFNEY

Audacious—a headline term used to describe the exploits of Clinton escapee Michael Gaffney—was right on the money. Gaffney had led a life of crime in the Binghamton area, committing burglaries and robberies that sent him to Elmira, Auburn, and finally Dannemora. Through good behavior he became a trusty, which allowed some men to work on road gangs and other outside jobs.

Gaffney was assigned as cook in the lumber camp at Chazy Lake, a few miles west of the prison. One of the cook's duties, obtaining water for the camp, required regular trips to the private home of Thomas and Louise LaPlante, who shared their house with son Levi and his wife, Martha. For two years Gaffney completed the task without issue, confirming that he had been a good choice for trusty status.

But when financial temptation reared its head, he couldn't resist. In becoming quite friendly with Martha LaPlante, Gaffney learned that her mother-in-law kept $5,000 somewhere in the house. On one of his routine trips for water, he searched the home, stole the money, and returned to work.

It was unwise to delay lest the theft be discovered, so Gaffney escaped from the camp later that night and headed north, stealing some civilian clothes along the way. Seventeen miles northeast of the prison, he arrived at the village of Mooers, where he boarded a train heading west. For the thirty-five miles to Malone in the next county, his seatmate was a police officer, but since his escape hadn't yet been discovered, they traveled together without incident.

Gaffney then headed south a hundred thirty miles to Herkimer, where he bought a suit of respectable-looking clothes, purchased a cashier's check (using the alias James Walsh) for $2,500 at the Herkimer National Bank, and with the other $2,500 in his pocket [$34,000 in 2015], headed for Utica.

While partying there and tossing money around freely, he met a girl named Mildred Farmer from Harrietstown (Saranac Lake). Central New York's newest big spender went on a binge, buying clothes, a pearl necklace, a gold watch and chain, and a sealskin coat for his newfound girlfriend. After hosting a party in Utica, they moved on and registered at the Winchester Hotel in Syracuse. For the next several days, they partied, spent more money, and Gaffney even got into a bar fight, but managed to escape arrest. On his fifth day of freedom, they did more nighttime partying, going from place to place and spending as if he were a tycoon.

Stories about the stranger with wads of money filtered through the grapevine to Syracuse police, who had also received information about the recent Clinton escapee. After tracking him down, they followed Gaffney and Farmer to the hotel and burst in on them at 3:30 a.m. They offered no resistance, and were taken to the police station. Clinton Warden John Trombly, informed that his missing prisoner was in custody, sent an officer from Dannemora to bring him home for completion of his sentence.

1920: CHRISTOPHER AFENTIS

After serving time in Elmira, Greek immigrant Christopher Afentis returned to a life of crime in New York City. In 1915, when Judge Harry Lewis sentenced him to six years in Sing Sing for robbing a jewelry store, he called Afentis, "one of the slickest crooks that ever came out of Brooklyn." He was later transferred to Clinton and released in fall 1919.

Afentis found work as a candy maker in nearby Plattsburgh at the Laskaris Candy Kitchen, owned by fellow countryman Nicholas Sepherlis, who offered Christopher a job as a chance to redeem himself. A month later, Afentis robbed the store, hired a taxi, and headed west for Ogdensburg, but was arrested at Malone. He was convicted of larceny, which was also a violation of parole, and was sent back to Dannemora on December 2, 1919, barely a month after his previous release.

Eleven months later, as an inmate working in the boiler room, where he was sometimes left alone, Afentis somehow managed to get over the twenty-foot-high wall and escape into the woods. For nine months his whereabouts were unknown, until he was arrested in Washington, Pennsylvania, for a series of burglaries across three counties. During questioning, Afentis eventually admitted to having escaped Dannemora, where he was cell-bound a few days later.

1921: LAWRENCE HAWTHORNE

In 1919, at age twenty-one, Lawrence Hawthorne was accused of stealing from guests at New York City's Hotel Commodore, where he worked as a bellboy. No indictment followed, and Hawthorne found employment, again as a bellboy, at the Astor Hotel. In 1920, he was among a trio of thieves charged with breaking into a guestroom and robbing two couples of cash and jewelry. The three young robbers wore masks and carried handguns, but as they turned to leave, the two male victims jumped Hawthorne and captured him.

Pleading guilty to several charges earned him a harsh sentence of thirty to sixty years, which began at Sing Sing so he could testify at the New York City trials of his co-conspirators. On June 6 he was back in Sing Sing with a revised sentence of fourteen to forty years, and was transferred to Clinton a month later.

Hawthorne claimed to have tuberculosis, and after an examination, he was moved to the prison hospital, which had a protective fence but was outside the main wall. On September 20, just over two months after arriving at Clinton, Hawthorne grabbed a food cache he had prepared, walked from the hospital exercise yard to the baseball field in mid-afternoon, placed a board against the fence, climbed it, jumped, and ran into the forest.

As he later related, the next several weeks were nearly his undoing. The food from the hospital consisted of a dozen slices of bread. For thirty-one days, said Hawthorne, hungry and tired, he roamed through the Adirondacks, on several occasions nearly freezing to death. Avoiding highways, he stuck to traveling in woods and fields. At one point he found a cow in a shed and lived off its milk for three days. Encountering a rail line, he jumped a ride that eventually took him to Baltimore, and then to the Pacific coast. He claimed to have been arrested on the way by a local constable, but talked his way out of trouble.

In California, as planned, Hawthorne's wife joined him, and they set up housekeeping in the Los Angeles area. The only crime he knew was robbing hotel rooms, which in California provided them with a good living for a few years. After a long string of burglaries, the heat was on, so the Hawthornes moved north to San Francisco.

But police from both cities cooperated on the case, resulting in an arrest plan. Using the element of surprise, detectives burst into their hotel room, where the couple was chatting. In a flash, Hawthorne dove through an open window, grabbed the fire escape railing, and ran like hell amid a hail of bullets. Dozens of officers were called to the scene, and after a half-hour search, he was found hiding in a garage four blocks from the hotel.

Under questioning, Hawthorne admitted to robbing the Los Angeles Biltmore room of Mr. and Mrs. Charles Christian and making off with $10,000 in jewels [worth $134,000 in 2015]. Even without the confession, he was facing charges for several other crimes. In their room were furs, a large quantity of jewelry, and booty from a robbery at the Willard Hotel in Washington, D.C., including an $800 watch.

Hawthorne was initially charged with the Los Angeles hotel robbery, and was locked up in the San Francisco city jail until his culpability elsewhere could be sorted out. He was eventually returned to New York and sentenced to fourteen years at Auburn, from which he was paroled in 1935. But the nature of incorrigibles is that they just can't stay out of trouble, and two years after he was released, Hawthorne's life of crime nearly ended permanently. At the Seneca Hotel in Rochester, New York, he slipped into a couple's room, grabbed a watch and eight dollars in cash, and left. As he departed, the woman awakened and called the front desk.

Shortly after 5:30 a.m., Everett Rhodes, the night clerk, noticed a flashing light on the hotel's new security system, indicating someone had opened a ninth-floor stairway door. His suspicions aroused, Rhodes alerted the night auditor, Lee Clements, and together they investigated. Encountering a man identifying himself as R. D. Cole on the tenth floor, they began asking questions, but sensed that Cole (as Hawthorne was registered) was about to act. Both Rhodes and Hawthorne drew guns, but Rhodes was quicker. He fired twice, one bullet passing through Hawthorne's hat and knocking it from his head. He ran around the corner and fired twice in response before rushing to the ninth floor and hiding out in his room. The two men followed and stood watch at Hawthorne's door until police arrived. He was then arrested without any further trouble.

By the prosecutor's reckoning, Hawthorne faced a potential ninety-eight-year sentence, which included twenty-eight years for parole violation, thirty to fifty years as a repeat felon, plus time for the burglary and using a weapon. At age forty-one, he was sentenced to Attica for life.

1921: WILLIAM TAYLOR

William Taylor was sentenced to Auburn Prison in 1918 for eight and a half years, but was moved to Clinton Prison a year later. A transfer to Sing Sing followed, but in early 1921, showing symptoms of tuberculosis, he was returned to Dannemora.

Taylor was assigned trusty status and became a fireman in the boiler-room section of the powerhouse. In October of the same year, at about one o'clock in the morning, he escaped Clinton by bending an iron bar into a hook and attaching a rope to the other end. After slinging it skyward and managing to catch the rail atop Clinton's wall, he used a ladder to reach the dangling rope and climbed to the top. Pulling the rope up, he lowered it outside the wall, slid down to the end, and dropped safely to the ground.

When he was just minutes from the prison, the alarm sounded and the manhunt began. Taylor reached West Plattsburgh, about seven miles away, where he ate several apples from a shed and lay down to rest. The landowner, unaware there had been an escape from Clinton, found him asleep and ordered him from the property.

Near the shore of Lake Champlain, fourteen miles from the prison, he encountered the Bluff Point rail depot and hopped a freight train heading south. Once it began moving, Taylor likely felt great relief that he had made it. But Clinton authorities had cast a wide net early on, enlisting the aid of sheriff's deputies, U.S. Marshals, and city police to cover exit points around the Plattsburgh area. Five miles south of Bluff Point, when the train slowed for Beardsley's Crossing near the Little Ausable River, lawmen spied the escapee aboard a car and flagged the engineer to stop. Minutes later, rail employees captured Taylor and turned him over to prison guards, ending his bid for freedom, which had lasted ten hours.

1923: JOSEPH SORACE AND MARTIN VANICEK

Of all the men to escape Clinton, few had a flair for the spectacular like Joseph Sorace. He entered New York's prison system in 1919 at the age of twenty-one after a cigar-store robbery resulted in a clerk's death. For a non-shooting role in the crime, he was found guilty of first-degree manslaughter and sentenced to ten to twenty years. His term began at Sing Sing, where Sorace proved himself an extreme escape risk by making a memorable exit.

Less than two years after arriving there, he stuffed an old prison uniform with paper to make a dummy for his bed, cut through three iron bars with a file, and broke through a trap door to access the roof, where the real fun began. Using a telephone wire as a modern zip-line, he slid seventy feet to the ground, climbed two high walls, and dove into the Hudson River.

The odds against such a sequence of events falling perfectly into place were astronomical, but with a convict in the water, ten carloads of armed men dispatched around the area, and dozens of volunteers joining the hunt, it began to look like an easy capture. He had, after all, just a five-minute head start. But Sorace somehow made it, and for a week no one knew his whereabouts.

Eight days after the escape, detectives in New York City trailed Mrs. Sorace to a secretly arranged meeting with her husband, and there he was arrested. He had done it all, said Joe, just to see his wife and child. After being returned to Sing Sing, a year was added to his sentence, and Sorace was later transferred to Clinton, which escape artists found a much tougher challenge.

In January 1923, he gave it a try, though the timing was

questionable, for Dannemora's weather can be brutal at that time of year, often dipping below zero for days at a time. The idea he came up with to get atop the wall was brilliant. He and a partner, Martin Vanicek, were riding in the back of a truck inside the prison. Sorace pulled a knife on the driver, a fellow inmate, and ordered him to drive close to the wall. As he did so, the two men climbed atop the truck's cab and from there jumped to the top of the barrier. It all had to be done quickly, for armed guards were in place, watching for anything unusual—and Sorace's plan was just that.

Officers at Posts Four and Five ordered them to halt, but both men dropped more than twenty feet to the ground outside the wall as the guards opened fire. Vanicek was struck in the hip and couldn't continue, but Sorace ran, even though the long drop from the wall injured one of his legs. He didn't get far before encountering Officer Herbert Short, who tackled Sorace and succeeded in capturing him. Neither inmate was seriously wounded. For his effort, Sorace had four years added to his already lengthy sentence.

In the late 1920s he was moved to Auburn Prison, and then to Great Meadow Prison at Comstock. In 1932 he was released, but was immediately rearrested at the gate to serve punishment time for the escape from Clinton a decade earlier.

But Sorace filed a habeas corpus writ based on a technical error during his sentencing back in 1923. The judge also considered that nine years had passed, during which Sorace had maintained a clean record. A suspended sentence was ordered on condition he support his family and report monthly to the Clinton Prison chaplain.

1924: MICHAEL WASILIA
(ALIAS JON SMERNOSS, JOHN SAZZANOV)

In mid-November 1916, a gang of five men robbed mining foreman and boarding-house operator Bladis Comminsky at Witherbee, New York, an iron-mining village near Lake Champlain. Comminsky died after suffering six gunshot wounds. His wife, coming to his defense, was shot in the leg by one of the men, Michael Wasilia, who escaped the scene.

Hundreds of circulars with his picture were distributed in New York City, and after ten months on the run, he was recognized by a man at an employment agency—ironically, the same agency that had originally sent the men north to Witherbee for mining jobs.

When Wasilia was captured in September 1917, two of his partners were already on Sing Sing's death row for Comminsky's murder, awaiting execution. A month later, his trial was held in Essex County, with prosecutors confident of a conviction and the death penalty. Mrs. Comminsky was a very effective witness, describing how Wasilia stood over her while her husband was being killed, and then deliberately shooting her. The defendant also took the stand, claiming he was drunk at the time of the shooting and therefore retained no memory of it. Amid a public outcry of injustice, he was found guilty of second-degree murder and sentenced to twenty years to life at Dannemora. Of the three men charged with murder in Comminsky's death, he was the only one to avoid the death penalty. Wasilia was in a Clinton Prison cell when his two partners were executed in May and June 1918.

At age thirty-three, Wasilia's tiny stature—three inches shy of five feet tall—earned him attention as the smallest inmate at Clinton. By refraining from infractions, he achieved trusty status and was given a job in the tuberculosis hospital. During the noon dinner hour on July 25, 1924, he executed a simple plan: wearing a blue serge suit and a black hat instead of a convict uniform, he simply walked away from the prison. Notices were issued across New York's northern counties and in New York City, where he had been captured after the Essex County murder. Expectations were that he would soon be back in Clinton, which was the fate of nearly all inmates who left the hospital, farm, or road crews.

Two weeks later, a man believed to be Wasilia was captured in Peru, fourteen miles southeast of Dannemora. The captive readily admitted to being an escapee, but when the warden received a physical description of the man, the height was clearly a mismatch, for he was much taller than the diminutive Wasilia. By odd coincidence, the man, Joseph Krauss, was a former Clinton inmate who had been transferred to Great Meadow. He was wanted for robbery and assaults, but was also an army deserter who had recently been incarcerated in the guardhouse at Plattsburgh, from which he had escaped, leading to the capture in Peru. So Krauss, a double-fugitive, was now in custody, but Wasilia was still on the loose.

Seven months after the escape, a Newark, New Jersey, saloon keeper was beaten and robbed by two men, John Sazzanov and Frank Horan, who stole his gold watch and twenty dollars. The perpetrators were caught, and in April 1925, Sazzanov received a hefty sentence of five to twelve years for assault and battery, and eight to twelve years for carrying a concealed weapon. The sentences were to run consecutively, so he was looking at a decade in prison, and probably much more. "Much more" turned out to be correct, for it was soon discovered that John Sazzanov was actually Michael Wasilia. Rather than foot the bill to imprison him for a lengthy term, New Jersey authorities decided to wait and let New York finish punishing him first. The four-foot-nine criminal was shipped back to Dannemora, where he was still imprisoned fifteen years later at age fifty.

1926: Frank Lang

For a third-degree burglary conviction on April 21, 1926, twenty-eight-year-old Frank Lang was sentenced to two and a half to five years in Clinton Prison. Just over four months later, on August 26, Lang was working as a trusty on the prison's outer wall when he quietly slipped away. During the past few decades, it had become commonplace for trusted prisoners to skip out on various work crews. Most were quickly recaptured, and two days later, a man matching Lang's description was spied boarding a freight train at Plattsburgh. A call was made to the Port Kent station twelve miles south of the city, where the suspect was removed from the train and brought back to Plattsburgh. A guard was summoned from Dannemora to pick up the prisoner, but upon arrival, he discovered that the captive was not Frank Lang.

Another month of searching turned up no evidence at all on Lang's whereabouts, and he became one of Clinton Prison's few cold-case escapes.

In 1941, fifteen years later, police in Elizabethtown, New Jersey, received an anonymous tip that an employee of Allied Steel Products was a fugitive from justice. When detectives questioned him, the man, who identified himself as Frank Lang, said he was through running, and confirmed that a burglary at Hudson Falls had landed him long ago in Clinton Prison. After escaping back in 1926 and finding various jobs in New York, he moved to a boarding house in Linden, New Jersey, found a steady job at Allied, got married, and fathered a daughter.

Following his arrest in New Jersey, Lang waived extradition, said goodbye to family and friends, and with a promise from Allied that his job would be waiting for him, headed north in custody of Clinton Prison officials. He still owed New York State more than two years of imprisonment, but on December 22nd, after serving nearly ten months, he was pardoned by Governor Herbert Lehman, who said that Lang "has attained a remarkable position in the esteem of his employers and of the community in which he lived."

1926: PAUL ROSSMAN

Paul Rossman came to America as a teenager and turned to burglary as his favorite pastime. In 1908, at the age of seventeen, he was sentenced to twenty years at Elmira for manslaughter, having killed Kingston Milbur at Mamaroneck, New York. After less than eighteen months, Rossman was released, but for such a small man (five feet two and 120 pounds) he was big trouble wherever he went. Heading to Baltimore, he stole a number of valuable jewels before moving to White Plains, New York, where he took a job delivering baked goods to several upscale neighborhoods.

After gaining familiarity with his customers, Rossman delivered baked goods during the day and robbed their homes at night. For possession of a stolen vase, he served ten days in the New Rochelle jail in early August 1912. When he was finally caught for the nighttime burglaries a few weeks later, police found in his apartment several suitcases of silverware, gems, vases, fine clocks, and other goods valued at $10,000 ($252,000 in 2015]. Rossman described using motor boats to access some luxurious homes, and mewing like a cat to determine if houses of the well-to-do had guard dogs inside.

He had no stories, though, to elicit any mercy in court. The judge sentenced him to twelve years, which he began serving at Sing Sing, but was later transferred to Clinton. He was released in 1922, and decided to ply his trade in the North Country. Shortly after leaving Clinton, Rossman was arrested for robbing summer cottages in Saranac Lake. He was sentenced to work on the Franklin County jail farm, but after escaping, he was recaptured and sent to Clinton in late 1922, this time for five to ten years.

Good behavior earned him trusty status, placing him in charge of the fire-engine house. But Rossman had an escape plan, which he executed in September 1926, using a rope to scale Clinton's wall and heading north into the thick forest. His freedom lasted for nearly two days and six miles, ending near the tiny settlement of Jerusalem. A tip that he was seen near the state mill there brought prison guards to the area. Several were put on watch, and Rossman was captured when he was seen exiting the woods.

He pleaded not guilty in court, but an appointed attorney advised him to admit guilt and ask for the court's mercy. Remarkably, it worked. Despite the fact that he was thirty-seven years old and had a criminal record dating back twenty years, Rossman was given a suspended sentence. He was later transferred to Comstock for completion of his term.

1928: Herbert Mackie and Otto Sanford

In early 1924, a twenty-year-old and an eighteen-year-old, both first-time offenders, were sentenced to ten to twenty years at Sing Sing for a series of robberies in Brooklyn, New York. They confessed to being the accomplices of Herbert Mackie, twenty-six, whom the assistant district attorney called, "the coolest, cleverest, and most successful bandit that has ever operated in Brooklyn."

Exaggeration or not, Mackie had been a busy man, stealing thirty-nine cars to commit more than fifty armed robberies in a five-week period earlier in the year. The trio seldom used the same car twice, abandoning the vehicles after escaping so as not to leave a trail.

After the gang broke up, his two former partners killed a man during a robbery, breaking Mackie's rules of shooting only when absolutely necessary, and aiming for the legs to prevent murder charges should they ever be caught. While they both went to prison, their former leader's whereabouts remained a mystery.

Authorities finally discovered that Mackie was imprisoned in Rahway, New Jersey, where they arrested him at the completion of his term in March 1924. In the face of strong evidence, he provided details on the crimes the trio had committed in Flatbush. He also confessed to having driven the car carrying away $180,000 [$2.2 million in 2015] worth of platinum stolen from the U.S. government in Tennessee a few years earlier. Mackie earned $12,000 [$159,000 in 2015] on that job, and said the Brooklyn robberies yielded about $160 each, or a total of about $8,000 [$111,000 in 2015]. When the courts were finished with him, Herbert was shipped off for twenty years to Sing Sing, where unruly behavior earned him a transfer north to Dannemora.

Mackie's musical talent as a cornet player, which was wasted on the outside, was further explored as a member of the Clinton Prison band, well known for excellence. Every Sunday afternoon he attended practice, and in the summer played with the band during Clinton Stars baseball games held inside the prison.

But on July 29, 1928, on the way to the ball field with other convicts to open for the game against Loon Lake, he asked permission to return briefly to his cell for some forgotten item. Later, when the ten-minute musical session ended, roll call was taken and Mackie did not respond to his name. His cell was checked, and when he couldn't be located, the alarm was sounded.

A more thorough investigation concluded that he was still somewhere inside Clinton's wall. At five feet four and 135 pounds, Mackie could hide in small spaces, so every nook and cranny was ordered searched and re-searched. Posters were distributed to sources outside the prison in case he had somehow escaped, but Clinton officials believed he was still within the confines. That theory was supported by Mackie's record, for he had once similarly disappeared inside Sing Sing for an extended period before being found.

By the fourth day of the internal manhunt, officials disclosed that Mackie was carrying a food package when he vanished, and that the escape had likely been in the planning stages for some time. Because resourceful inmates

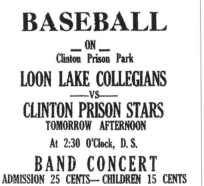

BASEBALL

_ ON _
Clinton Prison Park

LOON LAKE COLLEGIANS
—vs—
CLINTON PRISON STARS
TOMORROW AFTERNOON

At 2:30 O'Clock, D. S.

BAND CONCERT
ADMISSION 25 CENTS— CHILDREN 15 CENTS

Mackie disappeared during this baseball game against Loon Lake from Clinton's past had hidden beneath floors, many sections of flooring were ordered torn up in an effort to locate him. Piles of lumber and coal were moved to ensure they didn't mask a secret passage, and walls were drilled to locate possible hiding places. Nighttime was virtually eliminated at Clinton by searchlights that lit the grounds from evening until dawn, while nine men stood guard atop the wall, and twenty others roamed the prison's interior, ready to cut short any sudden dash for freedom.

Even after a week, Clinton's administration believed Mackie remained inside, and that he would likely be starved into submission soon. It was suspected that other inmates were somehow supplying him with food and water, so guards paid close attention to the movements of convicts who normally associated with Mackie, and continued performing facility-wide searches.

By Day 10, concerns mounted that the inside pursuit had been a waste of time. In Mackie's home turf of Brooklyn, police began looking for him, guided by one simple directive: shoot to kill. On August 9, Day 12, Warden Harry Kaiser asserted that no outside clues had been found, and that evidence within led them to believe Mackie had prepared a hidden cache of food to tide him over until the search subsided, at which time he could escape unnoticed.

The inside effort to ferret him out continued, but as days and weeks passed, prison officials looked more and more foolish standing by their belief that Mackie remained inside Clinton's walls.

Then, on the morning of Friday, September 7—Day 41 of the manhunt—a guard overseeing a crew of inmates repairing the outside of Clinton's wall found a rope attached to the top of the wall by a hook. The alarm was sounded, and a head count revealed the absence of inmate Otto Sanford—cornet play, leader of the prison band, and Herbert Mackie's best friend.

A search of Sanford's cell revealed a hole dug in the wall, and a tunnel leading to a sewer pipe, which ended at a manhole in the prison yard. It appeared Sanford took that underground path, exited the manhole, and followed the west and south halls to where the wall connected with the warden's residence. There he threw the hook to the top of the wall, ascended and descended without being discovered, and disappeared.

Further investigation underground led to a shocking discovery:

beneath Sanford's cell was a secret hideaway, furnished in relative comfort. The room held a homemade electric stove and a light, both connected to the prison's wiring. There was a mattress, bed clothing, magazines, food, cigarettes, matches, and other items. The only conclusion to be drawn was that Mackie had lived beneath Sanford's cell for six weeks, and after the interior search for him waned, they made a break for it together. The best test of that theory was to hunt down Otto Sanford. His escape wasn't discovered until the following morning, so the eight-hour head start he enjoyed was much longer than most inmates who had escaped Clinton in the past.

But Sanford's fate once he was outside of Clinton's wall was typical of most escapees: a brief stint of freedom, followed by capture. By Friday night, sixty men had surrounded an inmate a few miles south of the prison, and at about ten o'clock, Herbert Mackie was taken into custody. The posse pressed on, and at 1:30 a.m. on Saturday, Sanford was captured.

Many details of the escape were subsequently verified by the two convicts. Over time, after loosening a stone in the floor of Sanford's cell, Mackie created an opening by removing dirt in their pockets on a daily basis. He eventually scoured out a living space beneath Sanford's cell, and then tunneled to the large sewer pipe, which led to the manhole in the prison yard. This allowed Mackie to disappear in broad daylight by descending through the manhole and accessing his private crypt. While the search for him dragged on, he improved the passage and waited for the right moment for Sanford to join him. In the meantime, the loose stone in Sanford's floor was used to supply Mackie with food once his initial supplies ran low. Success was a matter of maintaining secrecy and waiting for the heat to die down, which took well over a month. The escape was completed during the night, when fewer guards were on duty. A key component allowing them to dig and escape was knowing the habits of guards who slept on the job or neglected their assigned rounds on a regular basis. Similar claims were made by David Sweat in 2015.

While the plan was ingenious, it remained a mystery why the two men hadn't put more space between themselves and the prison after scaling the wall and heading south. Mackie, after all, was captured by Eli Gonyea at Pickett's Corners, just four miles south of the prison wall.

Shortly after the breakout was first discovered, four Clinton guards were suspended. A week after the escapees were recaptured, Warden Kaiser confirmed that two of the suspended guards had been fired for negligence.

In late November, Mackie pleaded not guilty in court, but reversed it to guilty and was sentenced to the maximum of fourteen years as a second offender under the Baumes Law. He avoided a life sentence as a four-time felon when it was confirmed that two of his convictions in New Jersey were misdemeanors.

Opting for trial, Sanford was quickly convicted. Under Baumes he faced life, but demanded proof that he was a four-time felon, admitting to arrests in Connecticut, Massachusetts, and New Jersey, but claiming one was for a misdemeanor. However, witnesses from Clinton, Sing Sing, Massachusetts State Prison, Connecticut State Prison, and the New Jersey Reformatory testified that the same Otto Sanford before them had served terms at those institutions under aliases. Photographs, fingerprints, and lists of convictions were presented as evidence. The jury agreed that all inmates described were one and the same—Otto Sanford—and he was given the mandatory life sentence.

But their stories didn't end in Clinton Prison. Otto was transferred to Auburn, and the first entertainment there since the two riots in 1929 was presented by Otto Sanford and his Melody Boys. He wasn't just an ordinary talent. Despite a lengthy criminal history, his background included attendance at the oldest music school in Germany, the Conservatory of Music founded by Felix Mendelssohn. He was also once assistant musical director on a 950-foot-long ocean liner, the S.S. *Vaterland*, which the U.S. seized in 1917 and renamed the *Leviathan*.

In 1932, Auburn Prison's bandleader, who had also trained in Europe's music conservatories, fell dead in the yard of a heart attack, leaving Otto to take over his position. With Sanford sentenced to life, the music program appeared to be in great hands for years to come, but since the Baumes Law had been revised, he sought a sentence reduction in hopes of returning to his family in Germany. In late November 1937, Governor Herbert Lehman commuted his sentence so Otto could be deported to the homeland.

Meanwhile, at Dannemora, Herbert Mackie had assumed Otto's

former position as leader of the Clinton Prison band. The incredible escape he engineered in 1928 was the only blemish on his record, but it carried a mandatory fourteen-year sentence, due to begin after his original twenty-year term ended in June 1935. But changes in 1932 altered the severe terms imposed by Baumes, and many sentences had been reduced. With optimism, Mackie applied for a hearing.

On the day before Christmas 1934, he received an unexpected gift. His entire escape sentence was commuted, said the judge, "This, on one condition. You must promise to go straight!" Six months later, Clinton's famous escapee was a free man, returning to live with his parents in Brooklyn.

But he didn't honor his promise to the judge. On August 13, 1940, Mackie's leg was grazed by a police officer's bullet during an arrest for an attack on the owner of an auto sales company. He was jailed at Riker's Island, and transferred the next day to the Raymond Street Jail. If he were found guilty of assault, attempted robbery, and grand larceny charges, Mackie faced time in New York City, followed by a return to Clinton for violation of parole. As things stood, he might never see the light of day again.

But on September 5, the charges became irrelevant when Mackie was found dead in his cell, face down on the bed. The breakfast tray of food he had picked up earlier remained untouched. His death was attributed to natural causes.

The Clinton Prison Band

1928: John Little

John Little was convicted of second-degree burglary and sentenced to Sing Sing in 1922. In January 1926 he was transferred to Clinton, where he became a trusty assigned to the boiler house.

In the early morning hours of August 21, 1928, during a period when no guards were atop the wall, Little threw a hand-made rope to the top of the barricade, scaled the wall, and descended to freedom on the outside. About fifteen minutes later the alarm was sounded, giving Little only a brief head start.

The manhunt looked at all possibilities, but the focus was east of the prison, with more roads, more homes to access for supplies, and the potential for leaving by train, boat, or car. Guards were posted at rail depots and on all roads leading out of the area, while search teams worked from the prison eastward.

For several days, the area between Plattsburgh and Dannemora was searched and monitored without producing any evidence. Concerns mounted that he had left the area, but on Day 11 of the manhunt, a thoroughly exhausted John Little was found four miles west of the prison on the shore of Chazy Lake. He described an unexpectedly difficult struggle through the thick forest, and of nearly starving on a few berries, which were all he found to eat after devouring a loaf of bread he had carried over the prison wall.

Little's condition required hospitalization, but it appeared he would have ample time to heal. When the issue of punishment was argued in court, the prosecution claimed he was a four-time felon and faced an automatic life sentence. The defense argued that he was a first-time offender.

But witnesses and documents from New York's prisons brought clarity to a muddled issue. As many convicts had done, John Little had used an alternate name at other prisons to avoid the mandatory punishments provided in the Baumes Law. The evidence was irrefutable: fingerprints, photographs, and witnesses from Sing Sing, Comstock, and Clinton back in 1917 identified John Little and John Burke as the same man. As such, he was sentenced to life in Dannemora as a four-time felon.

His official sentence was fifteen years to life for second-degree robbery and escape, but there's an addendum to Little's story. He regained the boiler-house job and maintained a clean record, even standing guard there during the 1929 riot. A year later, in July 1930, he received shockingly good news—a commutation of sentence by the governor for him and three co-workers,

> ... as a reward for services rendered by them during the riot at Clinton Prison.... These men, at considerable risk to themselves, both for the present and the future, saved the entire equipment in the boiler room of the prison from destruction, as well as the lives of the persons in the boiler room.

The governor set them free, acknowledging their good deeds, and understanding that remaining in prison left them open to potential retaliation from leaders of the riot.

1974: Bernard Charles Welch and Paul Marturano

On the evening of September 5, 1974, two inmates in the hospital exercise yard climbed a section of a twenty-foot-high chain-link fence and escaped. Bernard Welch and Paul Marturano were participants in the Adirondack Correctional Treatment Evaluation Center (ACTEC) located outside of Clinton's main wall, in what is known today as the Annex. Marturano was serving twenty years for murder after beating Theresa Brush of Syracuse in 1972 and leaving her face down in a bathtub. He had also been acquitted earlier of strangling an eighteen-year-old Oswego girl. Welch was doing fifteen to twenty years for burglary and robbery convictions committed across six western New York counties.

Bernard Welch

Both men had been transferred from Attica to Clinton. Their escape, discovered thirty minutes after the fact, launched a huge manhunt, with bloodhounds, helicopters and hundreds of lawmen converging on northern New York. During the first several days, a stolen car ran a roadblock, and a few sightings were reported near Lewis, New York, thirty miles south of the prison. But no hard evidence was found, and in time the search was scaled back.

Nearly two years later, Marturano was captured in Charleston, West Virginia, and returned to Clinton County to face escape charges. He was sent back to Clinton Prison, transferred to other facilities, and eventually paroled in October 1989.

Welch remained at large for more than six years, until the night of December 5, 1980, when he was interrupted while burglarizing the home of Washington, D.C., cardiologist Dr. Michael Halberstram, whose brother David was a nationally known, Pulitzer Prize-winning journalist. Welch pumped two bullets into Halberstram's chest and then fled. The doctor hurried to his car, and with his wife beside him, began driving to a hospital. When she spotted Welch on a sidewalk, Halberstram went after him with the car, running him down before continuing towards the hospital. But he didn't make it, passing out behind the wheel, crashing into a tree, and dying shortly after arriving at the emergency room.

While still lying injured in the street, Welch was arrested, and in the days to come, stunning details of his life on the lam were revealed. He had lived in several locations and used about ten aliases. Most recently, he had been living for three years with a woman and three children in the affluent Washington suburb of Great Falls, Virginia. In their $350,000 home [$860,000 in 2015] was found stolen property from more than three thousand burglaries—booty that was worth an estimated three million dollars. To get around town he drove a $40,000 Mercedes. Known among lawmen as the Standard Time Burglar, Welch tied up many of his victims and raped several of them, including a seventy-four-year old. FBI and police from several states had been trying to catch him for years, a pursuit that finally ended when Halberstram brought him down.

When Welch was found guilty of murder in 1981, he was sentenced to life in prison under terms that made parole possible after 143 years served. Still, he was summoned in April 1982 from the federal penitentiary in Marion, Illinois, to face escape charges in Clinton County court. He still owed Clinton Prison sixteen years, most of which would never be collected due to his lengthy federal sentence, but they did get ten weeks of it back. Welch was locked up in Dannemora until July, when the escape charges were officially dropped, allowing his return to Marion, where parole awaited—in the year 2123.

Dannemora's Famous, Infamous, Dangerous, and Unusual Inmates

George Appo

For decades, George Appo was one of the best-known swindlers in America. Fame for a swindler makes life difficult, for being recognized hinders their ability to trick people out of their money. Like many such crooks, he was particularly well known among lawmen, and his exploits were followed eagerly by newspaper readers.

At the age of thirty-eight, Appo admitted he had been a crook for thirty-two years. When he was just a few years old, his Irish mother died and his Chinese father, Quimbo Appo, was imprisoned. Relatives offered little help in raising George, and he became a child of the streets. His father was a famous criminal with murders to his credit, and on his own, George was becoming famous as well, developing into a very proficient pickpocket.

In 1874, as a fifteen-year-old, he was sent up the river to Ossining. Said Appo,

> I did not know the ABCs of crime when I entered Sing Sing. When I came out I was familiar with the entire dictionary. I was only a pickpocket when I went there. Since, I have been a flim-flammer, or flopper, as they call it now, a pennyweigher, handshaker, green goods swindler, burglar, and nearly every other kind of a criminal that crooks call 'rough graft' men … those who do their jobs with more or less risk in them—risk not only of being speedily caught, but of the operator losing his life. I have been such a persistent pickpocket and general

pilferer that my right hand has taken on an unnatural form. The ringers now remain permanently in the positions which they are in while creeping into the pockets of other men— the first two crooked forward and the other two bent inward against the palm of the hand. It would be hard to tell just how much property belonging to other people I have taken with that right hand, but I am sure that $200,000 [$5.8 million in 2015] would be a low estimate.

Still, he claimed that after each sentence—in six state prisons and four penitentiaries—he promised himself to go straight. But it never took, in part because prisons were the best place to learn about crime and how to get away with all sorts of wickedness. At Sing Sing, besides the criminal tricks he learned, George was introduced to the system whereby men with money could purchase a much better life in prison, paying for special treatment, outside food, and other perks.

He also learned about cruelty, which had followed him much of his life as a half-Chinese and half-Irish citizen, facing epithets and frequent physical abuse. Severe punishments were imposed on him at Sing Sing, including paddling. As bad as it was, Appo said, he saw much worse at Clinton, where men were driven insane and even killed by the devious work of brutal keepers. Beatings at Dannemora left him with a broken arm, four teeth lost, and languishing in a dungeon. As an opium addict with no access to the drug, his screams during withdrawal kept other inmates awake at night.

But Clinton Prison also provided a higher phase of criminal education. Well-schooled crooks there taught him the ins and outs of becoming a convincing,

George Appo

smooth-talking swindler. Those skills, combined with the forgery expertise he picked up at Sing Sing, proved a potent and lucrative combination. Even as his fame grew, Appo still managed to pull off major swindles.

But there was never much honor among crooks, and George was victimized more than once. While pulling a swindle in Poughkeepsie in 1893, he lost his right eye to a bullet fired by one of his victims who had been tipped off to the scam. Appo nearly died, but refused to rat on the shooter. Upon conviction a few months later, he received a three-and-a-half-year sentence. After three weeks at Sing Sing, he was transferred to Clinton, but before the trip north began, he sneaked a knife into his clothing. While handcuffed to another prisoner, George drove the blade into his own side, but it bent from striking a rib. Although he bled heavily, there were no serious injuries.

After release the following year, he provided extensive testimony to the Lexow Committee, which was probing police corruption in New York City. Newspaper coverage of Appo's sensational revelations spanned the country, and George became a celebrity of sorts. On the witness stand, he described methods used to purchase police protection, and how swindlers operated. Such a betrayal angered crooked lawmen and swindlers alike, and a few months later, Appo was found drunk, with his throat cut. He survived the attack, which was believed the work of a dirty cop or a swindler, motivated by revenge. The case was never solved.

Near the end of 1894, lawyer and author Edmund Price wrote a play titled *In the Tenderloin*. George was chosen as the perfect man to play himself, a green-goods swindler. The show made the rounds in New York City theaters and opera houses, where with no little irony, wealthy people paid to see George Appo perform—a man who famously made a living swindling wealthy people.

In April 1895, he ran off to Buffalo after assaulting a New York City police officer, but was captured, convicted in October, and sentenced to six months in the penitentiary. In July 1896, during a drinking binge, he stabbed a reporter in a case of mistaken identity. The judge believed Appo was becoming mentally unhinged, so George was committed to the Matteawan Hospital for the Criminal Insane, where the oddest of reunions occurred.

His father, Quimbo, widely feared as a violent criminal, had eventually been confined to Matteawan. Now, with the arrival of George, father and son came to know each other after more than three decades apart. The story sheds a bit of its charm through location—a hospital for insane criminals—but when George was released three years later, it was believed he wasn't insane after all, instead being driven to bouts of wildness by drug addiction and withdrawal.

When he wasn't committing crimes or locked up, Appo worked with reform organizations to stamp out crime and corruption, and wrote his own life story. His book was incorporated into *A Pickpocket's Tale: The Underworld of Nineteenth-Century New York*, written by Timothy J. Gilfoyle in 2006.

How good was Appo at scamming people? The *Pittsburgh Dispatch* reported that during a break in testimony at the Lexow hearings on crime and corruption, George sat in a room with lawyers, investigators, and Dr. Charles Parkhurst, a reformer. Using small talk to put everyone at ease, Appo matter-of-factly asked Parkhurst, "Could you let me have two tens for a five? I need some change."

"Certainly, certainly, to be sure. I guess I've got it," replied Parkhurst. He passed the twenty dollars on to Appo, who handed the doctor a five-dollar bill as the group conversation continued. But hardly a man in the room could keep a straight face for long, and Parkhurst soon realized he'd been had. In the retelling, the newspaper ended with, "A man who plays with fire is very apt to be scorched."

MATTHEW ARMER

In 1936, at age seventeen, Matthew Armer of East Greenbush was arrested for stealing a car. While being chased by police, he shoved a young girl from the vehicle, and was later captured at gunpoint. A grand larceny conviction sent him to the New York State Vocational Institute at West Coxsackie, a prison with experimental programs aimed at putting troubled youths aged sixteen to nineteen on the straight and narrow.

But after attaining trusty status, he stole a car from the institution and left the state. Following recapture and the completion of his sentence, Armer stole a new Ford truck in March 1938. An investigation revealed he was operating a stolen-car ring, which earned him five to ten years in Clinton Prison.

He seemed to learn nothing from incarceration. In 1946, a short time after release, he was again found guilty of auto theft and possession of a gun. During questioning, he threw water in an officer's face and attempted to escape, but was caught. Before returning to Dannemora, he repeatedly expressed hatred for police.

When he wasn't locked up somewhere, Armer worked on the family farm, where he took over operations after release from his latest term at Clinton. This opened for him a new criminal endeavor—stealing cows and selling them at cattle auctions. He was soon wanted in Pennsylvania on several charges related to stolen vehicles and livestock, but also operated in New York, Connecticut, and Massachusetts. It was later learned that during this brief period, he stole more than seventy head of cattle.

In December 1950, Armer stole a truck in Newtown, Connecticut. Six months later, he used it to steal a cow, but was pulled over near Oneonta by State Police Corporal Arthur Diffendale, who may have noticed that the truck had mismatched front and rear license plates.

Moments later, as Diffendale approached on foot, Armer stepped from the vehicle with a rifle at the ready, and before the officer could draw his gun, Armer shot him dead at close range. He then sped away from the scene, abandoning the truck on a dead-end road not far from where the shooting took place.

Evidence pointed investigators towards Armer, who became the subject of a massive manhunt. Unique to his case was the use of television for the first time ever by New York State Police in tracking down a suspect. Photographs of Armer and the truck were broadcast, with a request that the public provide any information about either.

On Day 11, intelligence placed him on the family farm, and at about 6 a.m., nine cars carrying eighteen troopers were posted at discrete locations near Armer's East Greenbush residence. The plan was to arrest him when he left, but with his mother in the car, Armer drove past them and veered onto a back road.

Giving chase, police pulled up alongside him with guns drawn, and Armer, perhaps bowing to his mother's advice, pulled over and surrendered.

The explanation was simple: he and Mom were on their way

to Sunday mass. Why the sudden turn onto a back road? He lacked a license and didn't want to risk a ticket. But police weren't buying it. He was handcuffed and taken to jail despite claims of innocence.

In the days to follow, he steadfastly denied shooting Corporal Diffendale, insisting that on the day of the killing, he was at home fixing a chimney. But Armer eventually entered a plea of guilty to second-degree murder, and in September 1951 was sentenced to sixty years to life at Dannemora.

Parole remained a possibility, but killing a state trooper diminished the

Matthew Armer (1951)

likelihood of being granted freedom. He was transferred to less-stringent Green Haven Prison, a maximum-security facility, from which he and a partner escaped in late October 1974. They were captured before year's end and saddled with additional sentence time.

Armer was paroled in January 1984, but was back in prison by mid-August for criminal possession of a forged instrument. After release in February 1988, he was returned to prison ten months later for criminal possession of a weapon and stealing a car.

In April 1992, at the age of seventy-three, he was released, with a stipulation that he report to a parole officer the next day, which—wasn't it obvious?—didn't happen. He was on the lam only briefly, for just two months after leaving prison, Armer was hauled into court on charges of possession of stolen property, criminal mischief, and reckless endangerment.

His fate hinged on a state law requiring parole violators to serve up to the maximum of any previous sentence. Armer was found guilty in August, and on September 3, 1992, he was shipped off to Great Meadow for his seventh prison stint. There would be no further paroles and no further crimes. He died there in October 2001, having spent roughly sixty-five of his eighty-two years in prison.

It appears his greatest accomplishment was living eight decades without ever getting a job.

DAVID JUDSON ARMITAGE

David Armitage was the shortest inmate ever imprisoned at Dannemora, and also filed one of the most unusual lawsuits ever against the state of New York.

Unlike most Clinton inmates, he arrived at prison through the crime of arson. In 1885, the Cramer Hotel in the Saratoga County town of Charlton burned under suspicious circumstances. Judson, as he was generally know, was indicted for arson along with Fred Pulling. Both men pleaded not guilty, but Pulling turned state's evidence and spilled the beans, admitting he had been convinced by Armitage to attempt the scheme. Together they had upped the building's insurance, and after a proper waiting period, removed the cigars, liquor supplies, and best pieces of furniture, storing everything in Armitage's house at Mosherville. Judson alone then set fire to the building, destroying it.

The 1887 court case attracted lots of attention, not only because of the crime, but because of Armitage himself, who was considered something of an oddity. Seated in a chair, he looked ordinary, possessing a normal-sized upper body. But his legs were tiny little stubs about six inches long, with feet said to have been turned backwards—which mattered not at all because his legs were useless—and yet he got around as well as any person with two normal legs.

Armitage's mode of ambulation was a marvel of ingenuity and tremendous strength. Grasped in each hand was a solid wooden block thick enough to elevate him above the floor. Arms became legs and blocks of wood became feet as he propelled himself with ease, while his mini-legs were encased in a protective wooden brace. Being half-sized in a full-sized world was a challenge, but he was capable of working just as well as anyone—even crooks.

In this case, his criminal associate was Judson's undoing. In July

1887, he was found guilty of arson and sentenced to seven years in Clinton Prison. He denied guilt and sought a new trial, but the court refused and Judson was shipped off to Dannemora.

Prison life was difficult for Armitage, who was often treated as a sideshow freak. He complained about it while at Clinton, but under threat of punishment, he was forced to perform, showing prison

David Judson Armitage

visitors his deformities and demonstrating his unique method of locomotion. He threatened to sue the state, and did so following release in mid-1892.

Unlike most inmates who sought damages for brutality, Armitage petitioned for $20,000 [more than half a million in 2015] as punitive compensation for cruel indignities forced upon him time after time. But with no proof and no witnesses on his behalf, the lawsuit went nowhere.

FREDERICK BANKERT

On November 23, 1895, a horrible crime took place in Amsterdam, New York, about twenty-five miles northwest of Albany. Twenty-three-year-old Frederick Bankert was infatuated or in love with Cora Harrison, a twenty-year-old, up-and-coming actress who lived just down the street. He tried repeatedly to spend time with her, but Bankert's strong feelings were not reciprocated.

Distraught and out of control, he carried a pistol and knife to the Harrison home, where he shot Cora three times and cut his own throat in an attempted murder-suicide. But he failed completely in the effort, for both survived. In February 1896, he pleaded guilty to first-degree assault and was sentenced to eight years in Clinton.

While Bankert was doing time, Cora fell in love with William Green, nineteen, also of Amsterdam. They married in January 1899 and moved to a home on Elizabeth Street, occupying the second floor above the family of Mr. and Mrs. James Whitney. As Bankert's release loomed, Cora expressed worry over the jealousy that had driven him to nearly murder her in the past. She contacted the local police, who promised to speak with Bankert and take stock of his intentions. Still uneasy, Cora began carrying a pistol, and the couple slept with a loaded, double-barreled shotgun at the foot of the bed.

When Frederick was released in June 1901, police followed up, receiving his assurance that no harm would come to Mrs. Green. He worked on farms during the summer and was largely absent from the city, but was secretly seething all the while with a rage that finally boiled over.

In the early morning hours of November 2, he executed a well-thought-out plan, arriving at the Green home with a gun, hatchet, and rope ladder. Bankert removed his shoes to ascend quietly, and tossed the ladder upward to where it hooked on a protrusion. Climbing to the second floor, he located a window, worked it open, and entered the house. While quietly looking around, he located the master bedroom where Mr. and Mrs. Green were asleep.

Police who reconstructed the scene determined that Bankert initially attacked them with the hatchet. William tried to fight back, but was struck several times. He was found with his skull caved in and one leg dangling from the bed. A bullet to his neck was most likely a precaution to ensure death. Cora's skull was also severely damaged, and she had a bullet wound to the shoulder.

There was no getaway plan. After assaulting the couple, Bankert placed the gun tightly against his chest and killed himself with one shot to the heart. The Whitneys from the first floor discovered the carnage, with blood everywhere about the room, and two men dead. Between them was Cora, unconscious but somehow still alive. She survived until late afternoon.

ARTHUR BARRY AND BOSTON BILLY WILLIAMS (REAL NAME JAMES FRANCIS MONAHAN)

Arthur Barry and Boston Billy were two of the most famous thieves in America during the Roaring Twenties. With Prohibition and criminal gangs dominating the media, these two still managed to stand out from the crowd. Where guns and knives were the preferred tools of criminals, they became known as gentlemen bandits, politely mixing with society's most affluent members by day, and stealing from them by night. Above all, they were the thinking man's criminals, operating in Connecticut, Florida, New Jersey, New York, and Pennsylvania.

Arthur Barry was a slick operator, once touted in headlines as "the nation's super thief," but claimed that Boston Billy was the brains behind the operation. They were long suspected of many crimes against the high-society folks of Nassau County, but the elusive pair was even more audacious than investigators believed. The details only became public knowledge when, courtesy of anonymous tips, one Arthur Gibson was taken into custody at Ronkonkoma, Long Island, in 1927 with a box full of jewelry in his possession. Under questioning, he confessed to multiple crimes and named Boston Billy Williams not only as his partner, but as the man who had planned it all. Authorities put out an eight-state alarm and offered a $5,000 reward for his capture.

Police eventually learned that Gibson was an alias of Arthur Barry, whose burglary record dated back to 1910. He was jailed as the suspected shooter of a Connecticut policeman in 1922, but escaped and had never been recaptured. Barry, however, was not a man often associated with bloodshed—unlike his partner, who was known to let bullets fly when the situation called for it, but planned crimes so well that violence was seldom an issue.

Boston Billy was nothing short of ingenious in conjuring schemes and paying attention to details. After committing a number of crimes together, they turned their attention in the early 1920s to major thefts, targeting the wealthy. To select victims, they combed the society pages for reports on wealthy matrons sporting jewels. Suits and tuxedos were their criminal uniforms. They crashed parties, blending in while assessing possible theft targets.

At the casino near Central Park, Barry described following a diamond-clad woman to her car, where he made note of the license-plate number. Then, posing as an officer handling an accident, he called the traffic bureau to secure the name and address linked to the plate number, setting up another job.

They always thoroughly scouted the homes of potential victims, and sometimes wore socks over their shoes so as not to leave footprints. Arthur was known as the best second-story man, a thief who entered homes through upper-floor windows, often completing a job while the inhabitants remained unaware on the first floor. He and Billy also mixed it up, sometimes striking at the finest hotels, where most guests were of considerable means and carried valuables to be worn at special events.

Among their victims was the daughter of F. W. Woolworth, relieved of $685,000 in jewels [$9.25 million in 2015] at the Hotel Plaza, and William Durant, automobile manufacturer, who lost $100,000 in gems from his New Jersey home. Percy Rockefeller's Connecticut estate was hit for $19,000 worth of loot. Anyone on the social registry was a potential victim.

Their total take together was estimated at $2 million [about $27 million in 2015]. While engaged in such a lucrative criminal operation, they lived among their victims, hobnobbing with the best of society and spending lavishly. Arthur claimed Harry Houdini and Prince Edward among his friends, and took a vacation to Europe in 1924. Billy had luxurious homes in Palm Beach, Florida, and on Long Island, plus a Park Avenue apartment in New York City. Crime did pay, at least for a while.

But with the arrest of Barry in 1927, authorities knew they'd struck gold when he admitted to the famous Livermore jewel theft committed on May 29, just a week earlier. He and Billy had entered the estate of Mr. and Mrs. Jesse Livermore ("the Lone Wolf of Wall Street") at Kings Point in Nassau County, oozing charm while relieving them of goods valued at $100,000 [$1.4 million in 2015]. They treated the couple kindly, complying with their requests to leave behind certain possessions of personal value.

Arthur Barry

For that crime, Barry pleaded guilty on July 2 and was sentenced to twenty-five years in prison. Among those to testify was Mrs. Livermore herself, who said, "You'll have to admit he was a charming man!" He was also a snitch for claiming his unnamed partner was not only the ringleader, but also a cop killer operating under the alias Boston Billy Williams. Clever sleuthing by detectives over a period of weeks uncovered his real name— James Monahan. The information from Barry led to Billy's arrest after a shootout, ending forever one of the most famous criminal partnerships in the country.

Billy, who suffered a minor gunshot wound to the leg during his capture, was angry that a trusted, longtime partner had squealed. He denied being the criminal mastermind, and said that Barry was the violent one who had shot and killed a police officer in Scarsdale.

There appeared to be nothing Billy could do to avoid prison, though he certainly tried. After a failed jailbreak using a key fashioned from a spoon, he set fire to the mattress in his cell, and later tried a hunger strike. But nothing worked, and he soon ran out of options.

With a hopeless case before him, Billy pleaded guilty. For burglary and grand larceny, he was sentenced to a total of fifty years and shipped off to Dannemora. Barry, rumored to be planning an escape, was transferred from Sing Sing to Auburn. This set the stage for some of the most chaotic moments in New York's prison history.

On July 22, 1929, a riot took place at Clinton, leaving three inmates dead, many injured, and parts of the prison destroyed. Six days later, a riot erupted at Auburn, leaving two prisoners dead, several injured, and a number of buildings burned. No one escaped during the Clinton riot, but four men were missing from Auburn. Among them was Arthur Barry.

The Baumes Law and prison conditions were cited as causes behind the rebellions, which some state officials maintained were masterminded by Barry and Monahan at their respective facilities. Even knowing that Boston Billy was in solitary confinement, away from Clinton's general population, some investigators believed he had still played a role.

But at Auburn, little doubt was expressed about Barry's part in leading the uprising. It was he who chose to attack the arsenal, from which the convicts secured weapons. With guards firing machine guns, Barry and a few friends ran across the yard, accessed the main wall, disabled the guards, and reached the streets outside, where they hijacked a car and drove away. By keeping on the move, they successfully eluded capture.

Two years later, a woman who believed Barry was the kidnapper of the Lindbergh baby (in March 1932) revealed he was living in Newton, New Jersey, five miles from where the child's body was found. He was arrested there and interrogated about one of the twentieth century's most famous crimes. A private detective cited six factors that he felt linked Barry to the child's death, but authorities concluded the evidence didn't make a strong case.

Under heavy guard, he was lodged in Auburn to complete more than twenty years of sentence time that remained when he escaped. To everyone's astonishment, including the judge, Barry was later found innocent of charges that he fomented the Auburn riot. Judge Kennard Underwood called the jury's decision "the height of error."

But among the punishments he suffered for escaping were five years in solitary—twenty-three hours a day in a six by eight cell—a stint that would have driven many men insane. During that time he saw twenty screaming inmates taken out in straitjackets. At one point he was tossed into a dungeon, far worse than solitary, but emerged ten days later intact.

In 1948, after studying law while in prison, Barry claimed that a court error from sixteen years earlier entitled him to resentencing, but the plea was denied. He then sought parole, but at age fifty-three, he still had a half-dozen indictments waiting, including one for the Livermore heist. A deal was struck requiring a guilty plea to all pending charges in exchange for a suspended sentence, as long as he went straight for the rest of his life. Barry was released in November 1949 after serving nineteen years, and died in July 1981, having kept his word to the very end.

*   *   *   *   *

Following Boston Billy's conviction back in 1927, he was imprisoned at Sing Sing, but after threatening to escape, he was sent in shackles to Dannemora and kept in isolation. When detectives arrived a year later to question him on the whereabouts of highly valued booty that had never been recovered, they found that Billy had been declared insane as a result of dreadful treatment received at Clinton Prison.

He had certainly suffered terribly, but may have intentionally exaggerated his own plight. Less than a year later, Eddie Kane, an old crony from the Livermore burglary, was arrested and faced trial. No one knew more about the case than the perpetrator, Boston Billy, but insane persons were not allowed to testify in court.

Soon enough he was declared sane again, after offering to tell all in a Mineola, New York, courtroom and provide prosecutors with an easy conviction. Prison officials were suspicious it might be an old ploy used by Clinton inmates: since the place was virtually inescapable, any opportunity to set foot outside of Dannemora's wall represented a chance for freedom.

During the trip south in January 1929, police described him as upbeat, smiling a lot and enjoying the attention. But he expressed no interest in seeing former partner Arthur Barry, whom he referred to as a rat. Then, from the witness stand, Billy reneged on his promise, instead claiming that Kane wasn't present at the Livermore estate the night of the robbery. From the prosecutor's perspective, bringing their star witness south had been a complete waste of time.

On the return trip, the four guards accompanying him expected Billy would try something, and that perhaps his best behavior had been a ruse all along to put them at ease. They weren't wrong.

As the rail car was being switched at Albany to travel north, he suddenly slipped from the handcuffs, knocked a guard down, ran to the car's bathroom, and locked the door behind him. Tearing the curtain off a window, he kicked the glass out and tried to wriggle through the opening.

The officers gave chase but were unable to enter the bathroom. Rushing to their own berth, they opened the window and began shooting in Billy's direction, forcing him back inside. Other guards then broke down the door to the bathroom and rendered him unconscious. Although head bruises and cuts from the window glass were the worst of his injuries, many erroneous reports said Billy had been shot through the head.

A few hours later he was placed in solitary at Dannemora. Despite being there during the riot six months later, he was still believed by some to have masterminded the darkest day in Clinton's history. Either way, he paid a steep price, spending over ten years in the prison's isolation cells.

In 1948, Billy applied to Clinton County court, claiming his sentences of forty and ten years were supposed to be concurrent, not consecutive. The court disagreed. In 1952, he tried again in Nassau County court, but was rejected. Near the end of his term, he was moved to Sing Sing, where parole was granted in 1956. But he owed time to Massachusetts for a car theft from decades earlier, and was imprisoned at Walpole. Release finally came in 1958.

To counter stories that Barry had told the media about their exploits, Billy granted interviews in early 1960 and gave his own version of events from long ago. Six months later, he died at the age of sixty-two.

There's no doubt the two men were quite different from each other. A detective who worked with both convicts saw it this way:

> While Barry had been sullen and morosely stubborn when captured, Monahan was facetious and scornful; Monahan was cynical, where Barry was sentimental; Monahan was domineering, where Barry was easily led; Monahan was keen of intellect, sharp-witted, ready to take advantage of every point—he was the sort whose intelligence would have to be appealed to; whereas, it had been possible to "get at" Barry through his chivalry and affections.

FERDINAND BAUMGART

Ferdinand Baumgart led a troubled, unruly childhood and ended up in the State Industrial School (reform school) at Rochester. In 1926, at age sixteen, he escaped the school with a friend and drove a truck to Odessa, seventy miles away, where they were arrested and returned to Rochester.

During multiple arrests in the years to come, he sometimes gave his name as Ferdinand, and other times as Fred. In 1936, he was arrested for assaulting his wife's ex-husband. A little over a year later, in mid-1937, police solved a two-week-old stickup of the Royal Café in Niagara Falls with the arrest of twenty-seven-year-old Ferdinand and his brother, Albert, thirty-two. The total stolen was only $450, but because it was Ferdinand's second felony conviction, he was sent to Attica for thirty to sixty years.

In 1940, he filed a lawsuit on the grounds that he was never convicted of a specific charge, explaining that the original indictment back in 1937 covered four counts: first-degree robbery, second-degree grand larceny, first-degree assault, and criminally receiving stolen property. The jury determined he was "guilty of the crime whereof he stands indicted," which was nonspecific.

Baumgart had no luck at first, but after a transfer to Clinton, he used the prison library to study law and prepare his own legal papers. He met with success after filing a lengthy, hand-written habeas corpus suit in 1947. A judge agreed that a defendant had the right to know specifically what he had been convicted of, which wasn't stated clearly in Baumgart's court documents. The judge during his trial had presumed the guilty verdict addressed robbery, which prompted the lengthy sentence.

With a judge now declaring his conviction a decade earlier illegal, Baumgart filed for immediate release. The assistant district attorney said that obtaining witnesses for a new trial would be nearly impossible, and since Ferdinand had already served ten years, the indictment should be dismissed. That suggestion was unexpected, for the original sentence was thirty to sixty years. But the judge agreed, and Baumgart was a free man. He thanked the court and was quoted in the *Buffalo Courier-Express* as adding, "I will never be seen in any court again."

In a small way, he broke that promise quickly, for a year later Baumgart paid one of the highest fines in Tonawanda court for a collection of traffic tickets. But in February 1954, six years after gaining freedom, he broke the promise in a big way.

In Uncle Dud's Grill at Niagara Falls, people were gathered near the bar when a fight involving Albert Baumgart erupted. It was reported that Ferdinand Baumgart's wife had been insulted, and shortly after, from three feet away, Ferdinand shot another patron, Alphonse Kulik, dead. The brothers then fled in a car, but crashed, and were arrested.

After indictment on murder charges, they were tried separately. Albert's charges were reduced to a firearms violation and accessory to felony, sending him to prison for fifteen years to life. Ferdinand's defense hinged partially on claims he was too inebriated for premeditated murder, suggesting that manslaughter was more appropriate. The jury didn't agree, finding him guilty of second-degree murder.

Because of previous convictions, he was sentenced to forty years to life. In 1970, after sixteen years in prison, the New York State Court of Appeals denied a request to overturn his conviction.

DAVID BERKOWITZ (BORN RICHARD DAVID FALCO) (ALIAS SON OF SAM, ALIAS THE .44-CALIBER KILLER)

David Berkowitz was a serial killer known worldwide in the 1970s for shootings that terrorized New York City. There seemed no rhyme nor reason to the crimes he committed, and for good reason. His writings suggested a disturbed, demented mind, typified in the following letter (verbatim) he sent to Captain Joseph Borrelli of the New York City police:

Dear Captain Joseph Borrelli,
    I am deeply hurt by your calling me a wemon hater. I am not. But I am a monster. I am the "Son of Sam." I am a little "brat."
    When father Sam gets drunk he gets mean. He beats his family. Sometimes he ties me up to the back of the house. Other times he locks me in the garage. Sam loves to drink blood.
    "Go out and kill," commands father Sam.
    Behind our house some rest. Mostly young—raped and slaughtered—their blood drained—just bones now.
    Papa Sam keeps me locked in the attic, too. I can't get out but I look out the attic window and watch the world go by.
    I feel like an outsider. I am on a different wavelength then everybody else—programmed too kill.
    However, to stop me you must kill me. Attention all police: shoot me first—shoot to kill or else keep out of my way or you will die!
    Papa Sam is old now. He needs some blood to preserve his youth. He has had too many heart attacks. Too many heart attacks. "Ugh, me hoot, it urts, sonny boy."
    I miss my pretty princess most of all. She's resting in our ladies house. But I'll she her soon.
    I am the "Monster"—"Beelzebub"—the "chubby behemouth."
    I love to hunt. Prowling the streets looking for fair

game—tasty meat. The wemon of Queens are prettyist of all. It must be the water they drink. I live for the hunt—my life. Blood for papa.

Mr. Borrelli, sir, I don't want to kill anymore. No sur, no more but I must, "honour thy father."

I want to make love to the world. I love people. I don't belong on earth. Return me to yahoos.

To the people of Queens, I love you. And I want to wish all of you a happy Easter. May

God bless you in this life and in the next and for now I say goodbye and goodnight.

POLICE—let me haunt you with these words;

I'll be back!

I'll be back!

To be interrpreted as—bang, bang, bang, bang, bang— ugh!!

Yours in murder,

Mr. Monster

His victims included:

December 24, 1975: teenager Michelle Forman and an unidentified woman, stabbed with a hunting knife.

July 29, 1976: Donna Lauria, age eighteen, killed by one shot; Jody Valenti, age nineteen, struck in the leg by one bullet, survived.

October 23, 1976: Carl Denaro, age 25, suffered a bullet wound to the head, survived; Rosemary Keenan, minor injuries from a shattered car window.

November 27, 1976: Donna DeMasi, age sixteen, bullet wound to the neck, survived; Joanne Lomino, age eighteen, bullet wound to the spine, became a paraplegic.

January 30, 1977: John Diel, age 30, minor injuries; his fiancé, Christine Freund, died from two gunshot wounds.

March 8, 1977: Virginia Voskerichian, age nineteen, died from a bullet to the head.

April 17, 1977: Alexander Esau, age twenty, shot twice, died; Valentina Suriani, age eighteen, shot twice, died.

June 26, 1977: Sal Lupo, age twenty, shot, minor injuries; Judy Placido, age seventeen, shot, minor injuries.

July 31, 1977: Stacy Moskowitz, age twenty, shot in the head, died; Robert Violante, age twenty, shot in the head, blinded in one eye, mostly blinded in the other eye, survived.

* * * * *

During his crimes, Berkowitz wrote taunting letters to police, and his case received heavy media coverage. When he was arrested on August 10, 1977, he openly confessed to the attacks that left six dead and seven wounded, explaining that orders to commit the killings came from a demon speaking through a dog, Harvey, owned by his neighbor, whose name was Sam Carr. A search of Berkowitz's apartment revealed walls bearing Satanic graffiti. Within his diaries were notes on more than a thousand arsons he claimed responsibility for in New York City.

Nearly a year after his capture, in which a parking ticket played a key role, Berkowitz was convicted, but during sentencing, he began cursing loudly in court and attacked security guards, biting and kicking them before being subdued. The hearing was postponed, and measures were taken to prevent a recurrence.

For six murders and seven attempted murders, he was sentenced to a total of 315 years. On June 13, the day after sentencing, he was sent north to Sing Sing in the wee hours of the morning. In early afternoon, accompanied by several armed officers, he arrived at Clinton Prison for psychiatric testing to determine where Berkowitz would serve his time. Besides Clinton, the options were Attica, Auburn, Greenhaven, and the Marcy Psychiatric Center for the Criminally Insane in Utica.

Plattsburgh's *Press-Republican* described the aftermath of his arrival at Clinton:

> Security forces emerged from all directions in the village after Berkowitz was safely behind bars. They carried shotguns and small gymnasium-type bags that appeared likely to conceal more weaponry.

Without special psychiatric needs, it was believed he would remain at Clinton, but in early July, Berkowitz was declared mentally ill and in need of hospitalization. Shortly after, he was transferred to Marcy at Utica for four months, after which he was moved to Attica in November 1978, where his odd behavior led to the nickname

"Berserkowitz." An attempt to kill him in 1979 left fifty-six stitches in his neck, but Berkowitz wouldn't identify his assailant except to say he "was a pain in the neck."

In February 1981, after it was discovered he had fallen in love with a transsexual convict, who called himself Diane and took hormones to grow breasts, the inmate was

David Berkowitz

transferred to another prison. In July, because prison officials feared for Berkowitz's safety, he was sent back to Clinton and placed in segregation, apart from the main population.

In 1987, he received $118,000 for movie and book deals based on his story, but due to laws restricting criminals profiting from their crimes, a judge denied his claim for $120,000 in attorney fees and ordered the profits distributed among the families of eight of his thirteen victims.

While still at Clinton, Berkowitz claimed to have been "saved" by Jesus and was now the Son of Hope instead of the Son of Sam. He was transferred to Sullivan Correctional Facility in Fallsburg in 1987, where he remains today. His parole hearings are held every two years, but Berkowitz has been denied each time, the latest in 2014.

JOHN BERNAUER

In September 1912, John Bernauer burst into the headlines for the bold robbery of billionaire J. P. Morgan's mansion. The theft took place back in January, but wasn't publicized until Morgan offered police a reward for the recovery of missing items that were cherished by him personally.

During the investigation, officials believed they were tailing one of the nation's most notorious criminals, Reynolds Forsbrey, but when the capture was made, it was discovered that Bernauer, a relative unknown, was actually the culprit. He was branded the "Dutch house burglar," a name referring to thieves capable of robbing homes but leaving no trace behind. In his possession were several cigarette cases, watches, jewelry, and other items, several of them inscribed with "John Pierpont Morgan, Jr."

An item *not* in his possession was Bernauer's undoing—a silver cigarette case that he handled, but in favor of lighter loot was left behind with his fingerprints intact. Detectives photographed it, but after painstaking comparison to thousands of prints in their collection, they found no match.

During a series of pawnshop visits, they encountered a man selling many ritzy items. While questioning him, they found in his pocket thirty-seven pawn slips for jewelry. He was fingerprinted, and the results matched the print on Morgan's silver cigarette case.

Bernauer confessed, explaining that while robbing homes, he had found a back door of Morgan's house unlocked. He entered, took off his shoes, and explored the house without disturbing forty servants who were asleep in their quarters. Nothing interested him until he crept into Morgan's bedroom, where, with the financier asleep, he gathered the goods and made a clean escape.

With pawnshops being monitored, disposing of the items became a problem. He waited more than six months, committing many other burglaries in the meantime, but was still nabbed courtesy of the telltale fingerprints. In court, Bernauer admitted to the crimes, boasting of how he had ransacked Morgan's own drawers, but claiming his many robberies were committed under a hypnotic spell cast by a friend. He pleaded guilty and was sent to Sing Sing for five to ten years, leaving a pregnant wife to fend for herself.

Ten days after arriving there, he attempted to escape, but was eventually found hiding beneath a pile of rags. He was transferred to Clinton Prison as an incorrigible, but behaved well and became a trusty in the warden's house. Upon his release in 1918, Warden John Trombly prevailed upon New York City authorities to drop pending charges and allow Bernauer a clean start. He found employment for $12 a week as a porter, while his wife worked as an elevator operator.

But just six weeks after leaving Dannemora, he was arrested for stealing $5,000 worth of jewelry [$79,000 in 2015] from a Wall Street broker's home. During questioning he used an alias, but his fingerprints were compared to those from Morgan's silver cigarette case, confirming Bernauer's identity. When asked the reason for returning to theft, he said, "Well, I've got a wife to support."

Mrs. Bernauer was soon alone again and he was back in Dannemora. Within two years he again achieved trusty status and was assigned to a road crew in Hollywood, St. Lawrence County [in the modern town of Colton], some sixty miles west of the prison. In September 1920, he walked away from the job, the third man to do so that summer. Eight days later he was arrested in Saranac Lake after burglarizing a cottage while the family slept, stealing clothing, jewelry, watches, and a slew of other items. He was returned to Clinton Prison with a year added to his previous sentence.

Bernauer was transferred to Sing Sing shortly before his scheduled release in May 1924. At that time, New York City police were frustrated by a string of robberies that appeared to be the work of the Dutch house burglar, who, according to their records, was still locked up. In early June, a patrolman heard a scream emanating from the home of cotton broker Langdon Harris. Entering, he found two men engaged in a fight, and subsequently arrested George Weider.

At the station, police were shocked to discover that Weider was actually John Bernauer, a man they thought was still in prison. Sing Sing officials confirmed that he had been released several weeks earlier, which led to proof that initial suspicions were correct: the Dutch house burglar had robbed the homes of more than twenty wealthy folks during the past three weeks.

Before going to prison, he experienced a very awkward personal moment. Mrs. Bernauer brought twelve-year-old John Bernauer Jr. to court from a school for the poor, where he was housed because she couldn't support him financially. In a caged area at the rear of the courtroom, young John met his father for the very first time.

MARQUIS CURTIS, ROBERT MINFIELD, AND JOHN MURPHY (ALIAS CANADA BLACKIE)

"The man who was regarded as the most dangerous criminal in the state, became, through the same strength that made him dangerous, a loyal and trusted friend of the authorities…. The old prison system had seriously crippled him…. For many years to come, the name of Canada Blackie will be an inspiration to all who knew him, both within and without the prison." So wrote Sing Sing warden and prison reformer Thomas Mott Osborne about Canada Blackie upon his death in 1915. It's safe to say that most who knew Canada would never have imagined those words being used to eulogize him.

He had committed all sorts of crimes since youth, even robbing trains, but his famous gang of toughs was decimated after the murder of watchman Matthew Wilson in 1900 during a bank robbery at Cobleskill. During the trial, accomplice Sheeney Harris turned state's evidence, with devastating results: Whitey Sullivan and Goat Hinch were sent to the electric chair, while Dublin Ned and Canada Blackie were given long sentences at Clinton. Harris, the snitch who turned everyone in, was soon gone as well. After escaping the Schoharie County jail in 1903, he and a partner jumped a freight car. When a brakeman walked their way, both men climbed through windows and clung to the outside of the car, but Harris lost his grip and was chopped up beneath the train's steel wheels.

Canada Blackie bristled under Clinton's strict discipline and frequent humiliations. After several years, he joined with two of the most dangerous inmates in New York, Marquis Curtis and Robert Minfield, in a plan to dynamite the prison's main wall and escape. A snitch spoiled the breakout scheme and caused several men, including Canada, to suffer solitary confinement as punishment.

A year later, working with Curtis and Minfield, Canada tried again. Each man, using straight pieces and elbows of gas pipe, created makeshift guns incorporating matchheads, emery paper, and slugs of solder. The plan was to kidnap the warden and use him as a hostage to escape, but when they made their move, the warden wasn't in his office. A confrontation occurred with Prison Guard John Healey, who was shot three times by Canada, twice in the chest and once in the hand. One slug penetrated the chest, while the other solder pellet was too weak to break the skin. That lack of power likely saved Canada from a murder charge. Healey returned fire, and though no one was hit, the commotion brought several guards running. The escape effort failed, and the trio was locked up in solitary.

Months later, when they faced charges, Canada admitted to making all three guns and shooting Healey, but it made no difference. Curtis, acting as his own attorney, was given ten additional years, and the other two cases were deferred until the next court term. In the meantime, they were all confined to screen cells as punishment.

But this was a trio that defined incorrigible. While being moved to the exercise yard in July, two months after the court appearance, they attacked guard William Whipple, striking him in the head with a hammer and grabbing his gun. A melee ensued, with a fourth inmate, Alexander Devoe, attacking Officer Thomas Reid, and Minfield shooting Officer Whipple twice. The gunfire brought several guards rushing in to quell the rebellion. Minfield ran to his cell but remained a problem, firing the gun at any approaching officers until he finally ran out of ammunition.

All three leaders of the uprising paid dearly in Clinton's infamous dungeons, which were banned long ago but remained available for special cases. Canada spent twenty months there—no light, no conversations, no furnishings, and suffering from tuberculosis. His condition deteriorated until a transfer to Auburn was ordered. He was again placed in isolation, which included a bed and toilet—heavenly accommodations compared to the hell he suffered at Clinton, according to Canada. But he remained in terrible physical condition—blind in one eye from the constant darkness at Dannemora, and slowly wasting away.

For two years at Auburn he remained a troublesome inmate, but in time became familiar with rehabilitation programs through an inmate friend. He was also visited by Tom Osborne, whose ideas seem to take hold with Canada. Two months later, he was released from solitary to begin participating in Osborne's reform activities, which had been adopted at Auburn. They exchanged letters frequently, and on the last day of 1914, Canada was transferred to Sing Sing at Warden Osborne's request.

A physical examination revealed that he was dying of tuberculosis, at which point Canada was given a room in the warden's own home by the prison wall. For his apparently whole-hearted reform, Canada was granted a full governor's pardon on February 16, 1915. On March 20, he finally breathed his last. After cremation, his ashes were returned to Sing Sing, where sixteen hundred attended the first funeral service ever held at the prison.

* * * * *

After the attempted breakout in 1911, Robert Minfield, considered a very dangerous man, was locked away in a Clinton dungeon, where he remained for seven years until release.

Marquis Curtis, like his now-deceased friend Canada Blackie, was transferred to Sing Sing to prove that even the worst inmates could be reformed. But he was hardly the best example, for on October 19, 1916, just a few days after Warden Osborne resigned, Curtis and five other convicts—all of them members of Osborne's Mutual Welfare League—escaped in a prison truck.

In a speech in New York City shortly after the breakout, former warden Osborne blamed the breakout on inmates' expectations that stringent rules would be imposed under a new state administrator:

> Mr. Carter has caused the men to fear that Sing Sing will fall back into the iron discipline of Clinton Prison—"Siberia," as the men call it—and that is what caused them to plan and effect their escape.

None of the escapees made it far, and Curtis nearly died in the attempt. He was hunted down on the estate of billionaire John D. Rockefeller and shot, suffering serious injuries. As punishment, he was given additional sentence time and sent back to Dannemora. During the next decade, he went from Clinton to Auburn, Sing Sing, Matteawan (the insanity hospital), Sing Sing, Auburn, and back to Clinton.

Even as he was held in isolation at Dannemora, Curtis was a busy litigator, and it wasn't all for naught. In 1920 he won a sentence reduction of two lengthy terms reaching back to 1908. Unfortunately, he still had lots of time to serve for other crimes, including escape. In 1930, he filed the latest in a long list of appeals to the court, seeking freedom, but was again rejected. At age fifty-five, he was forced to serve the remainder of his time.

FOLKE E. BRANDT

For five years early in the twentieth century, Clinton inmate Folke Brandt was one of the most famous prisoners in the country—a victim of money and power perpetrating a frightening miscarriage of justice.

Brandt was a young Swedish man who spoke little English, and was hired as a valet by Mortimer Schiff, the millionaire son of New York City banker Jacob Schiff. Mortimer claimed that Brandt wrote suggestive letters to Mrs. Schiff, and accused him of burglary for stealing a pin valued at $150. Schiff used a high-powered attorney to prosecute the seemingly trivial case, which should have been nothing more than a wealthy man getting rid of the hired help.

But Brandt, perhaps confused by language issues, entered a guilty plea, which required the judge to determine the circumstances behind the crime and confirm that the plea was correct. Brandt's answers to the judge's questions contrasted with his plea, instead indicating he was not guilty.

That could have, and should have, ended the proceedings, but Schiff's attorney pushed hard for a long sentence, and presented evidence addressing the defendant's character. Brandt, he said, had been fired by six previous employers for criminal conduct.

Judge Otto Rosalsky accepted Brandt's guilty plea to first-degree burglary for taking the $150 pin, and in 1907, for his first criminal offense, Folke Brandt was sentenced to thirty years in Clinton Prison. In the history of New York's criminal courts, nothing like it had ever happened before.

Brandt sought help from behind Clinton's walls, but was for some unknown reason restricted in the type and length of letter he was allowed to write. He appealed to the governor for relief, but Schiff's expensive attorney successfully lobbied the governor to deny clemency.

He finally gained the attention of Senator Knute Nelson of Minnesota, a fellow Swede who believed he smelled not just a rat, but several of them. During three years of hard work, it was proven that court evidence had been fabricated. Four of Brandt's previous employers confirmed that he possessed

Folke Brandt

excellent character, a fifth provided no assessment, and the sixth gave an answer different from what was presented in court—quite the contrast from the prosecution's claim that all six had fired him for criminal conduct. It gradually became clear that nearly the entire case had been concocted by an angry rich man to punish a virtually helpless poor man.

Two lieutenants were charged by the police commissioner with providing a false report and conduct unbecoming an officer. Judge Rosalsky was criticized by the appeals court for applying such a draconian sentence and ignoring Brandt's testimony, while a grand jury investigated the district attorney's role in imposing the excessive punishment. The transfer of a first-time offender from Sing Sing to New York's toughest prison, Clinton, was highly unusual, and was believed to have resulted from Schiff's intervention.

By early 1912 there were four ongoing court proceedings regarding Brandt's case: habeas corpus to get him out of Clinton; a conspiracy inquiry against judicial officers, lawyers, and police; a study of the facts to see if a pardon should apply; and a look at suspension or disbarment of Schiff's attorneys.

The DA admitted the original burglary indictment would fail if brought again to court because there were so many errors in it. Evidence proving attorney wrongdoing existed in a book at the Tombs jail in New York City—coincidentally, the first such book to go missing in ten years. Again, Schiff and/or his attorney, who both had plenty to lose should the book's contents be revealed, were suspected of causing its disappearance.

Embarrassed by the legal mess, Judge Rosalsky rescinded his original sentence, but the courts ruled that since Brandt had been legally sentenced, he must stay in prison. So much for justice.

Former Governor John Dix had refused to commute Brandt's sentence, but another plea for a pardon was presented to current Governor William Sulzer, detailing the court's derelict actions:

> Folke E. Brandt was arraigned before Judge Rosalsky and was induced to plead guilty to burglary in the first degree. After so pleading, he was examined under oath by the judge, and his answers and testimony show that he did not commit burglary, and that he never intended to commit burglary, and

that he had not burglariously entered the house where he was found, but had gone there for assistance.

Before his original court appearance, Brandt had also been convinced by Schiff's attorney that if he didn't appeal the guilty verdict, he would be released after only two years. It was a mix of deceit and coercion on behalf of Schiff to ensure Brandt remained in prison for the full term.

In January 1913, Governor Sulzer ordered Warden Kaiser of Clinton to accompany his famous prisoner to Albany, where Brandt was granted an official pardon. (The timing was fortunate—just nine months later, Sulzer was impeached.) Certain conditions were attached to the pardon, one of which required Brandt to go west with Senator Knute Nelson, his strongest advocate, and find self-supporting work.

He did just that, but was hounded constantly by detectives, who followed him everywhere. It was believed a harassment ploy by Mortimer Schiff to upset Brandt's life and find some legal charge with which to attack him. The annoyance seemed to work, for in February 1914, Brandt sailed for Europe. Almost exactly a year later, he was reportedly killed while fighting in the Russian army.

MARTIN AND WALDO "LAKE" CASEY

Martin Casey was the son of Lake, both of whom lived in Rensselaer County in Stephentown, about twenty miles south of Troy and within two miles of the Massachusetts state line. Father and son were involved in a multitude of crimes in both states, and in newspaper headlines their names were frequently linked with the word terror. Martin was about the loosest cannon anyone had ever seen in the region, frequently pulling a gun on arresting officers and cowing them into leaving empty-handed.

But what the father-and-son combination were best known for was a feud with the Rathbones, who were also residents of Stephentown, and very tough customers in their own right. The Rathbones seemed to prefer using their fists to settle things, while the Caseys always had a gun at the ready.

It's difficult to pinpoint where the feud began, but the first major eruption occurred in 1874 over a gambling dispute at a saloon in Berlin, north of Stephentown. On his way home, Martin was confronted by John and Orlo Rathbone, who accused him of cheating. A fight began, and while Martin was on the ground being kicked, he pulled a gun and shot both men, taking out one of John's eyes and hitting Orlo in the stomach. Both men survived, and Martin Casey served five years in Clinton Prison for the shootings. It comes as no surprise that, unlike most inmates, he earned no time off his sentence for good behavior.

Upon release, Casey joined his father in committing several thefts, generating warrants for their arrest in the towns of Hudson and Kinderhook. Six constables finally cornered them in the town of Berlin, but knowing the Caseys were armed and had a devil-may-care attitude regarding gunplay, the lawmen withdrew.

The fugitives lay low for a brief period, but then went on the rampage of all rampages. Reportedly well liquored up, they visited the West Stephentown homes of two men who had taken part in the recent gang rape of fifteen-year-old Mary Jenks, who died from injuries suffered during the attack by five men. At the first house, Martin was knocked to the floor by a punch, but then sprang into action beside his father. Together they clubbed the man with a piece of firewood and kicked him into unconsciousness. The second man wasn't home, but they destroyed all the furniture in his house. Encountering a third of the rapists in the street, Martin shot to kill, but missed the man's head as he ran for home. They confronted him there, but were met by a shotgun and decided to move on.

The first man they had beaten had since awakened and summoned the local constable, but he declined to attempt an arrest, fearing for his own life. The Caseys stopped at the home of a fourth attacker, but finding it unoccupied, they destroyed furnishings and ransacked the house.

Near the village post office, they attempted to assault another man, but a large crowd interceded. Martin and Lake pulled out their guns, cursed the crowd repeatedly, and left, promising to come back another day and "clean up the town."

Warrants were issued for their arrest, but the focus was on bringing Martin in for damages and previous crimes. For weeks the pair remained hidden in a remote mountain location. A posse of about ten lawmen, including some from nearby Pittsfield,

Massachusetts, quietly surrounded the cabin, where they captured Martin after dropping him with a shotgun blast. Fifty-seven-year-old Lake dove through a back window and escaped into the woods, but no one pursued him.

Martin was wanted for many crimes in both New York and Massachusetts. Since he was in custody at Pittsfield, he was tried there for a series of thefts, found guilty, and sentenced to ten years in the state prison at Concord.

He was released from Charlestown, Massachusetts on February 21, 1892, and eight days later, at a political town meeting in Stephentown, Martin shot Barber Rathbone, brother of John and Orlo, whom he had shot years earlier. There were many eyewitnesses among the several hundred men in attendance, but because Lake was also involved and may have fired a gun, there was confusion as to whether he or Martin had shot Rathbone. The ambiguity may also have been intentional, for father and son were loyal partners, and if Martin were prosecuted as the shooter, he might have faced life in Clinton as a repeat offender.

While his son escaped the bedlam that immediately followed the shooting, Lake was arrested and jailed. A week later, Barber Rathbone died, even as the shooter's identity remained nebulous. Sixty-six-year-old Lake, who was beaten and kicked during the fight with the Rathbones, failed to clarify what had happened. "I don't know if I fired or not. I was so excited and was being pounded so." But he also claimed ignorance of whether or not Martin had fired a gun during the battle.

The grand jury determined that Lake had done the shooting, and that Martin was an accessory. But nineteen months later, no trial had been held and Lake was still in jail, too poor to afford a lawyer. Martin, in the meantime, remained a free man, and had branched out into a new endeavor—hosting a coin counterfeiting operation in the Casey home.

In March 1894, Lake's trial for first-degree murder ended with a verdict of second-degree manslaughter. Having by that time already served two years in jail, he was sentenced to two years, nine months in Clinton Prison, and was released in mid-June 1896.

Both Caseys remained the bane of local lawmen to the ends of their lives, and had more enemies than just the Rathbone clan. In

1910, not far from his own home, Martin noticed Frank Carr standing in front of the Carr residence. From the seat of his buggy, Martin let fly with two bullets that came close to his longtime adversary. As he continued down the road, Carr rushed inside for his rifle and put a slug through Martin Casey's chest, killing him on the spot.

Threats of violence and revenge caused several police officers to attend the funeral, but nothing of the sort occurred. Carr confessed immediately after the shooting, and charges of first-degree murder were brought, but the grand jury failed to indict. His claim of self-defense after shooting someone in the back seemed unusual, but Martin had threatened Carr many times in the past, and had finally sent two bullets his way—the last of many shots he fired at enemies and policemen during a long life of crime.

Lake Casey lived on, finally passing away at his home in 1914 at the age of eighty-eight.

Robert Chambers,
(alias the Preppie Killer, the Preppie Murderer)

The Robert Chambers murder case attracted enormous media attention for sensational, lurid claims made by the defendant. In 1986, the half-naked body of eighteen-year-old Jennifer Levin was found in New York City's Central Park. She had been beaten, bitten, and strangled, and her panties were discovered more than a hundred feet away.

During the investigation, bar patrons linked her name to twenty-year-old Robert Chambers, who, when questioned by police, had several scratches on his arms and face, marks he attributed to a feisty cat. He proceeded to change his story several times, but really caught the media's attention with claims that Levin had demanded rough sex, which led to her death. According to Chambers, she tied his hands with her panties, injured his genitals, and roughed him up so badly that when he finally freed his hands, he accidentally killed her while trying to get away.

It was a wildly improbable story, and almost impossible to believe based simply on body size: Jennifer was five feet four, while Chambers was six feet five and two hundred twenty pounds, nearly twice her weight.

The defense plan included destroying the victim's reputation by portraying her as a wild sex fiend, while Robert, on the other hand, was a former altar boy who had attended prep schools. But he'd also been involved in several crimes linked to his drug and alcohol issues.

It was galling to the public that Chambers, through friends and religious connections that included ties to a New Jersey archbishop, was released on bail, and remained free during the two-year trial on two counts of second-degree murder. The defense forged ahead with the "rough sex" defense, which a prosecutor noted was the first time in a decade, covering more than eight thousand sexual assault cases, that a man had claimed to be victimized by a female.

With the jury still undecided after nine days of deliberations, Chambers pleaded guilty to lesser charges, including first-degree manslaughter, in exchange for a sentence of five to fifteen years. On March 25, 1988, he addressed the court, apologizing for his actions and what he had put everyone through. But the Levins described it as a memorized speech, not at all heartfelt. In Mr. Levin's own words, "He said nothing."

The arrogance and spoiled-brat persona of Chambers was well established for the public, but that image was forever cemented two months later with a video that aired on the television show *A Current Affair*. In one cringeworthy segment, Chambers is seen facing several girls in lingerie, with the camera behind him. He plays with a doll and then turns towards the lens, smiles, twists the head off the doll, and says, "Oops, I think I've killed it." Worse yet, the video was made *before* his trial, during jury selection. Said Jennifer Levin's mother, "I was horrified when I saw it, but in a way I was glad that he showed himself for what he really was."

Chambers was sent to Auburn Prison, where an inability to follow the rules earned him a ticket to Clinton Prison. He also did time at Green Haven, and was finally released in 2003 after serving the full term of fifteen years, having forfeited all of his good-behavior time because of rules infractions.

During the next several years, he was arrested for drug-related crimes, culminating in 2007 with charges he and a girlfriend were dealing cocaine from their apartment. Facing possible life in prison, he took a plea in exchange for a sentence of nineteen years and was sent to Wende Correctional Facility, east of Buffalo.

GERALD CHAPMAN
(REAL NAME REPUTEDLY GEORGE CHARTERS)

Near the end of his twenty-two-year career, Gerald Chapman's several reputations came together in headlines touting him as **SPECTACULAR MAIL BANDIT, JAIL BREAKER, AND CRIMINAL EXTRAORDINAIRE**. But above all, he was most often referred to as a "super-crook," placing him above the level of most American criminals, one whose exploits were followed closely by the public. A worldwide manhunt finally resulted in his capture in 1925, but a decade earlier, he did some hard time at Clinton Prison.

Chapman first ran into trouble in New York in 1908 and served a three-year stint in Sing Sing. After release, he was again arrested for grand larceny, and in January 1912 returned to Sing Sing, this time for ten years. As a brilliant criminal he could be a handful in any prison, and was soon sent north to Dannemora, where he assumed a gang leadership position. As the source of many problems for guards and administration, he was confined to an isolation cell, which at Clinton offered a very stark existence.

After several weeks, he was given a job in the prison laundry, where he formulated an escape plan with other inmates. Their intent was discovered, and Chapman was relegated to the dungeon, which eventually convinced him that serving time was the only way out. He was transferred to Auburn shortly before release in early 1920.

Eighteen months later, he orchestrated a legendary theft, robbing a government mail truck in New York City by scouting a special shipment, boarding the truck while it was moving, and directing it to a side street, where his gang completed the robbery. The total take was a stunning $2.4 million [$32 million in 2015]. He was caught several months later while living in luxury in New York City's Grammercy Park.

During questioning on an upper floor of the federal building, Chapman, a famous escape artist, disappeared. It was finally discovered that he had climbed out a window high above Broadway and crawled along a narrow ledge, planning to re-enter the building through another window and make his getaway. It almost worked, but he was spotted before getting back inside.

In August 1922 he was sentenced to twenty-five years in Atlanta's federal penitentiary. Security was tight, but he escaped seven months later. He was caught after two days of freedom, but a month later he broke out again, setting off a nationwide manhunt led by some of the best trackers in the country.

Six months later, two criminals about to blow up a department-store safe in New Britain, Connecticut, were surprised by Police Officer James Skelly. One of the thieves shot Skelly and ran, but the other was caught. The officer died, and the shooter was identified as Gerald Chapman. For three more months he eluded the law, but was finally caught in Muncie, Indiana, and sent back to Atlanta.

Connecticut authorities put him on trial for the murder of Skelly, and the jury arrived at a guilty verdict in less than an hour. He was sentenced to hang on June 25, 1925. It was widely reported that chief defense attorney Frederick Groehl, with tears in his eyes, reached for his client's hand and said, "Chappie, I'm sorry." With a squeeze of Groehl's hand, he replied, "Oh, that's alright." The two had become friends, of which Chapman had many, along with admirers, and there was strong hope among them for clemency.

But a policeman had died and justice must be served. No one had foreseen Chapman's colorful criminal career terminating at the end of a rope, but after repeated appeals, he was hanged in early April 1926.

STANLEY CHERO (ALIAS GEORGE MILLER) AND WILLIAM SCHEMNITZER (ALIAS JOHN WILLIAMS)

Chero, age twenty, and Schemnitzer, age nineteen, were Pennsylvania youths who, after working briefly in the coal mines and on steamboats in the Great Lakes, went on a crime spree in March 1931. From Buffalo to Schenectady they traveled, until finally being arrested by Corporal Edward Updyke in the Albany area on vagrancy charges. Suspicions were strong that they were driving a stolen car, which contained what appeared to be the loot from several break-ins. After appearing before a justice of the peace, they were ordered confined in the jail at Troy. Police Sergeant John Frey assisted with the transfer, Updyke taking Schemnitzer in the troop car, and Frey following him in the youth's car, with Chero in the passenger seat.

But hidden beneath the dashboard of the boys' car was a

.38-caliber handgun, which Chero pulled out and pointed at Frey, forcing him to stop the car and get out. Chero then drove away as Frey fired several shots, none of which took effect.

Driving down the road a short distance, he encountered Updyke's troop car, which was parked and waiting for Frey to catch up. Chero ordered him from the car and told Schemnitzer to steal the officer's gun. Taking the patrol car, the two young men reversed direction, and soon encountered Frey. An exchange of gunfire left the officer dead by the roadside, where Updyke found his body a few minutes later.

A manhunt was launched, but with no clues discovered after four days, the search was officially expanded to nationwide. Meanwhile, the boys had headed south, abandoning the car near Rensselaer and stealing another. While police searched the Albany area, the two fugitives arrived in Scranton, Pennsylvania, before heading northwest to Buffalo. Leaving the car behind, they hopped a freight train southwest to Canton, Ohio, where they stole another car and drove to Oklahoma, fifteen hundred miles from where Officer Frey was killed.

After nine days on the run—tired, out of money, and in need of gas for the car—they parked near a filling station on the outskirts of McAlester and went to sleep. The station owner became suspicious and notified police, who conducted a search of the car. After finding two handguns, one with engravings indicating it belonged to a New York State officer, the boys were taken to the local police station. Arriving at the door, they both made a break for it. Schemnitzer was dropped with a blow from a billy club, but Chero continued running and was shot in the leg and torso, suffering serious injuries.

New York authorities were contacted about the guns, one of which proved to be Officer Updyke's, and from there the story began to unfold. Under questioning, the two boys blamed each other for the shooting. Headlines proclaimed that Chero was dying, but doctors did manage to keep him alive. He reportedly rubbed newspapers against his open wounds, which may have caused the infection that was threatening his life. His conditioned worsened until doctors were forced to amputate Chero's leg above the knee.

His poor health, and red tape related to warrants for the boys in Oklahoma, Ohio, and New York, delayed their trial until early

1932, when both were found guilty of second-degree murder. That they killed Officer Frey was a given; the jury's job was determining whether or not it was intentional. The boys had most feared the electric chair, so a sense of relief flooded them as the judge delivered a stern lecture and a term of thirty years in prison.

Immediately after sentencing, they began providing details of their flight from the law, stories that the sheriff shared with the press. In Painesville, Ohio, they had engaged in a running shootout, firing eighteen times at a policeman. That same officer sat in the courtroom during their trial, waiting to relate the incident from the stand, but was never called. They also admitted to stealing five cars between New York and Oklahoma.

Both boys were sent to Dannemora, with Chero on crutches that became a hindrance in prison. Schemnitzer worked in the shirt-making department, but Chero still wasn't mobile. Within six months, he shed the crutches for a better alternative—a wooden leg he crafted using materials from a prison workshop.

Schemnitzer remained at Clinton, but Chero was transferred to Attica in 1934, and Green Haven in 1942. Both were paroled in 1952, but a few years after release, Chero was arrested for burglary in Pennsylvania. Two years later, he was sentenced to five years in prison for participating in an interstate auto-theft ring—which also violated conditions of his parole.

New York State was waiting, and upon release from the Lewisburg Penitentiary, he was turned over to authorities and confined to Sing Sing. From there he was moved north to Clinton Prison to serve the remainder of his original sentence for the killing of Officer Frey. Chero, in his fifties, filed suit at least four times in the 1960s, even seeking to vacate his original conviction back in 1932, but was rejected each time by the court.

EDWARD AND CELIA COONEY
(CELIA, ALIAS THE BROOKLYN BOB-HAIRED BANDIT)

During the 1920s, great public fascination developed around the love story of criminal couple Ed and Celia Cooney, similar to how the Bonnie and Clyde story caught on in the 1930s. But Ed and Celia were known as robbers, not killers.

Cecilia Cherison, a Manhattan native, met Edward Cooney, a navy veteran, at a laundry where they both worked. They married in May 1923, and a few months later Celia was pregnant. Ed found work as a welder, but was making only thirty dollars a week. Concerned that the baby would be born in a small, furnished room, they came up with an idea to make some quick money: robbery.

Celia, it must be noted, wore her hair in a bobbed style—cut quite short—which was controversial in the 1920s, signifying a rebellious, independent woman. Ed bought a couple of pistols, and on January 5, 1924, with Celia seven months pregnant, they hit Roulston, a chain store in Brooklyn, for $688 [$9,500 in 2015].

More robberies followed, with both Ed and Celia participating in every heist. When reporters carried on about the Bob-Haired Bandit, the Cooneys became media stars. Several of their thefts netted only small amounts, less than $100, but the quality was balanced against quantity—and the Cooneys were a very busy pair of crooks. During the first three months of the year, they successfully pulled off sixteen robberies. Police were red-faced that a pair of criminals remained at large after committing so many brazen hold-ups within the confines of Brooklyn—and annoyed about several taunting notes received from the female robber.

It seemed likely that Celia's delicate condition would bring an end to their run, but she continued committing armed robberies even at nine months pregnant.

With the baby due any day, a decision was made: one last job and they would move to Florida, buy a farm, deliver the baby in their new home, find legitimate employment, and live happily ever after. On March 31 they purchased

Ed and Celia Cooney

boat tickets from New York City to Jacksonville, where they were scheduled to arrive on April 4.

On April 1, the Cooneys attempted to hold up the National Biscuit Company in Brooklyn. Their guns had successfully intimidated previous victims, but this time something went wrong. While trying to thwart the robbers, employee Nathan Mazo grabbed for Celia's gun, and in doing so knocked her to the floor.

In response, Ed fired twice, leaving Mazo seriously injured. His immediate concern was Celia's health, but in lifting her to her feet and rushing outside, Ed left behind several thousand dollars of potential booty. Their seventeenth and last stickup was the first to result in failure.

They fled New York immediately and found lodging in Florida, where they anxiously awaited the baby's arrival. Katherine was born a few days later, but she didn't survive. Ed wired home to give his mother the terrible news—but it was a message she never received. Knowing that Celia would deliver soon, detectives were monitoring the wires for any birth-related information. By intercepting Ed's telegram and combining it with other clues, police were able to pin down their location in Florida.

Two detectives were sent south, and in the wee hours of the morning, with guns drawn, they kicked in the Cooneys' door. But with weapons by the bedside, Ed and Celia were quickly armed, resulting in a potentially deadly confrontation. Finally, Celia said, "Don't shoot," and moments later they were under arrest. She and Ed had prepared a murder-suicide pact in lieu of being captured, but in the decisive moment had abandoned it.

The public's fascination with the Cooneys was about to rise to a new level. Their plan—to rob stores for the baby's future, start over in Florida, raise baby Katherine in a homey atmosphere, and die together rather than be caught—played widely in the media. Drawing readers in above all else was the obvious love between Ed and Celia. When they were captured, she made a full confession:

> It was all through me that dear Edward went wrong. I am responsible. I am the Brooklyn Bob-Haired Bandit you're looking for. I shot Nathan Mazo. My husband did not do the shooting.

But during a separate interrogation, Edward also confessed, assuming the blame for everything. Efforts to protect each other suggested sincere and true love, and the public sensed it. When they returned north via New York's Penn Station, President Coolidge was departing before a crowd of five thousand. But when word spread that Ed and Celia had arrived, Coolidge's five thousand admirers swarmed towards the Cooney's car to catch a glimpse.

To end court procedures more quickly in hopes of being back together soon, they declined trials and instead opted to plead guilty. But the harsh realities of punishment hit them hard. Both received sentences of ten to twenty years, Edward at Sing Sing and Celia at Auburn, which housed a prison for females. When Ed was deemed too hard a criminal for Sing Sing, he was transferred to Auburn, with the consolation that just a month after sentencing, he was somewhere close to Celia.

Shortly after his arrival at Auburn, Ed was involved in an accident while operating a license-plate machine. His injury became badly infected, causing the amputation of his left hand. Celia was aware of his troubles, but husband and wife weren't allowed to interact at Auburn. He filed a lawsuit for $50,000 against the state, and not long after was transferred to Clinton Prison.

In 1930, for the first time in several years, Ed and Celia met

Celia and Ed Cooney in 1930. Ed lost his left arm several years earlier.

face to face. The occasion was a court session in Syracuse regarding his lawsuit, but for the media it was the return of two A-List stars. Celia cried a little when they hugged, and blushed when asked if she still loved him after seven years in prison. "Love him? Why, it's the only thing that has kept me going during these long days and months and years." Several Auburn inmates, officials, and Celia herself took the witness stand during the hearing, after which she and Ed returned to their respective prisons.

The lost hand wasn't Ed's only health problem, for at Clinton, he had spent an extended period in the tuberculosis hospital. But on the bright side, the possibility of parole for both of them was just six months away. On October 16, it became reality for Celia, and on the 28th, when the parole board met at Clinton, Ed was granted his freedom as of November 5th.

For the Cooneys, the holiday season would only get better. Just days before Christmas, Ed was awarded $12,000 [$187,000 in 2015] for injuries suffered at Auburn Prison, a good start for building a new life in Brooklyn.

RAYMOND, VERNON, AND HOWARD: THE DAFOE BROTHERS OF ST. LAWRENCE COUNTY

Had New York's prisons been operated like a modern airline, the Dafoes of St. Lawrence County would have been knee deep in frequent-flyer miles. They committed so many solo offenses, plus crimes in conjunction with other family members, that a link-chart was needed to sort it all out. The condensed version tells an amazing story of lawless behavior and Clinton Prison reunions.

The oldest Dafoe brother, Vernon, was portrayed in local media as the wild man of Jingleville, a settlement near Canton. He was arrested for robbery and gun issues in 1913, and went on a weeks-long robbery and shooting campaign in October 1914, which earned him five years and two months in Dannemora. Shortly after release in late 1919, he teamed up with brother Howard in committing multiple robberies. They were easily tracked in the snow and arrested, and both were sentenced to Dannemora (Vernon's time was four years and eight months). He was released in the mid-1920s, but teamed up with youngest brother Raymond in committing burglaries and grand larcenies. Both were sentenced to Clinton Prison in 1927, but under Baumes, Vernon was committed for life as a four-time felon.

* * * * *

Howard Dafoe was first sentenced to Dannemora in 1919 for crimes committed with oldest-brother Vernon. He was paroled in October 1921, but was arrested a month later with Raymond for grand larceny and burglary (selling furs, then stealing them and reselling to others). Both were sentenced to terms at Dannemora, where Howard served four years as a second offender. Shortly after release, he again committed crimes and was returned to Dannemora. Finally, in February 1931, for several incidents of forgery, Howard received a life sentence at Clinton under the Baumes Law for his fourth felony conviction.

*   *   *   *   *

In March 1922, youngest brother Raymond Dafoe, still a teenager, was sentenced to Clinton Prison for four years after burglary and grand larceny convictions for crimes he committed with oldest brother Vernon. Following release, Raymond was returned to Dannemora for violation of parole. In 1927 he received a six-year sentence at Clinton, again for burglary and grand larceny. After transfer to Attica, he escaped, but was captured and returned to prison on a third felony charge. In 1935, for burglary and larceny, Raymond was sentenced under the Baumes Law to fifteen years to life at Clinton. His offense? Stealing a cashbox after breaking into the store owned by another brother, Alfred.

Two years later, Raymond was resentenced on a technicality that he discovered while studying law in Clinton Prison's library. The escape charge, was, in fact, a felony, but didn't count towards a life sentence under a Baumes clause. The court resentenced him to fifteen years, ensuring that for an extended period, all three brothers would remain confined at Dannemora.

*   *   *   *   *

A threat to carry on the family tradition in 1938 was eighteen-year-old Clifford Dafoe, convicted of third-degree burglary for stealing a car and robbing a liquor store. Capturing him wasn't all that difficult—after robbing the store, he fell asleep in the adjoining telegraph office, where he was arrested. The judge gave Clifford four years' probation and a stern reminder that three of his uncles were already keeping each other company in Dannemora.

REYNOLDS FORSBREY

Reynolds Forsbrey was once known as the worst criminal in America. He was certainly a bad guy who committed many serious crimes, but was perhaps better described as the worst inmate in

America—totally uncooperative, and a proven escape risk at even the most secure institutions. What made him a media star of sorts was a story built around Forsbrey's powerful love for a woman.

As a teenager, he was arrested for forgery, and by age fifteen was in the House of Refuge, a New York City reform school. He was arrested in Indiana in 1905, served nine months in Albany County jail in 1906, and did time in 1907 at Elmira, where he learned the ins and outs of robbery. After release, he spent a couple of years burglarizing homes, but was caught and sentenced to two and a half years at Sing Sing, a term that Forsbrey later confessed was the source of his cocaine addiction.

It was believed, but never proven, that he killed Brooklyn store owner Walter Meneritz during a holdup—he took part in the robbery, but it was never proven legally who fired the fatal shot.

In 1912, when Forsbrey made the acquaintance of nineteen-year-old Margaret Ryan, nine years his junior, the two fell for each other hard. He struggled financially working as a plumber, and when they decided to elope, he needed cash.

On July 29, while attempting to rob a jewelry shop, he shot watchmaker Morris Schwartzkopf, but came away with no money. An hour or two later, he shot and injured Max Katz, a cigar-store clerk, during a robbery. Forsbrey was captured shortly after and confined in the Tombs, a New York City lockup with a reputation similar to Clinton Prison—tough on crooks and nearly inescapable. Schwartzkopf identified the shooter before dying in a hospital bed, and Katz, who survived, identified him as well. Margaret was questioned and professed undying love for Reynolds, but was released as an innocent who knew nothing of her boyfriend's crimes.

After about a month in the Tombs, Forsbrey was discovered using hydrochloric acid and saw blades on the bars of his cell. How did he obtain such tools under tight security? Margaret had paid him a visit, carrying the blades in the stay pockets of her corset and the bottle of acid hidden among the curls of her hair.

Following that close call, visitors were banned and he was moved to a secluded cell with an around-the-clock guard stationed nearby. Forsbrey laughed at their efforts, promising that even the Tombs couldn't hold him. They dismissed it as braggadocio, but four days later, his cell was empty.

In a story that became prison legend, he used suspender buckles to undo the screws on a ventilator grill while the guard was briefly away. He then removed the register, managed to climb up and squeeze into the airshaft, and where a duct angled straight down, he pressed against the sides and slowly lowered himself two floors to the carpenter shop. An older guard was there, asleep at his post, so Forsbrey exited quietly to the yard, placed a long board against the wall, climbed to the top, and jumped down into the busy traffic of Center Street.

Prison officials and virtually everyone else were stunned, and the next day's headlines gave Forsbrey full credit for an incredible accomplishment. Over the course of three weeks, the manhunt went from citywide to statewide, national, and international. As far away as Belgium and Australia, lawmen were alerted to his appearance and habits.

Finally, a month after the escape, Forsbrey was captured in the Bronx, living quietly with Margaret Ryan. In an interview, she acknowledged the serious crimes he was charged with, but espoused unwavering devotion. "I intend to marry Reynolds. I love him. He has always been good to me. Yes, I would marry him if he were sitting in the electric chair."

To lock Forsbrey up securely as soon as possible, prosecutors accepted his plea to second-degree murder and rushed him up the river to Sing Sing in late November, but for just a brief period. There was only one place for a man of his escape talents: Clinton Prison.

Separated by three hundred miles and a sentence of twenty-five years, he and Margaret maintained communications, exchanging letters as often as allowed. Forsbrey worked in the machine shop, and seemed to be keeping his nose clean, but Clinton guards were wary of his level of cunning.

In April 1913, after barely four months at Dannemora, he was already preparing an intricate escape plan when prison officials were alerted and aborted it. After fabricating a bomb using gasoline, two tin cups, a cap, and a fuse, he joined with a few co-conspirators in building ladders and hiding them in the basement of the tin shop. The last piece of the puzzle was the love of his life, Margaret Ryan, who had secured lodging at Chazy Lake, a few miles west of the prison. The plan was to detonate the bomb and cause mass confusion, during which Forsbrey and company would use the ladders to scale the wall and escape. Margaret awaited at the Chazy Lake hideout with changes of clothes and transportation to the Canadian border about fifteen miles away.

But the ladders were discovered, foiling the plot. Forsbrey took physical revenge on the officer who uncovered the scheme, putting him in the hospital for ten days. As punishment, he was tossed into one of Clinton's screen cells—enhanced solitary confinement, with an iron-barred door and fine-mesh steel screen preventing anything from entering or exiting. Escape was unimaginable.

Unimaginable, perhaps, to the thousands of criminals who came before him, but not to Reynolds Forsbrey. By December 1913, eight months after being confined to the screen cell, he was ready to complete another escape plan, again intended to culminate in running off to Canada with Margaret. Everything was in place, awaiting execution, when prison officials intercepted a letter between the two sweethearts, the contents of which were enough to launch an immediate inspection of his quarters.

Forsbrey, it was determined, could have already escaped, but was waiting for just the right day. A search of his cell revealed unexpected and remarkable ingenuity at work. The steel bars at the top of his solitary confinement exercise cell, located outside, had been pried loose, a feat that seemed impossible, especially with guards checking on him frequently. Forsbrey had used his cot as a tool source, laying the mattress against the wall in order to climb up, and employing a leg from the cot to pry the steel bars. He also reworked the bedsprings into a wire ladder.

To successfully prevent detection of the ongoing work, he rigged the cot in his cell to look normal, when even a bit of pressure would

Reynolds Forsbrey

have caused it to collapse. While the work went on, Forsbrey slept on the cold cement floor. Prison officials were amazed, having never seen anything like it.

The reward for such resourcefulness was a new cot poured of solid cement—no mattress, no springs, just cement. His next trick was to work on the cell door over a lengthy period. By the time guards discovered what he was up to, nearly the entire door was already unhinged.

Because he had predicted escaping the Tombs and stunned everyone by doing just that, there was a tendency to take Forsbrey at his word, which caused consternation at Clinton when rumors spread in 1915 that two revenge murders were in his plans. One involved a man who had reportedly stolen Margaret's affections, and for that he was the intended victim of Forsbrey's knife. The other was a guard who told prison officials that Reynolds had the knife and planned to use.

Margaret had, in fact, become a cabaret singer and taken up with a man named Lloyd Thompson, whom she had moved in with just two months previous. But wracked with guilt over cheating on her one true love, she wrote a note that said, "I am Margaret Ryan, the sweetheart of Reynolds Forsbrey. Let me say, 'The wages of sin is death.' Notify Thompson, Kayser Silk Mills. Forsbrey's address is No. 11, Van Campen Street, Danville, N.Y." She then ingested carbolic acid and some mercury tablets before turning on the gas and lying down to die. But the suicide attempt barely failed, and a week later, from her hospital bed, Margaret said she would live to marry Forsbrey, who still had twenty-two years of his sentence left.

And miracle of miracles, far away in Dannemora, Forsbrey began swearing that his love for Margaret had reformed him. He was inspired to behave, insisting there would be no more trouble after four years in solitary.

In late 1916, when the state prison superintendent visited Clinton, Forsbrey made a direct appeal to be removed from isolation, where ill health and interminable solitude threatened his sanity. The prison had never seen such a crafty inmate as Reynolds, who not only won removal from solitary, but was transferred to Auburn at the end of December and allowed to spend time in the main yard. Despite repeated promises that he wouldn't try to escape, he was watched closely by guards.

But with Forsbrey, anything was possible. Less than four months after arriving at Auburn, he pulled off a remarkable ruse. At mealtime, with men crowding into the mess hall, Reynolds held up a package he said was being sent from one keeper to another. The okay was given for him to deliver it to the office, where Keeper John Betts, an elderly man, was seated. As Betts reached for the package, Forsbrey unleashed a barrage of punches, knocking him unconscious. He then stripped the guard, bound and gagged him, and donned his uniform, complete with keys, nightstick, and revolver.

Walking in a manner that projected confidence, he entered the yard of the women's prison, but realized the uniform was a poor fit and might be noticed. Selecting an unmanned gate, he climbed it, jumped to the street, and walked away from the prison.

Forsbrey's absence went unnoticed for an hour, at which point a manhunt was launched. Dogs were used to track him, and at a brewery barn, their excited behavior gave his presence away. No shots were fired during the recapture.

He was placed in solitary confinement and scheduled for return to Dannemora, but remained at Auburn. Less than a year after escaping, he did it again in March 1918, this time by sawing through the isolation-cell bars and climbing over the prison's outer wall. Hundreds joined the manhunt, and Forsbrey was captured a few days later in a freight car near Locke, New York, about twenty-five miles south of Auburn.

On March 13, less than a week after escaping, he was back in a Clinton isolation cell by order of State Prison Superintendent James Carter—and Auburn Warden Harry Kidney was happy to see the troublesome inmate go. After getting to know Forsbrey a bit, Kidney gave an assessment of what drove him to escape.

> There is no doubt that the thing that makes him do all this is his love for that girl. He idolizes her. He can think of nothing else. If he talks to you for ten minutes he gets to talking of her. I think she is never out of his mind. He hopes against hope to get out and be with her again. I suppose it is something he can't forget. Don't know how one can blame him. It was thought best to cut off communication between him and her.

Anyone can see why it was done. But it hasn't helped matters much, as his escapes show.

Back at Clinton, Ryan Forsbrey's life became one of prison drudgery, so distrusted that he could never be left unguarded. All he could do was wait to get out and perhaps once again be with the woman he loved.

Because he remained behind bars for much of his life, Reynolds Forsbrey was unaware of how his name was linked to Margaret Ryan's in an unusual and amazing story. At different times in her life, she had used aliases, like Margaret Reynolds during a shoplifting arrest, and May Hays back in 1912 when she was considered an accessory in some of Forsbrey's crimes. But there was also a third alias, Jessie M. Ryan, that became headline fodder during a high-profile power struggle in court.

One side of that story involved a woman named Anna Dolly Ledgerwood, who had been raised in the household of wealthy banker Frederick Matters. Despite a forty-year difference in ages, when she was old enough, they married in October 1914.

In his will, Frederick named a total of forty-five heirs, including Mrs. Dolly Ledgerwood Matters, who would receive one-third of his substantial estate. If she bore him a child, that offspring would also inherit one-third of everything. But in January 1915, three months after they married, Frederick died. In July 1915, exactly nine months after they married, Dolly came home from an Ottawa, Canada, hospital with baby Irene—which meant Dolly controlled two-thirds of the Matters fortune instead of one-third.

Other heirs to the estate raised questions about the child's heredity, but the hospital's chief obstetrician, Dr. L. C. Emile Beroard, testified that he delivered the child. Providing confirmation was Head Nurse Marie des Rosiers, who attended in the delivery room.

The issue appeared settled until a young woman named Jessie M. Ryan came forward and claimed the baby was hers. She told of being in the poor wing of the hospital when Mrs. Matters was there, and of giving birth to a baby boy, who unfortunately hadn't survived. But not long after leaving the hospital, she was informed by a confidant that her baby was, in fact, a girl, and had been claimed by Mrs. Matters.

Despite professional verification of Mrs. Matters' story by the doctor and nurse, investigators who looked into Ryan's claims kept digging until the shocking, unlikely truth was uncovered. Both the doctor and nurse returned to court and recanted their previous testimony about witnessing the baby's birth. Mrs. Matters nevertheless battled to the end, but the court ruled that baby Irene, born on July 24, 1915, belong to Jessie M. Ryan. The "M" represented Margaret, who was said to be Margaret Ryan, the lover of Reynolds Forsbrey, criminal extraordinaire.

In subsequent interviews, she strongly intimated that Irene was fathered by Reynolds, but wouldn't state it outright so as not to taint the child's future. Irene was placed with a member of Margaret's family for proper rearing, and they seldom saw each other.

A flaw in Margaret's explanation passed unnoticed, but a close examination of his prison record proves that Forsbrey could not have fathered Irene. When she was conceived, he was languishing in a solitary-confinement cell at Clinton Prison after two unsuccessful escape attempts. It was in 1915 that rumors were publicized about Forsbrey's plans to kill a man who had stolen Margaret's affections. If she were actually the Jessie Margaret Ryan who gave birth to baby Irene in Ottawa, it's possible Lloyd Thompson was the father. It was nine months after the child's birth that Margaret had attempted suicide—while still living with Thompson, but professing her love for Forsbrey. A twisted tale indeed.

Reynolds Forsbrey's story didn't end after the two Auburn escapes and his transfer back to Clinton Prison. He behaved himself and melded into the system, hoping to at least escape the stringent atmosphere at Dannemora. Eventually there came a transfer to Sing Sing, followed in 1930 by a headline that prison authorities had never envisioned: **Prison Breaker Appointed Trusty**. After nine years of good behavior, the most feared escape threat in the country was entrusted with running errands in Sing Sing's hospital.

On July 15, 1931, at age forty-six, he was granted a conditional pardon by Governor Franklin D. Roosevelt, releasing him from prison on lifetime parole. Forsbrey told reporters he was finished with crime, and planned to live with his mother while working for his brother.

Former inmate friends at Sing Sing said Reynolds had often

spoken of Margaret, and they assumed the two would be together again, but he was now quoted as being "no longer interested" in her. Many newspapers claimed she had died years earlier, while others reported she was married and living at some unspecified location.

Despite claiming to have sworn off crime, Forsbrey began hanging out with old associates and gambling on the horses to support himself. After release from prison, his life free of crime lasted at most five months and three days, ending with the armed robbery of the Consolidated Ticket Office in New York City. The victim, Frank Pope, was left tied up in the office, but managed to reach a desk and dial the phone with his nose, ringing up his wife, who called police.

Using Pope's description of the thieves, lawmen in early January 1932 tracked Forsbrey and his accomplices to Miami, where he was found living with actress Dorothy Jordan. He offered no resistance during the arrest, despite possessing a sawed-off shotgun. Back in New York, three detectives handed him over to two dozen specially selected city policemen, who were on hand to prevent any escape attempt. Six guards were assigned to monitor his court appearances.

The crimes blamed on Forsbrey were robbing the Baltimore and Ohio Coach Company of $75, and stealing $5,000 after kidnapping the ticket-office manager from the street. Two months later he was found guilty of first-degree robbery, with the jury deliberating for just twenty minutes. Judge Charles Nott (yes, Judge Nott) excoriated the parole board for having freed Forsbrey months earlier.

> I am utterly at a loss to understand why the authorities turned this man loose on the community years before his time would have expired. As a result, people were humiliated by being stripped of their clothing and robbed, and three days were required for this trial. All this could have been avoided if this man had been kept where he belonged.

On March 10, 1932, with a dozen policemen surrounding him, Reynolds Forsbrey was sentenced to life in prison. He was taken to Sing Sing and later transferred to Clinton Prison, where he spent the last eleven years of his life, dying there on June 10, 1943, after a brief illness.

In early October of that same year, police puzzled over the case of a fifty-two-year-old Brooklyn woman, found dead in the Carleton Arms Hotel by a cleaning lady. The victim died of stomach injuries, strongly suggesting murder. It was verified that she and an unknown man had registered back on August 20 as "Mr. and Mrs. George Washington." A man named Fred Gebhardt identified the woman as his wife, Margaret Gebhardt. After investigating further, police said the deceased had a record that included "seven arrests and five convictions for larceny, prostitution, assault, and drug addiction."

Using fingerprints, they obtained positive identification of the victim as Margaret Ryan, the long-lost love of Reynolds Forsbrey.

ROBERT F. GARROW

Adirondack serial rapist and serial killer Robert F. Garrow didn't just serve time at Clinton: he was actually born a short distant from the prison's imposing wall. The family moved from Dannemora when he was very young and settled near Lake Champlain's western shore in the village of Witherbee, where the children were raised amid the rough background of an iron-mining town. The Garrow household featured beatings, alcoholism, and other negative behaviors. Robert became a farm hand at a young age, butchering a variety of animals for sale to local businesses—and also engaging in bestiality.

As a teenager he was sent to reform school, and in the years that followed held different jobs, including air force military policeman. Until he was booted from the service, most of his time was spent in military prisons. Garrow then moved to upstate New York, where he committed several crimes before serious sex offenses involving young girls in the Albany area landed him in Clinton Prison for a term of ten to twenty years.

By pestering the corrections system incessantly, he finally won a transfer to Auburn, close to his family in Syracuse. After his release, Garrow found work in the Syracuse area, but committed several rapes until one attack ended in murder. While court appearances were pending on sex charges, he traveled through the Adirondacks and killed twice more. His favored method was tying up victims and tormenting them with a knife before executing them.

Another trip to the mountains left a fourth victim tied to a tree and stabbed to death, but this time there were witnesses. Garrow abandoned his car and took to the woods with a rifle, launching one of the biggest manhunts in New York State history. For eight days he eluded hundreds of searchers whose goal was to capture him alive. Staying on the move in the thick summer woods, he survived by stealing supplies from remote camps.

After stealing a vehicle and surviving a wild car chase, he escaped the area and fled to Witherbee, where a three-day manhunt ended when Garrow was shot and captured. He survived wounds to the arm and back, but when doctors said he was well again, Garrow remained in a wheelchair.

During a high-profile trial, it was discovered that his attorneys had known the location of some victims' bodies well before police found them. That revelation caused an uproar nearly as big as the murder trial itself, and led to rulings that addressed certain basic tenets of the American legal system. The "case of the hidden bodies" is used in many law courses as an example of the difficult issues faced by attorneys dealing with capital crimes.

The trial received intense media scrutiny and featured lurid, sometimes sickening testimony, including that of Garrow himself, who described several rapes and homicides. He was eventually convicted of one murder and sentenced to twenty-five years to life in Clinton Prison. Within months, he accepted a plea bargain, admitting to murders in three other counties in exchange for sentences of fifteen years to life in each case.

But Robert Garrow's involvement in the legal system was far from over. From his Dannemora cell, he began filing appeals and new lawsuits against prosecutors,

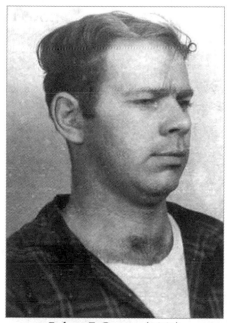

Robert F. Garrow (1961)

police, doctors, and even his own attorneys. It was all part of a strategy to win transfer to a prison with less-stringent conditions than those at Clinton. An accompanying tactic was frequent doctor visits to address his ongoing disabilities from being shot.

He was eventually moved to Auburn Prison, but the lawsuits continued, much to the annoyance of state corrections officials. Finally, after more than fifty assessments by doctors, he was transferred to Fishkill, which had been his goal all along. He remained in a wheelchair, and Fishkill had a medium-security wing for older and handicapped inmates.

As Garrow settled in, the doctor visits and lawsuits came to a halt—and for good reason. Officials soon discovered he had been faking the severity of his injuries all along. His bed was found empty one morning, launching an intense manhunt that spanned several states, caused chaos on the highways, and lasted for three days. He was finally discovered hiding near the prison grounds, but when cornered, he shot a corrections officer, causing serious injuries. Return fire left him deceased.

During the investigation that followed, it was discovered that Robert's son had sneaked the gun into the prison by burying it beneath gravy in a bucket of chicken, a violation that sent the young man to prison. As the result of Garrow's long and twisted story, substantial changes were made at Fishkill and to the corrections system statewide. (His life story is told in the book, *Terror in the Adirondacks: The True Story of Serial Killer Robert F. Garrow*, by the author of this book.)

LIZZIE HALLIDAY

A woman in Clinton Prison, upstate New York's well-known bastion of male criminality? Yes, the infamous Lizzie Halliday was the first woman ever incarcerated there. It happened during the period when Dannemora served as New York State's house of execution (1892–1913). Even the briefest sketch of Halliday's life explains why she was there in an era when females were only executed in extreme cases of brutality.

She was born Eliza Margaret McNally in Ireland, and came to America in 1867, seemingly to collect husbands. In 1879 she married

Charles Hopkins, bore him a son, and was widowed two years later. She next married Artemus Brewer, a veteran drawing a pension, but he died before a year passed. Hiram Parkinson, her next husband, deserted her in less than a year, and without divorcing, she married George Smith, another military veteran who was a friend of Brewer (husband number two). A few months into the marriage, she made a failed effort to poison Smith, after which Halliday went north to Bellows Falls, Vermont, where she married Charles Playsel. All of two weeks passed before Lizzie again moved on.

She was known to have been in Philadelphia, where she looked up the McQuillans, known by the McNally family when they were back in Ireland. She operated a small shop before turning to arson, burning her own store in a fire that consumed two neighboring houses. For that crime she was sentenced to two years in prison.

Around 1890 she was in downstate New York, where she married Paul Halliday and settled about twenty miles west of Newburgh. In early 1892, Lizzie took a team of horses and ran off to Newburgh with a male neighbor, who dumped her there. She was arrested for horse theft, and was placed in an asylum following an insanity plea.

After talking Paul into getting her released, she burned his house down in a fire that took the life of his handicapped son. In 1893, neighbors questioned the whereabouts of Paul, who hadn't been seen for some time. Concerned friends conducted their own search, leading to a grisly discovery—the bodies of Sarah and Margaret McQuillan, buried beneath a haystack in a barn. Shortly after Lizzie's arrest for killing the McQuillans, Paul Halliday's body was found beneath the floorboards of his burned home, prompting a third murder charge against her.

While held in jail, she refused food, which, according to *The Morning Star* (Glens Falls, New York), was just one of many issues.

> … it became necessary for the jail physician to force liquid food through her nostrils. In November, she tried to strangle the sheriff's wife. A few days later she set fire to her bedclothes. In December she tried to hang herself with the binding torn from the bottom of her dress. On December 15, she came near ending her life by gashing her throat and arms with glass broken from her cell window. For the last three months it has been necessary to keep her chained to the floor.

The newspaper also made note of Halliday's growing fame.

> During her time in the county jail, Lizzie became a national celebrity of sorts. The New York City newspapers, ever on the lookout for a sensational story, soon discovered the Halliday saga and gave it front-page coverage. Papers from around the country soon followed suit.

There was really no reason to sensationalize her story—the truth itself was awful enough. Some suspected Lizzie was actually London's Jack the Ripper, but she denied any connection, and no solid proof was offered.

She was convicted of murder in June 1894 and sentenced to die in the electric chair at Clinton Prison. On June 30, Lizzie arrived at Dannemora, where two matrons from the Ogdensburg state hospital looked after her in the condemned cell, an open cage consisting of iron bars from floor to ceiling on all sides, allowing full observation of the prisoner within. On July 13, three doctors appointed by the governor finished their insanity examinations, and a week later her sentence was commuted to life in the Matteawan asylum for insane criminals. Having been saved from the chair, she was transferred from Clinton on July 23.

At Matteawan she was a constant problem, frequently assaulting staff, attempting several escapes, and in fall 1895 tried to murder an attendant. In 1906, she killed nurse Nellie Wickes by stabbing her more than two hundred times with a pair of scissors. *The New York Times* referred to her as "the worst woman on earth."

Lizzie Halliday committed at least five murders, but the toll, which included some of her husbands, was suspected to have been much higher. She died at Matteawan in 1918.

LEON KRAEMER
(ALIAS LEON MILLER, LEON LISS, HYMAN PODERFSKY)

In 1927, Clinton officials uncovered a plot by inmates to blow up the prison's main wall. Amid growing unrest in facilities across the state, major jailbreak attempts backed by big-city gangs were one of the biggest fears in the system. At Dannemora, which hosted New York's most dangerous clientele, machine guns were posted on the street at each end of the prison and atop the wall. State-of-the-art floodlights were installed to illuminate all areas inside and outside the facility. Extra patrols circled the prison's perimeter, alert for any sign of an uprising.

Escalating fears at Clinton were not unfounded. In August 1927, a crate shipped by express from New York City arrived at Dannemora with the address, "H. M. Kaiser, Warden, care of Industrial Department." Inside were maps of the county, three bottles of liquor, four hundred rounds of ammunition, and six automatic pistols from which the identifying numbers had been removed. In September, a second crate arrived with more of the same, but some ID numbers remained intact, allowing the guns to be traced.

An escape planned around such weaponry could well have proven catastrophic, but a snitch, inmate Harry Ross, had intervened. In the prison yard, Leon Kraemer, the man behind the planned revolt, fashioned a spoon into a knife and slammed it three times into Ross, who was seriously wounded, but survived. Leon promised the man he would pay with his life.

At year's end, when governors commuted the sentences of certain convicts, Governor Alfred Smith included Ross among the choices, even though he had served just four and a half years of a thirty-year term. The official documents state that Ross divulged

> ... valuable information relative to attempts by outside groups to send revolvers, ammunition, alcoholic beverages, road maps, and other materials to certain dangerous groups in Clinton Prison. Through this information and assistance, the prison authorities were able to apprehend these shipments.

Commutation of his sentence allowed Ross to go before the parole board in early January and win very short-lived freedom. Leaving Clinton, he walked into the waiting arms of authorities from New Jersey, where he faced charges of possessing burglary tools. Because of fears that Kraemer's gang would waylay them and kill Ross, several officers accompanied him on the trip south.

Leon Kraemer had proven himself a very dangerous man many times over in America, but was a native of Poland, where he was born in 1892 as Leon Lis. His first sentence of any length was in Brussels,

Belgium, where he served eighteen months for robbery at age twenty-one. Two years later, Leon and his half-brother Jacob were deported from England as undesirables. Before reaching Poland, which at that point was under Russian rule, they escaped in Sweden and made it to the United States.

Authorities stateside had been alerted, and crimes matching Kraemer's style confirmed that he and Jacob had begun robbing safes in America. They avoided prosecution for an arrest in Detroit, and operated successfully for about six years. In 1921, an arrest in Baltimore sent them both to prison, where they met Dick Whittemore and developed a criminal partnership.

When the three of them were released in 1924, the famous Whittemore Gang was formed, specializing in jewel thefts. As partners, the Kraemers became fences extraordinaire, handling more than a million dollars in stolen gems ($14 million in 2015). Like many criminals, Whittemore spent wildly and enjoyed a lavish lifestyle. Gambling, partying, and living at the Embassy Hotel on Upper Broadway in Manhattan attracted the attention of lawmen, and proved to be his eventual undoing. He was arrested after several spectacular thefts in 1925, and the Whittemore gang was soon dissolved by court convictions and lengthy sentences.

During their trials, it was discovered that Leon Kraemer, the so-called brains of the operation, had been much smarter than his associates. He and Jacob had invested their criminal "earnings" in several tenement buildings and owned multiple overseas accounts. Police estimated each brother's worth at $500,000 ($7 million in 2015). To their underworld cohorts, the Kraemers were known as top-quality operators. One robbery, said to have netted them $350,000, was achieved by tunneling through a basement wall in order to leave burglar-alarm wires intact.

But the breakup of the entire gang sent the Kraemers to Dannemora. Whittemore was executed in Maryland in 1926 (some said Leon Kraemer had squealed on him), and other gang members were serving sentences ranging from twenty to sixty years. Leon's sentence of forty years meant he would be locked up in Clinton Prison for a long, long time.

In addition to that punishment, Leon was now suffering in solitary confinement for stabbing the snitch, Harry Ross, who had been rewarded with a pardon. But before leaving Dannemora, Ross was informed by Kraemer that he was a dead man walking.

In July 1929, six months after Ross's release, the worst uprising in Clinton's history occurred, leaving three inmates dead. The suspected mastermind was Leon Kraemer, who had engineered another breakout plan two years earlier—the one foiled by Harry Ross. Prison officials feared that no one would provide inside information about the recent riot, for Ross, the last man to speak up, had been stabbed several times as payback.

Months after the riot, Ross's fate was settled permanently. For nine months he had lived as a free man in New York's criminal underworld, but was arrested in October for gun possession and confined to the Tombs. It was his fourth felony, and Ross knew what that meant—a life sentence under Baumes Law, and incarceration at Clinton. That, he knew, was a death sentence, for Leon Kraemer anxiously anticipated his return. Tombs attendants reported he was frantic at the thought of what awaited at Dannemora. The day after his conviction in a New York City courtroom, Ross was found hanging from the upper cot in his cell, preferring suicide to death at the hand of Kraemer.

Leon, still suspected of playing a role in the riot, was transferred to Auburn to separate him from certain associates. He would never see his half-brother again. Jake Kraemer, having contracted tuberculosis, died at Clinton and was buried there in August 1932.

Escapes are always a big deal in prison news, with the more unusual stories making headlines that sometimes span the country. One such breakout took place in mid-September 1932 at Great Meadow Prison, located ninety miles south of Dannemora in Comstock, New York. A car belonging to a relative of Warden Joseph Wilson was repaired in the prison garage. Before trusty chauffeur Thomas Burke drove it off prison grounds, inmate Leon Miller wired himself to the bottom of the car. One reporter called the escape "unquestionably the most sensational in the history of the prison."

And it worked. A manhunt was launched, but Miller was nowhere to be found for a week, then two, then three. Week four arrived with astounding news—escapee Leon Miller was, in fact, Leon Kraemer, widely acknowledged as one of the most dangerous convicts in the country. Somehow Leon had altered his identity and finagled a transfer to Great Meadow, where security was lax compared to Clinton and Auburn. Prison officials were embarrassed and scared, having unleashed on the public a wealthy inmate with a criminal record on two continents and in four countries—a suspected murderer who once scared a man into committing suicide.

The chase intensified, but Kraemer was a cut above the average crook, and with the passage of several months, authorities remained mystified as to his whereabouts. After exiting the prison, Leon had abandoned the car at Saratoga Springs, where the trail police were following ran dry. He returned to New York City, settled into a luxury Manhattan apartment, and rejoined the criminal underworld. Apparently he wronged someone in a very big way, for Leon hired a young man to act as bodyguard. Police could only surmise parts of what happened next, but nine months after the escape from Great Meadow, Kraemer's apartment was entered by supposed gangsters, who machine-gunned him and his bodyguard, Leo Schneider.

Kraemer, struck three times and bleeding heavily, identified himself to police as Hyman Poderfsky. Schneider made it to the street and half-walked, half-crawled for nearly a block before collapsing. After Poderfsky was hospitalized, police determined through fingerprints that he was actually Leon Kraemer, one of the most wanted men in America.

His apartment was described as a virtual arsenal, and police suspected the shooting was revenge related, with two possible motives—jealousy over a red-haired girl who for the past two weeks had lived with him, or a grudge against the old Whittemore gang, another member of which had recently been shot and killed.

Kraemer survived his wounds, but his bodyguard, Schneider, died the next day. Although both had told police they were attacked by unknown men, Kraemer was charged with killing Schneider. The case was later dismissed, but Leon was in enough trouble already. He was returned immediately to Great Meadow to fulfill his original lengthy sentence, and shortly after arriving there, he was transferred to Clinton.

But Kraemer wanted out, and would do anything to leave prison—even snitch on some very famous crimes and criminals. While serving time at several prisons, he had accumulated inside information that, if shared, could get him killed, but he was now willing to use it. Through a convict friend on the outside, he became the subject of many secret communications with the Department of Justice. Among the names he mentioned were Lucky Luciano, Dutch Schultz, Alvin Karpis, and the Barker clan, plus three cases of great national importance: New York City's Judge Crater, who had famously gone missing; the high-profile kidnapping of Edward Bremer (a personal friend of President Franklin Roosevelt); and the Lindbergh baby kidnapping.

However, freeing one of the nation's most infamous inmates

BARKER-KARPIS GANG
$2,000.00 REWARD

Kraemer offered information on the Barker-Karpis gang to the Justice Dept.

in exchange for cooperation was a sticking point. The department wanted information, but noted in writing, "Of course it is impossible to promise any action will be taken in connection with anyone serving a sentence in a state penitentiary, and this is the objective the informant is seeking." Receiving no assurances from the government, Leon remained at Clinton.

In 1935, two more years were added to his sentence as punishment for escaping Great Meadow. Nothing of the sort was going to happen at Dannemora, where post-riot changes and improvements made Clinton Prison one of the most secure facilities in the country. There he completed his term, and was released in September 1949 at age fifty-seven.

WAYNE LONERGAN

In the 1940s, it took a sensational murder story among New York's high society to temporarily snag front-page space that was dominated by coverage of World War II. The victim was an heiress to a family fortune, and the perpetrator was her husband, but there was more—much, much more—that would leave tongues wagging for a long, long time.

The accused murderer was Wayne Lonergan, twenty-five, a

native of Toronto, Ontario, Canada, born there to American parents in 1918. In 1938 he moved to New York City, where he worked at Abercrombie & Fitch, and then became a rickshaw operator at the 1939 World's Fair.

But it was in Cannes, France, where he met William Burton and his daughter, Patsy, who were operating a military canteen. William was a painter who had attended the Yale School of Fine Arts. He was also a millionaire by inheritance from his father, Max Bernheimer, who for years was president and treasurer of a brewing company. (When the United States joined World War I, William Bernheimer and his brother, George, changed their name to Burton because of the unpopularity of all things German.)

William's background included a marriage in 1920 to Lucille Wolf. Their daughter, Patricia, was born in New Jersey in 1921, and just weeks later, the family moved to Paris, where they remained until 1926, when Lucille's divorce from William was finalized. The grounds were cruelty, but the principal issue was desertion: William was frequently absent, preferring the company of handsome young men, referred to as his "protégés." But he remained Patsy's father above all, and was on friendly terms with Lucille.

William's homosexuality was known within social circles in New York City, and in 1939, his latest companion was Wayne Lonergan. They remained an item until Burton died in 1940. Lucille happened to be overseas at the time, and couldn't return until two months later to be with Patsy. She discovered that Wayne Lonergan, her husband's former lover, had stepped in to comfort Patsy, and the two had grown quite close. Lucille didn't approve of the burgeoning relationship, so she took Patsy on a trip to California. But Lonergan trailed them there, met up with Patsy, and they eloped to Las Vegas.

As close as Wayne and Patsy had seemed, the marriage was by all accounts a disaster, although they did share a son, Billy. Tenants of the same apartment building prayed the Lonergans would move out and spare everyone the ongoing screaming and fighting. In an effort to keep Patsy as his wife, Wayne tried to enlist in the U.S. Army, but was rejected twice because of his homosexuality. He then went north of the border and joined the Canadian Air Force. But it was no use. The violent fights continued, and in planning for a divorce, Patsy revised her will, dropping Wayne and leaving everything—a fortune worth millions—to their infant son.

They were a real partying couple, hitting the hot spots of the rich and famous—Wayne at 21 Club, and Patsy at the Stork Club—but she was with other men, and he, like her father, was with other women *and* men.

In late October 1943, Captain Peter Elser of the U.S. Marine Corps, and former star football player at Harvard, arrived to pick up Patsy at her three-floor brownstone for a dinner date. When the governess caring for eighteen-month-old Billy couldn't get into Patsy's bedroom, Elser forced his way in. Before him on the bed lay Patsy, naked and lifeless, her head badly battered.

Police began the difficult task of sorting through her many friends, relatives, and acquaintances for possible suspects. With money and jewelry left in the apartment, robbery as a motive was ruled out. The victim's hands were partially blocking her face, suggesting she had been resisting, which was confirmed by bits of human skin found under her fingernails.

It wasn't long before witnesses related the nature of the Lonergans' relationship and police began looking for Wayne. He was located in Toronto, but denied any connection with her death when Ontario police paid him a visit. When asked about the scratches on his cheek, chin, and neck, he said they had happened while shaving.

Officials discovered that he had flown to Canada shortly before Patsy's body was discovered, but Lonergan had a story ready. Wearing his cadet uniform, he had gone to New York City on military leave. Why, they asked, did you wear a regular suit on the return trip to Canada? Wayne said he had hooked up with a soldier, but they had an argument, and his uniform was stolen—which left authorities wondering why an American soldier would express anger by stealing a Canadian soldier's uniform. When pressed for more information, he provided a name: Maurice Worcester.

Canadian police agreed to send Lonergan south so New York officials could probe his story further. During a long interrogation session, Wayne was unable to identify a man brought before him at the station. That man, police informed him, was an honorably discharged soldier from Bridgeport, Connecticut—Maurice Worcester. It was a name Lonergan had plucked out of thin air, and police had called his bluff. The rest of his unlikely story quickly unraveled into a full confession.

On the night before Patsy's death, they had both partied, separately as usual. Wayne went to her apartment in the morning, and although Patsy was asleep, she let him in and returned to bed. They made snide remarks back and forth about each other's hell-raising, and then he asked about seeing the baby. Some other time, she said, because Billy was asleep.

According to Wayne, as he was about to leave, Patsy yelled, "You're not going to see the baby again—ever!" He lost control, seized a brass candlestick, and beat her on the head until it broke. Grabbing a second one, he resumed the beating, but Patsy fought back furiously, and as she tried to get up, he strangled her. Leaving the scene, Wayne went to his apartment for a change of clothes. After putting iron weights in a duffle with his bloodied uniform, he tossed it into the East River. Using pancake makeup to cover the scratches on his face and neck, he then kept a lunch date with an unemployed showgirl before catching a flight to Toronto.

Patsy's will was filed in court a week after her death, confirming that Wayne was to inherit nothing. She had expunged his name two months earlier, which, along with her plans to divorce him, represented probable cause for her untimely and violent death.

The charge against him was first-degree murder, which carried with it the death penalty. His attorneys went to work, claiming the dictated confession had never been signed by Wayne (which proved true), and that at any rate, it had been beaten out of him. But they also advised him to plead guilty to second-degree murder in exchange for a twenty-year sentence. Lonergan, however, insisted on going to trial, which promised to be interesting. During the investigation, police had announced that, "the background of the case was sordid, with unpleasant relationships developed in sex crimes." If nothing else, it ensured the courtroom would be packed every day.

The trial certainly started in bizarre fashion: for the first two days, Lonergan's attorney, Edward Broderick, was a no-show, much to the judge's displeasure. A telegram conveyed that he was investigating some very important leads in Toronto, but the court was not amused. (After the trial ended, Broderick was found guilty on four charges of contempt and sentenced to 120 days in jail.)

Testimony delved into the partying habits of the wealthy,

mentioning in matter-of-fact fashion that Patsy had been out all night on each of the three days preceding her death. Wayne's homosexuality and bisexuality were discussed, and despite the details of Patsy's final minutes offered in his confession, the story widely circulated was that Patsy was found naked because their volcanic relationship had led to sex that morning when Wayne visited her. The reason he beat her was because she had bitten him—some said bitten *off* part of him—during oral sex, which prompted brutal retaliation with the candlesticks. That part of the story has never been proved, nor disproved. Much of the testimony regarded as sexual in nature was closed to spectators.

To her mother's outrage, Patsy was portrayed by defense attorneys as wild and promiscuous, which they claimed led to at least one abortion. It was an apparent attempt to blame the victim for her own murder, as if she had it coming.

On March 29, 1944, without Wayne having taken the stand, the defense rested after only two and a quarter hours of presenting evidence. Following nearly ten hours of deliberation, the jury found him guilty of second-degree murder. He was sentenced to thirty-five years to life and taken to Sing Sing, but was later transferred to Clinton Prison. With time off for good behavior, it was estimated he would still serve about a quarter century. Because of the felony conviction, he was dishonorably discharged from the Royal Canadian Air Force. Lucille adopted baby Billy and changed his last name from Lonergan to Burton, severing any obvious link between father and son.

In 1965, after serving twenty-one years, Wayne filed a writ from inside Clinton Prison, seeking a new trial. His arguments hinged on claims of irregularities related to his confession back in 1943. Seeking to vacate his conviction was a veiled effort to get at the family inheritance, valued now at more than $10 million. It was all in the hands of his son, who had grown up as William Burton, with no connection to the name Lonergan. The court rejected his plea.

Nine months later, in December 1965, Wayne was released from Clinton Prison with the stipulation that he leave the United States immediately. After being delivered to the Rouses Point customs office, twenty-five miles east of the prison, he entered Canada and headed west to Toronto.

In the 1970s, he began a fourteen-year relationship with

comedian Barbara Hamilton, known as the funniest woman in Canada. Always looking for a laugh, she was said to have introduced him to party-goers as "the lady-killer." Lonergan died of cancer on New Year's Day, 1986, at age sixty-seven.

CHARLES LUCIANO (REAL NAME CHARLES LUCANIA)
(ALIAS SALVATORE LUCIANO, LUCKY LUCIANO)

To some, Lucky Luciano is the greatest crime boss ever in the United States. During the 1920s, he and several other youthful hoods known as the "young Turks" became criminal icons. By killing off gang leaders, they replaced the "mustache Petes," a reference to the longstanding, old-time Italian bosses. After a series of shrewd, dangerous, and near-deadly moves, Luciano became the man who truly "organized crime" by forming the Commission, an umbrella consortium that embraced crime families from several cities, each running their own operations.

Among those looking to make a name for themselves politically in the 1930s was Special Prosecutor Thomas Dewey, who harangued and harassed New York's leading criminals. At a meeting of top crime bosses, an exasperated Dutch Schultz vowed to murder Dewey. The Commission refused permission, with Luciano arguing against it as a sure way to invite the worst police crackdown possible. But Schultz stormed out of the meeting and was apparently going rogue, which led to his execution. Many attributed his death to an order issued or recommended by Luciano.

Lucky's operations in New York City covered bookmaking, drug trafficking, extortion, loan sharking, and prostitution. Dewey targeted Luciano's prostitution network with a major raid in February 1936. Among more than a hundred men and women held in jail after their arrest, some talked, attributing the business to Luciano. Several months later he was tried on more than sixty counts of forced prostitution, and with seven accomplices was convicted of having "placed women in houses of prostitution."

A review of his previous criminal record was impressive, with many arrests and convictions, but no punishments remotely resembling what came next. On June 18, 1936, he was sentenced to thirty to fifty years, sending Lucky and his crew up the river that same day to Sing Sing on the Hudson's eastern shore. New York State Corrections Commissioner Edward Mulrooney ordered that the gang be broken up, and on July 2, Luciano was sent north to Dannemora, accompanied by David Betillo, his first lieutenant, whose sentence was twenty to forty years.

Inmates with financial means could make life in prison more bearable, which Lucky did. Betillo acted as his personal cook, and Luciano prevailed upon New York City connections to send goodies north, including fish from his man Joe "Socks" Lanza, who ruled over the Fulton Fish Market. For certain items that weren't allowed, Lucky had the resources to pay whatever bribes were necessary. He didn't live like a king, as some have said, but he did better than most.

His status as a crime boss—*the* crime boss in America—made life easier as well. He maintained good behavior, worked daily, and enjoyed his own section of Clinton's "courts" in the prison's northwest corner, where outdoor comfort was available.

It's puzzling how someone in Lucky's line of work could be religious, but at sentencing he claimed to be a practicing Catholic. When the famous St. Dismas Church was built within the prison by inmates at Dannemora, he donated the Appalachian red oak used to create the pews.

He still managed "the business" from Dannemora, being consulted by his lawyers and associates on any major decisions.

Luciano provided the Appalachian red oak for the pews of St. Dismas Church

Otherwise, day-to-day operations in New York were handled by Frankie Costello.

But like most other inmates, Luciano's main interest at Clinton was getting out. Barely a month after arriving, he filed a suit claiming the law he was convicted under was unconstitutional. Representing him was James Noonan, the lawyer who had once won freedom for Dutch Schultz, the mob man whose last move was to defy Lucky. Appearing in the county courtroom at Plattsburgh, Luciano was shackled to one officer, seated near two others, and watched closely by more than a dozen state troopers and city policemen. The large contingent was to preclude any breakout plans his men from the city might have prepared.

Two weeks later, his plea was denied. An appeal failed as well, followed by new charges against Lucky for tax evasion. In May 1937, his appeal for a new trial, based on the recanted testimony of three prostitutes, was rejected. In April 1938, other appeals made on different grounds were tossed.

In 1940, Luciano made headlines in New York City, where he was publicly accused by Brooklyn's district attorney, William O'Dwyer, as having ordered in 1934 the slaying of Sam "Muddy" Kasoff, for cutting into Lucky's narcotics action at the time. In all, O'Dwyer attributed more than thirty killings to Murder, Inc. But for Lucky, stuck in Dannemora, it was nothing more than a distraction.

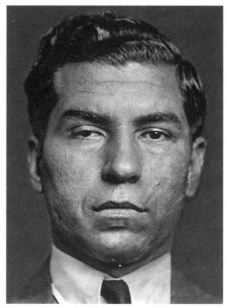

Lucky Luciano

On February 9, 1942, two months after the Japanese attack on Pearl Harbor, Lucky's luck changed in a big way. At a dock in New York, one of the three largest and fastest ships in the world, the *Normandie*, was being refitted for war when it caught fire and eventually flipped on its side. With America having just joined the war, it was feared this was the work of an enemy.

To avoid future problems, naval intelligence officers met on March 7 with New York County District Attorney Frank Hogan, requesting his cooperation "in connection with matters affecting the national security." They spoke of convoy movements, and the possibility that enemy ships were being refueled by sympathetic foreigners working on the docks. Other important issues were discussed, after which Hogan agreed to help. The codename for the endeavor was Operation Underworld.

Weeks later, a second meeting was held, this time including Lieutenant-Commander Charles Haffenden, head of the Third Naval District Investigative Section. After further discussions about security issues, he approached various men working on the docks, including Socks Lanza, who steered him towards the only man wielding the type of power Haffenden sought: Charles Luciano.

DA Hogan, approached about arranging such a meeting, gave the okay to Luciano's attorney, Moses Polakoff. State Correction Commissioner John Lyons in Albany was asked to cooperate with the DA's office and the navy in allowing Socks Lanza to meet with Luciano. Everything fell nicely into place, except that Lucky inserted a stipulation—he wanted out of Clinton Prison.

Haffenden met another mob boss and close friend of Luciano, Meyer Lansky, who acted as go-between. Looked at in retrospect, with dates provided by documents from the Thomas Dewey Papers, the sequence of events in early 1942 is clarified: the *Normandie* incident, February 9; navy meets with DA Hogan, March 7; navy seeks meeting with Luciano, March 25; meeting with Correction Commissioner Lyon, April 29; and Lucky Luciano transferred to Great Meadow, May 12—just forty-eight days after the navy sought his help.

Haffenden and the military sought certain assurances: that no one from the docks would aid or cooperate with enemy ships; that no strikes or work stoppages would occur during the war; and that military supplies would be protected from sabotage and theft.

Lucky continued meeting with Lansky and others at Great Meadow, where he found the accommodations luxurious compared to life in Clinton. In February 1943, he applied to Justice Philip McCook for sentence modification. McCook, who had sentenced him in 1936 to thirty to fifty years, considered Lucky's behavior as a model prisoner for six years, his aid to the United States Navy, a job awaiting with his brothers, and plans "to be married and to be simple and respectable folk"—and wrote, "Application Denied."

The wording of Justice McCook's three-page denial suggested no intent to allow a reduction anytime soon. Two years later, in spring 1945, Lucky tried bypassing the judge by seeking executive clemency—an application, it turns out, that was wrapped in great irony. In 1935, when Dutch Schultz vowed to kill Special Prosecutor Thomas Dewey, Luciano had Schultz killed instead. The following year, Prosecutor Dewey sent Luciano to prison for thirty to fifty years. And now Dewey, as current governor of New York State, could, and did, grant Luciano clemency.

After nine and a half years behind bars, Lucky was finally free—from prison, but not from prosecution. Deportation papers required him to leave the country, and included the phrasing, "… if he re-enters the United States, he shall be deemed an escaped convict," which meant he would be arrested and returned to Clinton for the remainder of his original thirty-to-fifty-year sentence.

Luciano remained involved in organized crime, and died of a heart attack at Naples, Italy, in January 1962. But he did fulfill the dream of returning to America, which he considered home. Lucky's body was buried in St. John's Cemetery in Queens, New York.

CARL PANZRAM

A word commonly associated with the name Carl Panzram is nightmarish. It is terrifying that people like him exist, sociopaths who rage through life with no sense of empathy or mercy. But rather than accept this definition of Panzram, form your own judgment from his written words.

> In my lifetime I have murdered 21 human beings, I have committed thousands of burglaries, robberies, larcenies, arsons, and last but not least I have committed sodomy on more than 1000 human beings. For all of these things I am not the least bit sorry. I have no conscience so that does not worry me. I don't believe in man, God, nor devil. I hate the whole damed human race including myself.

He was born in Minnesota in 1892 and led the early life of many criminals: in trouble at home and school, breaking laws at a young age, and being sent to reform school. This preceded a horrific life of crime and brutality that is beyond most people's imagination.

During one of his many periods of incarceration, Panzram was befriended by a jail guard who encouraged him to write about his life. The result was a chilling story of evil so dark that publishers avoided it for decades.

At the Minnesota State Training School, one of two reform schools he attended, Panzram was admittedly miserable:

> Right there and then I began to learn about man's inhumanity to man. They started me off by trying to beat the Christian religion into me and the consequences were that the more they beat and whipped me, the more I hated them and their dam religion. They beat me and whipped me for doing this and not doing that. Everything I seemed to do was wrong. Just at that time I was eleven, twelve, or thirteen years old, I was just learning to think for myself. I first began to think that I was being unjustly imposed upon. Then I began to hate those who abused me. Then I began to think that I would have my revenge just as soon and as often as I could injure someone else. Anyone at all would do. If I couldn't injure those who injured me, then I would injure someone else. From that day to this I have followed that line of thought.

He described a school building called the Paint Shop, where severe whippings were enhanced with salt water to intensify the pain once the skin broke. Sexual abuse of the boys was common as well. The lessons he came away with were not the ones intended.

> We were all supposed to go to school a half a day and work half a day, and the rest of the time learn how to love Jesus and be good boys. Naturally, I now love Jesus very much. Yes, I love him so dam much that I would like to crucify him all over again.... I had been taught by Christians how to be a hypocrite, and I had learned more about stealing, lying, hating, burning, and killing. I had learned that a boy's penus could be used for something besides to urinate with and that a rectum would be used for other purposes than crepitating.

He finally listened to other boys who shared the best way to escape the school: pretend you've reformed. After a stretch of good behavior, he used contrived pleas of piety to win release. Left behind in his wake were some very disturbing actions, including trying to poison the food of an administrator, and burning down the Paint House. He retaliated in less violent ways as well.

> I was too dumb to learn anything in school so they took me out and put me to work all day washing dishes and waiting on table in the officer's dining room. Right there I began to get a little revenge on those who abused me. When I served the food to some of the officers, I used to urinate in their soup, coffee, or tea and masturbate into their ice cream or desert and then stand right beside them and watch them eat it. They enjoyed it too because they told me so. I wish they could read this now.

Besides the sexual abuse at the school, he was likewise attacked twice by hobos—on a train, and in a small town he visited while traveling on his own. From it all, sodomy became a key theme throughout his life.

When he was fifteen, an arrest at Miles City sent him to the Montana State Reform School, where, he said,

> They worked me hard and beat me harder. You see, they were trying to make a good boy of me. They took me in the hospital and operated on me by clipping my fore-skin off to stop me from the habit of masturbation. So they said, anyway, but how the hell they figured that would stop me is more than I could see. I can't yet.

After escaping the school with a friend, they went from town to town, stealing from churches, many of which they burned. Arson became a big part of his life, and years later, when he visited Houston, Texas, during a raging fire, Panzram's impressions while walking the streets were far from the norm:

> ... enjoying the sights of all the burning buildings and listening to the tales of woe, the moans and sighs of those whose homes and property were burning. I enjoyed it all very much.

276

After a period spent in northern Mexico, he raised hell from Yuma, Arizona, to Fresno, California.

During this time I was busy robbing chicken coops and then touching match to them. I burned old barns, sheds, fences, snowsheds, or anything I could, and when I couldn't burn anything else, I would set fire to the grass on the prairies or the woods, anything and everything. I had a pistol and I would spend all my spare change for bullets. I would take pot-shots at farmers' houses, at the windows. If I saw cows or horses in the fields I would cut loose at them. At night while I was riding the freight trains, I was always on the lookout for something to shoot at or trying to stick up the other hobos that I met on the trains. I looked 'em all over and whenever I met one who wasn't too rusty looking, I would make him raise his hands and drop his pants. I wasn't very particular either. I rode 'em old and young, tall and short, white and black. It made no difference to me at all except that they were human beings.

During a stay in prison, where there were two men per cell, he relished in the opportunity presented.

Each man could choose his own cellmates and get a new one anytime he wanted one. I used to want a new one pretty regular. At that place and time I got to be an experienced wolf. I knew more about sodomy than old boy Oscar Wilde ever thought of knowing. I would start the morning with sodomy, work as hard at it as I could all day and sometimes half of the night. I was so busy committing sodomy that I didn't have any time left for to serve Jesus as I had been taught to do in those Reform Schools.

His penchant for crime followed Panzram overseas as well.

… from 1918 to 1923, I was in 31 different countries, had stole and spent thousands of dollars, had committed many murders and robberies and other crimes….

In 1923 he was sent to Sing Sing for robbing an express office, and was transferred to Clinton, where he spent five years as a very uncooperative inmate. He tried making a time bomb and attempted to burn down a prison shop. During an escape attempt, he "broke both ankles, both legs, twisted my back, and ruptured myself." After six months in solitary, an attack on another inmate led to more months in the hole.

Panzram then entered the prison hospital for a serious health issue.

> My ruptured testicle had been bothering me, and a new doctor came to the prison. He took me in the hospital and cut one testical out. Five days after my operation, I tried to see if my sexual organs were still in good order. I got caught trying to commit sodomy on another prisoner. For that I was thrown out of the hospital and put in the segregation building, or the isolation. I stayed there until my time was up, two years and four months later.

Pent-up rage from the harsh punishments at Clinton erupted in a frenzy of crimes. During the next five weeks in Philadelphia, Baltimore, and Washington, he committed a dozen burglaries and one murder before being arrested and confined in the Washington Asylum and Jail. It was there that he met guard Henry Lesser, who encouraged Panzram to write his autobiography.

Besides the details of crimes, abuses, and prison tortures, he assessed the past.

> I started out in life enjoying it and hating no one. I am winding it up now by hating the whole human race including myself and having no desire to live any longer. For all the misery and tortures that I have went through, I have made other men go through many times over, only worse.... From the time I was twelve years old I have been in jail almost continuously until now, when I am thirty-six, I have spent twenty years of my life in prison.... I have lived thirty-six years in this world and soon I expect to leave it.
>
> All that I leave behind me is smoke, death, desolation, and damnation.... I am sorry for only two things. These two things are: I am sorry that I have mistreated some few animals in my lifetime, and I am sorry that I am unable to murder the whole damed human race.

Admitting to the killing of two boys led to his conviction and a sentence of twenty-five years at Leavenworth Federal Penitentiary, where he promised to "kill the first man that bothers me." Four

months later, on June 20, 1929, he murdered the foreman of the prison laundry and was sentenced to death.

His hanging was scheduled for September 5, 1930. Just how much had Panzram mellowed by age thirty-nine, after so many years of extreme violence? The quotations from his last moment vary slightly, but as the noose was being adjusted, he spat in the executioner's face and said, "I wish the entire human race had one neck and I had my hands around it!"

Carl Panzram

The request for any last words elicited one final gem. "Yes, hurry it up, you Hoosier bastard! I could kill a dozen men while you're screwing around!"

OLIVER CURTIS PERRY

Oliver Curtis Perry became the 1890's version of a rock star by virtue of his daring criminal exploits. Newspaper readers across the country followed his career, and women sent flowers to him in both jail and prison. His story includes many unusual twists and bizarre elements.

Perry had many run-ins with the law, and once attacked a jail guard, cutting the man's arm, but suffering a serious cut to his own chest. He was well known in criminal circles, but two particular incidents involving trains put him in the spotlight, elevating his status to legendary among New York's crooks.

In the early 1890s, Perry worked on the Delaware & Hudson rail line running north from Troy, a job that provided knowledge useful to his criminal future. On September 30, 1891, as the New York Central ran from Albany to Utica, a thief sneaked onto the train, sawed a hole through the upper panel of the express-car door, climbed inside, and donned a mask. Stealthily making his way to the center of the car, he got the drop on express agent Burt Moore. After robbing the car of cash and jewelry, the thief cut the air hose that triggered the brakes, and as the train slowed, he jumped off and made a clean getaway. Moore's story of the robbery seemed so improbable that he was considered a prime suspect, but he remained so adamant that Pinkerton detectives looked further and came up with another possibility—Oliver Curtis Perry.

A manhunt began, and in late November, headline stories widely reported that Perry, the man with fourteen aliases, had been captured in southern Vermont. Days later, the embarrassed detectives were forced to backtrack. The man fit Perry's description, but it wasn't him.

Unbeknownst to them, he had embarked on a long journey that passed through Louisiana, Texas, Mexico, Arizona, Montana, and Canada. He claimed knowledge that Pinkerton men were in pursuit, but he stayed on the move to avoid capture. From Guelph, Ontario, he sent letters to the express company after learning that express agent Burt Moore's job was in jeopardy. The missives explained that Perry himself was responsible for the robbery—and to prove it, he included a package containing a few gems he had stolen. Detectives took it as a taunt, but the public saw Oliver Curtis Perry as a standup guy—a crook, yes, but a nice crook who worried that a man might unfairly lose his job.

He returned to the West once more, but when traveling and living comfortably devoured his profits, Perry returned to New York and began planning a second heist.

On February 21, 1892, at Syracuse, he secretly boarded a freight train destined for Rochester and Buffalo. About twenty miles west of Syracuse, agent Daniel McInerney was facing an express-car safe, preparing his checklist. With the shattering of glass, he turned towards a broken window, where he saw a masked man aiming a gun at him. It was a shocking sight, achieved by some amazing acrobatics. Riding atop the train at about fifty miles an hour, Perry hooked a rope ladder to the car's roof and lowered himself to the window level, where he hung from one hand while using the other with the pistol to smash the window glass. Ordered to put his hands up, McInerney instead grabbed the whistle rope and was immediately shot in the wrist. He reached for his pistol, but was struck by two more bullets, causing non-fatal injuries.

Perry entered the car and was going through the express packages when he was approached by the conductor and brakeman, who had been alerted by McInerney's light tug on the whistle rope. He yelled at them to keep the train moving, and fired a shot that sent both men running.

The train soon slowed for the Port Byron stop, where a crowd had gathered after word of a holdup had spread. It was believed that the thief jumped from the train after being sighted, but the conductor then noticed a familiar face among the crowd—a face he had seen at the Syracuse station before departure. The brakeman provided confirmation, and the crowd surged towards Perry, who stopped everyone in their tracks by pulling out two guns.

Holding them at bay, he ran to a nearby track where a six-wheeled locomotive was ready to go. Chasing the engineer and firemen off, Perry opened the throttle and drove away.

Conductor Emil Lass ordered his engine uncoupled, and with a crew aboard the faster machine, he gave chase. As his pursuers closed in, Perry slowed and then threw it into reverse. When the two parties passed each other in opposite directions, they exchanged gunfire, but to no effect. Lass then reversed, but as he closed on his quarry, Perry changed directions again, shooting out his rivals' windows as they passed, but causing only minor injuries. Lass and crew by this time had run out of ammunition, forcing a return to the station while Perry made his getaway.

But he didn't get far. The train soon ran out of steam, after which he abandoned it and stole a horse. By this time the countryside was in an uproar over the wild events. Perry was finally cornered and captured by a posse of farmers and lawmen.

Found in his valise were the rope ladder with grappling hooks attached, some burglar's tools—and a bottle containing a human ear. He was known to have killed at least two men, one of them out west in Montana. The second murder victim was a black man, selected by Perry for the good luck charm he coveted—a black man's ear.

Despite that distasteful, disgusting story, women sought to catch a glimpse of Perry while he awaited trial. Many even brought flowers, food, and sweets to him at the jailhouse. At just twenty-six years old, he enjoyed the attention, having achieved celebrity status as a handsome, daring crook.

When he appeared for trial, there was chaos among spectators who packed the courthouse. But the excitement faded quickly when he pleaded guilty to four indictments and was handed a sentence of forty-nine years and three months.

When Perry left Lyons, New York, for Auburn Prison, the streets were crowded with excited onlookers. At the train, Perry and his chaperones fought their way through two thousand spectators, who then rushed into the rail cars in what the *Weekly Auburnian* called "a surge of humanity."

The same newspaper reported that his arrival in Auburn

> ... caused the greatest sensation that has occurred on State Street in years.... Since the Kemmler electrocution, a larger and more excited crowd has not been seen about the prison.... The mob pushed and jostled each other restlessly.

Like his trip to the prison, Perry's time at Auburn was eventful, to say the least. For trying to kill an inmate (who was sentenced for murder), he was placed in a special basement tier of cells in the prison's north wing. There he managed to dig through a brick wall, crawl through the adjoining cell, and disappear for eight hours, causing a panic in the city until he was found hiding, but still inside the prison wall. Resisting to the last, he was subdued by several officers and hauled off to a screen cell. At that point he had been at Auburn for only five months.

In May 1893, after refusing to vacate his cell, he was blasted continuously with a high-powered hose. Instead of giving in, Perry placed his pail (slop bucket) over his head to block the flow, and was near suffocation when several keepers rushed in to overpower him.

He was soon declared insane and transferred to the Matteawan State Asylum at Fishkill, but for Perry, crazy like a fox was a more apt description. In April 1895, from the isolation ward holding Matteawan's most dangerous cases, he led the escape of four other inmates by attacking a guard and reaching the chapel roof. They crawled to the edge and followed the gutter to a waterspout, on which they slid down to the ground before climbing the outer wall to freedom and going their separate ways.

Perry made it to New York City, but after a week on the run he was captured in Weehawken, New Jersey, warming himself by a bonfire with several strangers. He was returned to Matteawan and then sent to Auburn in June 1895.

Three months later, he intentionally blinded himself in gruesome fashion.

> I fixed up a machine which was heated, dropping two sharp pointed weights into my eyes. I lay on my back and watched the needles because I wanted to make a good job of it. I had obtained some opium—it was easy then to get opium— and the pain was deadened. In fact, I went to sleep after the weights dropped, and when I came to I couldn't see at all. A little light, however, gradually crept into my eyes, and I was glad—glad because I had a little more to destroy.

He later finished the job by chewing glass pieces to dust and rubbing it into his eyeballs. Why did Perry do it? Initially, he reasoned that blindness would prevent him from committing crimes, and the governor would probably pardon him.

Instead, he was transferred back to Matteawan for aberrant behavior, where he later said, "I blinded myself to keep from seeing these brutes punish men without provocation." There were many complaints that the asylum had become a house of horrors. In late 1897, he went to the newspapers with charges of filth, cruelty, and assorted tortures at Matteawan. The facility was only five years old, but already the cemetery had seventy-two graves, many of whose occupants it was charged had died from abusive treatment.

In March 1901, Perry launched a bizarre attack, biting, scratching, and nearly strangling an inmate soon to be sent home to Germany. The only explanation offered was that he wanted people in the man's homeland to know about Oliver Curtis Perry.

In June 1902 he was transferred to Clinton, which had a new hospital for insane criminals. But he remained very uncooperative, and in 1903 began refusing to take food or water, claiming he would never eat again unless the prison food was improved. In November, as he approached starvation after dropping from 180 to 120 pounds, Perry was fed through a nose tube. He also stopped wearing clothes. One of the few items he continued sporting was a narrow white bandage over his eyes.

He stopped using his bed, lying instead on the cold cement floor. Even with temperatures at twenty to thirty degrees below zero in

Oliver Curtis Perry

the dead of winter, Perry persevered. He was still naked much of the time, but wore a groin towel, his eye-band, and a short pair of socks when greeting visitors. His only physical complaint was bad teeth, a problem he solved by having them all extracted.

He began reciting poetry in his cell, and became obsessed with exercise, building himself into such an impressive physical specimen that Dr. North called Perry the most powerful man in the prison. His strength was due in part to the feeding tube, which produced an unexpected result: he regained all the weight lost and then some, reaching two hundred pounds.

But he was forever difficult, taking a stubborn, unyielding stance against rules and treatments. After an inspection in 1912, state prison officials confirmed that Perry was "one of the most troublesome men with whom they have ever had to deal." He finally agreed to wear clothing, but only undergarments.

Perry was pronounced near death by several newspapers in 1924, but he finally passed away on September 5, 1930, after thirty-eight years in prison, the last twenty-eight having been spent at Dannemora.

Decades earlier, he claimed the Utica express robbery netted much more booty than officials admitted to, and that somewhere west of Little Falls was buried a quantity of gems, including diamonds.

Ralph "Bucky" Phillips

Ralph Phillips served three years at Auburn for second-degree burglary, and ten to twenty years at Great Meadow on multiple burglary and grand larceny convictions, a term that ended in November 2005. But a drug conviction months later constituted a parole violation, presenting the uncertainty of freedom or another extended punishment in prison. On April 2, 2006, a few days before his scheduled hearing, Phillips opted to escape, busting out through the roof of the Erie County Correctional Facility in Alden, New York, east of Buffalo.

Police assisted in the search, addressing several area crimes believed to be the work of Phillips. But on June 10, ninety-five miles southeast of Alden, Trooper Sean Brown was shot, launching the New York State Police into the biggest manhunt in department history. It began in innocuous fashion in the town of Veteran, south of Watkins Glen, when Trooper Brown stopped to check on a car that had pulled onto the roadside. As he approached, the operator shot him for no apparent reason and sped away.

The shooter was believed to be Ralph Phillips, described by police as "a forty-four-year-old career criminal." Beginning in June 1980, his arrests covered burglary, criminal possession of marijuana, criminal possession of a weapon, criminal use of a firearm, grand larceny, menacing, reckless endangerment, and unauthorized use of a motor vehicle. He had threatened police in the past without ever taking action, but the shooting of a trooper elevated him to number one on New York State's wanted list.

Phillips would prove a very elusive target, much like the other two subjects of New York's most extensive manhunts, James Call in the 1950s and Robert F. Garrow in the 1970s. Call and Garrow took refuge in the rugged Adirondack terrain, while Phillips made similar use of the wooded areas in southwestern New York. But he had one advantage the others didn't: a network of family, friends, and prison pals who repeatedly helped him avoid capture.

Early in the manhunt, people were resentful of police intruding into their lives with roadblocks and property searches for a man they considered little more than a common burglar and car thief. As the search dragged on, Phillips was elevated to local folk-hero status by the selling of T-shirts imprinted with, "Run, Bucky, Run" and "Where's Bucky?" It's a safe bet that people doing those types of things were not among the criminal's victims. And there was nothing funny about what he had done, especially shooting a police officer.

Many resources were brought to bear, and in time the manhunt included police from New York and Pennsylvania, the FBI, U.S. Customs and Border Protection, U.S. Marshals, the U.S. Drug Enforcement Agency, the New York National Guard, the New York State Division of Parole, the state DEC, several sheriff's departments, plus city, town, and village lawmen.

Overall he was sighted nine different times, but Phillips proved difficult to pin down, especially with his knowledge of the region's terrain and his ability to steal vehicles. During the ninety-one-day manhunt, he stole nearly thirty, including cars, trucks, motorcycles, ATVs, and bicycles. Between April 2, when he escaped, and June 10, when the manhunt was launched, Phillips made four trips to Flatgap, Kentucky. Throughout the summer the pace of travel continued, but to many other locations. On one vehicle alone he racked up more than 2,500 miles. He frequently returned to the area comprising Chautauqua, Cattaraugus, and Niagara Counties, but also made confirmed trips to Michigan, Ohio, Pennsylvania, Tennessee, and West Virginia. Recognizing his penchant for stealing vehicles, New York's police resorted to an unusual tactic: planting bait cars and ATVs in strategic locations, hoping he would take one.

Nearly three dozen burglaries were attributed to Phillips during his time on the run, including the theft of more than fifty firearms ranging from pistols to rifles, some with armor-piercing bullets. On August 19, while riding a motorcycle, he was followed to a private residence, which he entered. Unsure of the man's identity, but suspecting it was Phillips, the observing officer called for a registration check. The desk officer realized that backup was needed, but while other officers were en route, Phillips jumped from a second-story window and ran into the woods.

Twelve days later, the fugitive put one of his many stolen rifles to deadly use near the home of Kasey Crowe, who was his ex-girlfriend and the mother of Phillips' daughter. At about 6:15 p.m., two officers hiding on watch near the house exchanged gunfire with Phillips, resulting in serious injuries to Donald Baker and Joseph

Longobardo. Baker, who survived, spent nearly three months in the hospital. Longobardo's leg had to be amputated, but three days after the shooting, he died in a Buffalo hospital.

The manhunt intensified, and on September 6, Phillips was named the latest addition to the U.S. Marshals' "Fifteen Most Wanted" list. On September 7 he became the 483rd person added to the FBI's "Ten Most Wanted Fugitives" list. Together they brought the reward money offered for his capture to $250,000.

On September 8, a vehicle pursuit was reported in Warren County, Pennsylvania, on the New York border south of Jamestown. An hour later, the same thing occurred in New York's southern Chautauqua County, where the driver leaped from the moving vehicle and ran into the woods. State Police K-9 handlers tracked the fugitive south into northern Pennsylvania, where a sighting at 9 a.m. led to one shot fired in Phillips' direction. A dog was released, chasing him to a steep embankment that the dog couldn't climb. Other K-9 units assisted, but it wasn't until eleven hours later that he was sighted, monitored by a helicopter, surrounded by New York and Pennsylvania police, and forced to surrender.

On November 29, 2006, Phillips pleaded guilty to aggravated murder and attempted murder, and confirmed that he intended to kill all three police officers that he shot.

He served six tumultuous years at Clinton Prison, most of it in segregation, facing discipline more than twenty times for a range of violations including threats, damaging property, and the common, vile acts of spitting or throwing urine and/or feces at guards. In 2011, a sweatshirt in his cell was found stuffed with bedding, suggesting the preparation of a bed dummy used during escape attempts.

In 2012 he was transferred thirty miles northwest of Dannemora to Upstate Correctional Facility at Malone, New York, and held in the special housing unit known informally as "the box."

JOEL RIFKIN

On June 28, 1993, a truck crashed into a utility pole in Mineola, New York, ending a high-speed chase that began when police noticed a vehicle with no license plates. What began as a minor traffic stop escalated far beyond anyone's imagination. Beneath a tarp in the bed of the pickup was the decomposing body of a twenty-two-year-old woman whom the driver, Joel Rifkin, had killed several days earlier. The arresting officers felt he was too blasé about a situation most people would find very disturbing—and they were right that this wasn't the first dead body Rifkin had toted around. After a few hours of questioning, he began revealing details that identified him as New York's most prolific serial killer, having admitted to the murder of seventeen prostitutes.

A few of Rifkin's victims died from heavy blows to the head, but most were strangled after he paid them and engaged in sex. Some bodies were dumped whole, four of which were stuffed into oil drums, while some of his victims were dismembered. Some parts and full bodies were disposed of on land, while others were dumped into the Harlem, Hudson, and East Rivers, plus Coney Island Creek and Newtown Creek. Such a wide dispersion area made it difficult for investigators to link various crimes. The head, legs, arms, and torso of a single victim were sometimes dropped at different places. According to Rifkin, cutting up the bodies was for ease of disposal without getting caught, and not related to some obsession or rage.

During his confession in 1993, Rifkin told police where to find the head and legs of his first victim, whom he called "Susie." A severed head and other parts had been found on a New Jersey golf course back in 1989, but it was not until 2013, twenty-four years later, that "Susie" was identified as Heidi Balch from the recovered parts.

The names of some victims remain unknown, and it's uncertain how many women he actually killed. Despite having confessed to slaying seventeen women, he was found guilty in 1994 of nine murders and sentenced to 203 years to life. After serving four years in Attica, most of it in twenty-three-hour-a-day isolation cells, he was transferred to Clinton Correctional, where he is still held in a segregation unit away from the general population.

Rifkin filed a lawsuit against Glenn Goord, State Corrections Commissioner, seeking damages of $77 million—$50,000 for each of 1,540 days he spent in solitary confinement. In 2000, New York's highest court ruled against him in no uncertain terms.

A prison's internal security is peculiarly a matter normally
left to the discretion of prison administrators.... We reject the

contention of petitioner that the more restrictive placement violates his right to equal protection. Equal protection does not require absolute equality or precisely equal advantages.... We also reject the contention of petitioner that his placement in administrative segregation constitutes cruel and unusual punishment. Segregated confinement involving neither intolerable isolation nor inadequate food, heat, sanitation, lighting, or bedding, does not fall within the category of conduct so below civilized norms as to be cruel and unusual punishment no matter what its provocation.

Max Shinburn (real name Maximillian Schoenbein) (alias Mark Shinburn, Count Shinburn, the Baron)

"Shinburn is the leading professional criminal of the age. He is undoubtedly the greatest bank, safe, and vault burglar that has ever been known in police history." So said William Pinkerton of the world-famous detective agency when he finally nabbed one of the world's slipperiest crooks in 1895.

Max Shinburn came to America around 1861 as a man both mechanically and criminally inclined. In preparation for a very lucrative line of work, he took a job with the Lilly Safe Company, considered among the best in the industry. There he learned everything there was to know about the construction of locks and safes, and became so attuned to the twisting of dials that he could detect when the tumblers fell into place. That talent would vastly simplify robberies that normally required the use of dynamite to open safes.

Media attention and public fascination with the exploits of criminals made many of them cult heroes. Among the greatest of the nineteenth century was Shinburn—polite, gentlemanly, the best in the game, and a gambler who lived extravagantly, enjoying the fruits of his labor.

His first major crime was a massive score at a Maryland bank, but one that ultimately failed, for in lieu of prosecution, he made full restitution of $140,000 [$2.7 million in 2015].

In 1865 he was arrested at Saratoga Springs, New York, for robbing the Walpole Savings Bank in New Hampshire. Police recovered only a portion of the loot and shipped Shinburn off to

Concord, but he escaped from the Keene jail the night after he was convicted.

Two years later he was arrested during an attempted bank robbery in St. Albans, Vermont, and was sent back to New Hampshire, where he was again imprisoned at Concord. After nine months, he pulled off a remarkable escape with the help of an inmate friend and burglary partner. They somehow managed to drill holes in a wooden section of the prison gate, badly weakening it, but leaving the overall gate intact. Arrangements were made with friends on the outside to have a wagon waiting, and the next day, while marching through the yard in lockstep with other prisoners, they broke rank and ran for the gate. Quickly knocking out the drilled section, they climbed through the hole and made a clean getaway.

He next surfaced at Whitehaven, Pennsylvania, and perpetrated a brilliant scheme against the Lehigh and Wilkes-Barre Coal Company. Twice he entered the office and opened a safe, but found no great quantity of cash. Each time he stole only small amounts, but finally hit it right on the third attempt, which occurred just after the payroll deposit of $40,000 [$687,000 in 2015]. Several weeks later, he was arrested in New York City and taken by detectives back to Pennsylvania, where Shinburn achieved one of the major building blocks of an amazing career.

He provided a fake confession that pointed the blame at several other men, and while everything was being investigated and sorted out, he was locked in a hotel room, accompanied at all times by a detective. Due to his penchant for escape, Shinburn slept handcuffed to a detective sleeping next to him. The cuffs were of the latest ratchet design, and to ensure that no one was going anywhere, the clothes of both men were locked in a closet every night. With everything in place, one final security measure was added: in the next room slept the superintendent of the detective agency. Shinburn was as slick as they came, so nothing was left to chance.

And yet one morning, the detective woke up alone. Max's specialty was locks, and after all, that's what handcuffs were. Hidden in his mouth was a small piece of metal, which he dropped into the ratchet mechanism just before the bolt locked into place, so the cuff outwardly appeared secure, but wasn't. Once the detective fell asleep, Shinburn eased the cuffs off, slipped from the bed, entered the room

Max Shinburn

of a nearby guest, selected a new wardrobe, and escaped the hotel. It was perhaps the greatest demonstration of his legendary ingenuity.

Shortly after the successful escape, he began planning the robbery of Ocean Bank in New York City, which he and a gang of confederates completed in 1869 to the tune of a million dollars [$18 million in 2015]. To execute that and other large robberies, he pioneered smaller and very effective burglary tools that became the new standard for crooks.

Some lawmen claim he also assisted with the Boylston Bank robbery in Boston, which may have been true, although no proof was provided. Shinburn next hit the West Maryland Bank for $25,000 [$470,000 in 2015], and then fled to Belgium, which had no extradition arrangement with the U.S., making it safe for him to settle down and enjoy the fruits of his illegal labor.

After living in Brussels, he purchased a country estate and part ownership of a silk mill, joined high society, and adopted the title Count Shinburn. With the passage of more than a decade as an aristocrat, his funds began running low, in part due to a passion for gambling. A meeting with one-time burglary partner "Piano Charley" Bullard sparked plans to rob the Provincial Bank of Verviers in Belgium. Bullard was a pro who operated a Parisian saloon, and like Shinburn had escaped a U.S. prison and fled to Europe.

To case the joint, they conducted a surveillance break-in, which required the removal of several screws from a door lock. When it was time to leave, one screw was missing, and during the delay to find it, they were caught. After nearly talking their way out of trouble, the screw was found stuck to a piece of wax in Max's pocket (he was famous for using wax to take key impressions), providing evidence against both men that a bank robbery was the ultimate goal. They were tried, convicted, and sentenced to seventeen years in prison, where Bullard died before his term expired.

But Max served his time and circulated word that he, too, had died. Little is known of his travels at that time, but he went to England, and within two years returned to the United States, where his death had been widely reported. This gave him anonymity, a marked advantage for any robber. In the early 1890s, a number of successful bank thefts were executed that baffled detectives. To their knowledge, Shinburn was the only man capable of such detailed, successful schemes, but he had died years earlier.

Over time, information was developed that an older man with a German accent was a participant in many of the robberies. Eventually, from convict photographs, a banker recognized that man as Max Shinburn. Among those hunting for him were the Pinkerton Agency, Scotland Yard, the Paris Secret Service, and Frank Kelly, considered one of the world's greatest bank detectives.

In 1895, after two more years of work, detectives arrested him for robbing the Middleburgh, New York, First National Bank. During Max's trial, a New Hampshire sheriff waited to arrest him for sentence time owed in that state if he were set free, but the jury found him guilty in January 1896, sending Shinburn to Clinton Prison for four years and eight months.

Nearly all the state's worse criminals did time at Clinton, but so did the best—and in the public's estimation, Max Shinburn had long been the best bank robber in the world. He enjoyed the attention that came with the territory, but living in prison was cramping his style, so after two years, he successfully appealed for a new trial. It was one of those rare instances where winning backfired. Shinburn was found guilty again, but was sentenced to three years and one month—which meant he would end up serving a year longer than if he *hadn't* filed for a new trial.

Max, one of the best-behaved men at Dannemora, was released in October 1900. Waiting for him at the prison gate were several Pinkerton men and one anxious New Hampshire sheriff, ensuring he finished the sentence he escaped from more than thirty years earlier. Max did his time, and after release in 1908, he lived in Boston's Home for Reformed Prisoners, where he died in 1916.

Besides the thefts already mentioned, he was implicated in robberies at the First National Bank of Griswold, Iowa; the Phoenix Bank of Phoenix, Maryland; banks in Milan and Sandusky, Ohio; the Thomaston National Bank of Thomaston, Connecticut; and the St. Hyacinth Bank of Montreal. No one can ever know how many banks he robbed or for how much money. Most estimates by lawmen of the day ran into the millions of dollars, which today would translate to $25 million to $50 million.

ALPHONSE STEPHANI

For the better part of four decades, millions of readers around the world followed the story of Clinton inmate Alphonse Stephani—physically alive but declared civilly dead, and believed to be the wealthiest prisoner in the country.

His father, also Alphonse, lived a classic rags-to-riches success story achieved through hard work. Arriving from Italy around 1835 with just pennies in his pocket, he used a basket to peddle various fruits. The business grew into a fruit stand, a store, and finally a company importing fruit and wine. He became wealthy by investing the profits in real estate.

Of his two sons, Alphonse was a smart investor, but also a big spender and emotionally erratic, while his older brother was more inclined to save money and spend carefully. When the father died in 1888, Alphonse was disappointed that the entire family fortune, valued at $200,000 [$5 million in 2015], was left to Mrs. Stephani, while he was handed control of the family business operations and properties. At times he removed cash from the business and invested in bonds and other securities—and funded his flashy lifestyle.

Learning that $60,000 had been removed from the business coffers by her son, Mrs. Stephani became alarmed. She contacted a lawyer, Clinton Reynolds, and together they met with Alphonse. Instead of reaching an agreement, they argued until her son struck the lawyer and stormed out. He later argued with his mother and struck her as well before leaving angrily for Europe, with a promise she would never see him again.

When he finally returned to the United States, Alphonse learned that his mother had taken legal action to prevent any additional expenditures by him. In May 1890, after securing a hotel room, he went to visit her lawyer, but another argument broke out, ending when Stephani pulled out a gun and shot Reynolds. Office workers came rushing in, fighting Alphonse until one of them smashed a chair against his head, knocking him unconscious. The most damning witness to the attack was Clinton Reynolds, who described the incident before dying from his injuries five days later, leaving Alphonse to face a murder charge.

His trial became a bizarre event, with Mrs. Stephani doing everything she could to protect Alphonse, including hiring William Howe, one of the country's best defense attorneys.

An insanity plea was decided upon, and young Stephani, who had been for years running a profitable business, was suddenly described by friends and family as behaving erratically at times in the past, and attempting suicide on more than one occasion. His neat grooming as a businessman was now replaced with a regimen of no bathing, no shaving, and no haircuts. When asked by a psychiatrist why his hair was so long, Alphonse said he believed hair was a nonconductor of electricity, and thus long hair would prevent the electric chair from killing him by rendering useless the electrodes attached to his head. That doctor pronounced him insane. Others did, too, while some said he was faking mental illness.

Mrs. Stephani took the stand and confessed to her son's peculiar behaviors: he had never kissed her, had exhibited unusual mannerisms since he was a child, thought family members were trying to poison him, had fits of depression, frequently struck her "quite hard," and acted oddly enough that she sent him to Germany for a cure.

The jury wasn't swayed, finding Alphonse guilty of second-degree murder. In April 1891 he was sentenced to life in prison.

In 1893, Mrs. Stephani filed suit to gain access to the account Alphonse had established, but the court refused her request. He continued serving time at Sing Sing, and was transferred to Clinton Prison's Hospital for Insane Criminals in January 1903 when doctors determined Alphonse's mind was failing.

For more than a decade, family members had expressed no interest in his well-being or even acknowledged his existence. That situation changed drastically with the revelation that when Mrs.

Stephani died in April 1902, she left her entire fortune to Alphonse.

Newspapers far and wide reported on Dannemora's millionaire convict who was serving a life sentence. Suddenly, long-lost relatives were popping up everywhere, and Alphonse skyrocketed to the top of their popularity—or rather unpopularity—list.

Because of a life sentence, he was declared civilly dead, which carried with it the loss of most civil rights. Self-perceived heirs began filing suit to control his financial worth, estimated at $120,000 [$3.3 million in 2015]. Some wanted it placed in a trust until he died, at which point it would go to them. The stakes were high, but for a dead man, Stephani put up quite a lively fight.

A 1904 headline read **INSANE CONVICT AT DANNEMORA HEIR TO FORTUNE; GETS OVER $125,000**, but that was just the beginning, for it addressed only his inheritance. There was also the matter of Alphonse's personal account, the one protected from his mother by the court. Relatives virtually salivated when "The Dead Man of Wall Street," as he was portrayed in the media, was finally forced to open the safety-deposit box in 1906. Upon examination, it was found that the $31,000 in securities and $10,000 in stocks had since doubled in value to about $82,000 [$2.25 million in 2015].

But instead of his relatives winning access to the account, Stephani was permitted to resume using it by giving orders to the controlling entity, Trust Company of America. By 1911, from selling railroad bonds and making other investments, he had increased the account's value by another $10,000 [a quarter million in 2015], prompting an interesting *New York Herald* headline, **"DEAD," BUT ALIVE, HIS ESTATE GROWS.**

Prison rules allowed the use of only fifty dollars a month for an inmate to purchase amenities not provided by the state, but still he continued investing and growing his fortune.

In 1914, Alphonse's aunt from Germany sued for control of an account her sister (Alphonse's mother) had ceded to him. She appeared to have won, but he took the ruling to New York's highest court, which ultimately said, "When a trust fund is established for the benefit of a life convict, he is entitled to have the entire amount of the income held for his benefit, even if it is probable that he will die in prison."

Resentful towards American relatives who tried to usurp his

accounts, Alphonse hoped to donate much of his wealth to kinfolk in Germany, but the law denied him direct control of his fortune as long as he was legally insane. He began seeking a sanity assessment at Clinton in order to give his money away to the people he chose.

Through finance companies, Stephani continued growing his fortune, establishing accounts in Frankfort, London, and Paris. By 1919, his net worth was estimated at $500,000 [$7 million in 2015]. In 1927, he received an inheritance from a German aunt, adding $10,000 to his overall worth [$135,000 in 2015].

In 1935, when Alphonse, age seventy, died after twelve years at Sing Sing and thirty-two years at Clinton, the *New York Sun* carried an unusual headline: STRANGE CASE OF MAN 'DYING' TWICE. Despite being declared civilly dead in 1914, Stephani had successfully fought off all those who sought to steal his fortune.

But his part of the battle was now over. Relatives, some he didn't even know about, came seeking a piece of what he left behind. The question was, could a legally dead man leave behind a legal will?

It took another thirteen years to settle his estate. Alphonse had made wills at three different times, and all included some interesting clauses. One requested burial in Hoboken, New Jersey, his last home before going to prison. "I feel that after death, I should be free and without the confines of New York State, where I suffered so much— Woodlawn being too adjacent to Sing Sing, where thirteen years of misery were endured by me." He wished to be buried, "wrapped in a blue army blanket or heavy sail cloth and put in a wooden box."

Other clauses were aimed at the vultures he knew would come looking for a free meal. "I hereby disinherit all persons either blood relationship or otherwise, especially cousins, American or Scotch-American, from inheriting or demanding any sum, or suing for any part of the estate."

In another will, he left everything to the city of Frankfort-on-Main, Germany, stating that, "under no circumstance is any American to benefit hereunder." He also added having "severed all allegiance to the United States."

Still another stipulated, "It is not my wish or desire that any member of my mother's family, either sister or brother or the issue of my sister or brother, or my mother, Josephine Stephani *nee* Moehring, herself should inherit, receive, or derive any profit or benefit from either my own personal estate, or the interest I may have in the estate of my father ... or in any inheritance which I might get or receive if even from my mother's side. This distinctly, emphatically, and positively disinherits all and every party either bearing the name of Moehring or in whose veins one drop of Moehring blood flows."

The Germany-based will called for huge donations to charitable causes, financing a "bread line similar to St. Luke's Chapel bread line," and the establishment of houses or homes for the needy. But it's fair to say that most of the litigants didn't want his fortune to go to charity.

The players in the contest for pieces of his fortune were many, and most were contesting one or more of the wills. Included were: Frederic Stephani, said to be a German baron, World War I ace, Hollywood screen writer, and long-lost cousin of Alphonse; nephew Hans Stephani from Germany; Carl Stephani, an uncle from Germany; three friends and two cousins in Germany; cousins Sophie Moehring and Maria Baker Moehring of White Plains, New York; a Frankfort bank; and New York State, which sought $18,000 in taxes on the estate.

The court eventually divided his holdings among most of those listed, including certain relatives he specifically and emphatically stated should get nothing.

KATE TAYLOR

In 1903, Kate Taylor of Centerville in Sullivan County, about thirty miles west of Poughkeepsie, became the second woman ever to be incarcerated at Clinton Prison. She was held there in relation to a gruesome crime that captured headlines, packed courtrooms, and created many "fans" who sent her gifts and supported her claims of innocence.

In late 1903, Lafayette "Lafe" Taylor disappeared, and with suspicions aroused, investigators developed evidence that pointed strongly towards his wife, Kate, who was charged with first-degree murder. Her trial pitted two unusual witnesses against each other—Mrs. Taylor for the defense, and Ida May DeKay, her fourteen-year-old daughter, for the prosecution.

Ida May took the stand and testified to the ghastly events that occurred in the Taylor household on the night of January 26. In a foul mood fueled by alcohol, Lafe came home and disrupted the evening by yelling, complaining, and damaging pieces of furniture. After Ida May went to bed, she was awakened by a gunshot. She got out of bed and saw Lafe putting on his boots, and heard him promise to get out in the morning if Kate wouldn't shoot him anymore.

Ida May stepped outside, and a few minutes later heard a second gunshot. Following her mother through the kitchen door, Ida saw her stepfather lying on the floor. Kate stood over him and pulled the trigger repeatedly, but the gun didn't fire. She tried to reload, but stopped when Ida told her not to shoot anymore.

It was possible Lafe was still alive when Kate grabbed a nearby axe and proceeded to chop off his head and right arm. After soaking both with kerosene, she burned them in the stove. Next, she chopped off the other arm and both legs, stored them with the torso in a tub, and spent the next several days burning those parts as well. The skull and bones were pounded into bits, mixed with corn, and fed to the chickens. A deputy sheriff testified that Kate said she burned everything because she didn't want to throw the parts out and have the dogs carting them around.

Ida also testified to a pair of important conversations. A week after Lafe's death, during a visit with Kate's uncle, Peter Yerkins, Kate told him she had killed Lafe and burned him. The discussion, Ida said, was a follow-up to one five months earlier, when Yerkins asked if Lafe was still mean to her. When Kate said yes, he told her to kill Lafe when he was drunk, get rid of him, and Peter would let her live in a home that he owned nearby.

Other prosecution testimony told of four previous attempts by Kate to kill Lafe. On two occasions while he was asleep, she tried using chloroform held over his nose, once with a handkerchief, and another time with a sponge. She once struck him on the head with an axe, but only inflicted a bad scalp wound, and when he entered the barn shortly after, she locked the doors from the outside and set it on fire.

Among the evidence presented in court were parts of Lafe's flesh and bones, and even the bloody door he stood against when he was shot. Witnesses described finding the hidden axe, plus bullet holes in the walls, hidden by new pieces of wallpaper.

Kate refuted most of her daughter's testimony, claiming the shooting was accidental during a struggle for control of the gun. She offered no denial of dismembering Lafe's body, disposing of the parts, and feeding bits to farm animals, explaining that even though his death was an accident, people might not have believed her, so she tried to hide the evidence. She also had forty witnesses available who would testify to the many bruises and injuries she suffered from beatings dished out by Lafe, but since the claim was accidental death by shooting, those stories were not allowed into evidence.

Although the jury deliberated all night, the first vote was eleven to one against Kate. By morning she was declared guilty of first-degree murder. The judge sentenced her to die in Clinton Prison's electric chair on July 5, just five weeks away.

She was sent to Dannemora, where matrons were brought in to care for her needs in the all-male prison. It's very likely that Kate Taylor was the first Clinton inmate ever to engage in extended periods of needlework embroidery while confined there.

An appeal was filed by her attorneys, delaying Kate's execution. She waited on Clinton's death row, and was relieved to hear that on January 26, 1904, exactly one year from the day Lafe was killed, she had won the right to a new trial. The court of appeals was astonished that testimony of witnesses confirming terrible physical abuse by Lafe had been disallowed. Since Kate had claimed self-defense in a struggle for control of the gun, the court said those witnesses to abuse would have provided context for that struggle, perhaps convincing the jury that a fight over a gun was an expected event in an abusive relationship.

After seven months at Dannemora, Kate was transferred to attend her second trial, held in May 1904. It was an event with many surprises, particularly the revised testimony of Ida May, which caused an uproar in the packed courtroom and a sensation in the media. With her father lying on the floor, bleeding from a wound to his temple, said Ida,

> Mother then got an axe and chopped off Lafe's head. There was a fire in the kitchen stove, and she put the head in the fire. Then she cut off the right arm. Mother got a lantern and after lighting it, went out into the yard and moved the

lantern about her head three times. Soon afterward a man came in out of the darkness.

Questioning by District Attorney Frank Anderson about the man's identity provided several shocking revelations. It was Peter Yerkins, she said, and he helped cut up Lafe's body.

> Peter said, "Is Lafe dead? Did you do what I told you to do?" She answered, "Yes." Then they talked in German and I did not understand them. After a little while, mother got the axe again and began chopping Lafe's leg. Then Peter chopped up the bones and I went to bed. When I went to bed, mother was putting the body in the stove. Just after the legs were cut off, they were put in a tin tub and the body in a sack. The sack was out in the pantry. Next morning I saw mother take the skull out of the stove and break it up. Then she cut up the body into four pieces and put it in the tin tub. Afterward she buried the bones in different parts of the yard.

Ida May added that the axe handle was burned, a broom used for cleanup was destroyed, and the pounded bones were fed to the chickens. The tin and wooden tubs in question, plus the axe head and revolver, were then introduced as evidence.

She also related two other parts of the plan specified by Peter Yerkins: if anyone asked, they were to say Lafe was looking for work in Orange County; and if either Kate or Ida May said anything about the murder, he would kill them both. When the judge asked why she hadn't mentioned those items during the first trial, Ida May replied, "I was not asked." The entire murder story, compared to testimony from a year earlier, was now muddled even further.

For her part, Kate described many abusive incidents that were confirmed by the testimony of other witnesses. She also pointed out that Ida May had been living with Lafe's relatives since his death, and they had influenced her testimony, which was why it had changed so much. Kate added that the female detective guarding Ida May had hypnotized her to provide certain testimony, and that Ida May had also been threatened with prison if she didn't cooperate with the prosecution.

Another defense witness contradicted Ida May's story about

Yerkins, confirming that Peter was at the man's farm that evening until 9 p.m., and was awakened at 5 a.m. to begin work. Since the farm was located six miles from the Taylor residence, Yerkins would have traveled twelve miles during the night while pausing to help cut up and dispose of Lafe's body parts, a scenario that seemed unlikely.

The jury found Kate guilty, but of second-degree murder, saving her from execution. She was sentenced to life at Auburn, which housed a women's prison. In July 1907 she was transferred to the Matteawan State Asylum for Insane Criminals, where she died of tuberculosis four months later at the age of forty-four.